Hebrews Commenting from Erasmus to Bèze 1516–1598

by

KENNETH HAGEN

WIPF & STOCK · Eugene, Oregon

Wipf and Stock Publishers
199 W 8th Ave, Suite 3
Eugene, OR 97401

Hebrews Commenting from Erasmus to Beze
By Hagen, Kenneth

ISBN 13: 978-1-61097-350-2
Publication date 3/11/2011
Previously published by J. C. B. Mohr, 1981

Hagen, Kenneth:
Hebrews commenting from Erasmus to Bèze:
1516–1598 / by Kenneth Hagen. –
Tübingen: Mohr, 1981.
(Beiträge zur Geschichte der biblischen Exegese; 23)

TO

Aldemar
Carolyn
Susan
Erik

Table of Contents

Preface

This monograph is answer to a question put to me by a publisher in the Fall of 1974 about what happened to Hebrews after Luther's Lectures on the epistle (1517–1518). This project also allowed me to venture further into the little researched area of 16th century *exegetica*.

I wish to acknowledge the research stipends of Marquette University and the American Philosophical Society (Penrose Fund), which allowed me to travel in Europe the summer of 1977 for further bibliographic work. Also to be thanked for that summer is Rev. William J. Kelly, S.J., now chairman of Marquette University's theology department.

Special thanks for the preparation of the manuscript goes to Rev. Thomas Caldwell, S.J., for his linguistic and editorial expertise, to Olaf Roynesdal for help with the bibliography and the preparation of the Scripture index, and to Guy Carter (all three of Marquette) for the Name index. Secretary Camille is singled out for her courage and paleographical skills.

For the publication I am very grateful to the editor, Professor Cullmann, and the publisher, J. C. B. Mohr (Paul Siebeck) Tübingen.

Oslo, St. Hallvards, 1980 K. Hagen

List of Abbreviations

ARG	Archiv für Reformationsgeschichte
CH	Church history
CR	*Corpus Reformatorium* Halle, 1834 ff.
PG	*Patrologia, Series Graeca* 161 Vols., Ed. J. P. Migne. Paris, 1857– 1866
PL	*Patrologia, Series Latina* 221 Vols. in 222, Ed. J. P. Migne. Paris, 1844–1904
SCJ	The Sixteenth Century Journal
SVRG	*Schriften des Vereins für Reformationsgeschichte*
TZ	Theologische Zeitschrift
WA	*D. Martin Luthers Werke. Kritische Gesamtausgabe.* Weimar. 1883 f.
WA DB	*D. Martin Luthers werke. Deutsche Bibel.* Weimar, 1906–1961
ZKG	Zeitschrift für Kirchengeschichte

Introduction

Most treatments of Hebrews that approximate a commentary begin with an *"Argumentum,"* often so called. In this prefatory section the author usually summarizes the general importance of the Epistle to the Hebrews. Often the content or doctrine of the epistle is highly praised and compared favorably with other (Pauline) epistles, very often accompanied by claims of uniqueness with regard to Hebrews. Introductory items like authorship, purpose, audience, and structure are discussed. For the 16th century, the authorship question was quite critical, not only because conflicting views of the first five or six centuries were becoming increasingly apparent, but also because of Erasmus' critical and negative comments (1516) regarding Paul as author. Luther in 1522, Cajetan in 1529, Calvin in 1549, and Bèze in 1556 (1565^2, 1582^3), expressed serious doubts about Paul as author. The authorship discussion will be handled in terms of the commentator's use of authorities, type of argumentation and interpretation of Heb. 2.3 (whether Paul received the gospel directly from Christ as he claims in Gal. 1) and 6.6 (regarding the possibility of second repentance).

The purpose and importance of Hebrews is nearly always summarized in terms of the relationship of the Old and New Testament ("In many and various ways God spoke in times past to the fathers by the prophets; in these last days he has spoken to us by his son," Heb. 1.1). The advantage of concentrating on the *"Argumentum"* or its equivalent is that one can immediately get at the commentator's view(s) of this perennial issue, views which then color the entire piece of exegesis.

The scope of this study is a focus on the introduction *("Argumentum")* in as many printed commentaries on Hebrews as this author could identify, locate and secure copies of. Other possible approaches that were considered and rejected for this study include the following: treatment of all the pericopes in a few exegetes or a few pericopes in all the exegetes, or some compromise that would include some texts in some exegetes in some manageable time frame. None of these satisfied the original vision of seeing the whole scope of Hebrews commenting after Erasmus (1516) and Luther (1517/18). Calvin was a natural *ad quem*, but 1549 was only on the verge of the late reformation and besides Bèze's influential work was not far away. Bèze's editions developed and shifted and so work on Bèze (1556–98) and others during this time extended the work to the late 16th century. One way of presenting work on Hebrews from 1516 to 1598 that would provide some control on focus and length has been to focus on introductions (with, of course, the whole commentary in view), because they are first, they are a literary type (which changes), they often engage in controversy (both *humanistica* and *theologica*) implicitly and explicitly, and they discuss the controversial issue of authorship, often connected with authority, and lay out the theology of Hebrews, though after Calvin introductions often do more and other than cover content of the epistle.

The material is divided into two Parts, Erasmus to Calvin, Politus to Bèze[1]. Erasmus, Calvin, Bèze are known terminal points. There are good reasons to regard Politus as a *terminus a quo:* 1. 1551 is the next first edition to appear (after Calvin), 2. he was important in the church, 3. he was teacher of Sixtus of Siena, 4. he reaffirmed the medieval stance on authorship against Erasmus by implication and against Cajetan (1529) explicitly. The real reason, along with a need for a summary and breather after Calvin, is that in Politus and at this time there is the development of an expanded type of introduction.

This study also seeks to make a bibliographic contribution to 16th century *exegetica*. Only 12 out of my 64 date cards (first editions) refer to works only on the one epistle to the Hebrews. Considerable effort was given to identify every edition of a Hebrews commentary in the 16th century. Modern bibliographies are cited. Wherever biographical information was difficult to find, effort has been made to identify the exegete.

The material has been ordered chronologically in terms of exegete/text, in the order of giving (e.g. lecturing). There is some exception

---

[1] The beginning with Erasmus (in 1516) was deemed appropriate for two reasons. Hebrews commenting from Chrysostom to Luther (1517/18) has been treated by this author *(A Theology of Testament in the Young Luther: The Lectures on Hebrews* ["Studies in Medieval and Reformation Thought," Vol. 12; Leiden: Brill, 1974]). And, Erasmus' critical discussion of authorship at the end of his 1516 New Testament was widely discussed while Luther's lectures on Hebrews of 1517/18 were published in 1929 (from student notes) and were not discussed. Thus, even though Erasmus' *Novum Instrumentum* (1516) does not have an introduction, it does have the equivalent in an appendix and he is a major terminal point.

(with Zwingli and Oecolampadius, the date of giving could not be determined). The ordering is not significant because little attempt has been made to assess the historical influence of one exegete/text on another. Differences, similarities, parallels, controversies are dwelt on, but the "from" and "to" (title and subtitle) are not intended to suggest the development of Hebrews or the development of thought about Hebrews *in abstracto*. The natural weakness of the study, given the broad scope, is that each exegete/text could not be studied in the light of its historical context to the extent the author would have wanted. After a translation of the introduction, with the original text in a footnote, an analysis of the piece is given in the light of medieval and (earlier) 16th century exegesis of Hebrews.

Every temptation to treat the exegetes along denominational or sectarian lines has been avoided. In fact one of the by-products of this study is that such denominational determinants are largely nonexistent because of the control of the text (Hebrews). Interpretations differ. Polemics enter in. But in large areas, e.g. authorship, authority of the epistle, Christology, even soteriology, Old Testament hermeneutic, interpretations are not along confessional lines.

Part One

Erasmus to Calvin 1516–1549

Desiderius Erasmus (c. 1466–1536)[1]

The Argument of the Epistle to the Hebrews

No people resisted the gospel of Christ with more obstinate souls than the Jews, who were also particularly hostile to Paul, because he publicly declared himself an apostle of the Gentiles, whom the Jews detested as profane and impious, and because Paul seemed to antiquate the law of Moses, which they held as sacrosanct and wanted to spread around the whole world instead of the gospel. There were also those among the Jews who received the doctrine of Christ who thought that the observance of the law should be mixed with the gospel. There were those believers, therefore, in Jerusalem who were afflicted with various calamities by those who resisted the gospel (those in possession of public authority); they were thrown in prison, beaten and robbed of their goods. These, therefore, Paul consoles, partly with the example of the saints of old, the majority of whom were harassed with similar or else more severe calamities, by which their virtue was more certain and respected, and especially with the example of Christ; and partly Paul consoles with the hope of heavenly reward. Then he declares that already with the dawn of the gospel of Christ the shadows of the Mosaic law cease, repeating much from the Old Testament and pointing to Christ. He teaches that one cannot hope to be saved by the observance of the law, which was given for a certain time and which was imperfect, but by faith, through which most of all the ancients also were pleasing to God, they who proved to be most virtuous men, the memory of whom was sacrosanct to the Jews. In the end Paul gives certain precepts for the doing of Christian deeds.[2]

---

[1] *In epistolam Pauli ad Hebraeos paraphrasis per Erasmus Roterodamum extrema* (Basel: Johan Froben, 1521). Also in *Opera Omnia* (LB, 1703–1706; 1962), VII, col. 1165–98. For editions see Ferdinand van der Haeghen, *Bibliotheca Erasmiana* (Nieuwkoop: Graaf, 1961); "1re Série" for *Paraphrasis in epistolas Pauli* (pp. 143–46), "2e Série" for *Novum Testamentum* (pp. 57–66).

[2] In epistolam ad Hebraeos argumentum per Erasmum Roterodamum. Nulla Gens obstinatioribus animis repugnabat Evangelio Christi, quam Judaeorum, qui Paulo etiam peculiariter erant infensi, quod se Gentium Apostolum profiteretur, quas Judaei ut profanas et impias abominabantur, quodque Legem Mosaicam, quam illi sacrosanctam habebant, et Evangelii vice per universum orbem spargi cupiebant, antiquare videretur.

It is fairly well known that Erasmus devalued the Old Testament in relation to both the New Testament and the ancient civilizations of Greece and Rome both before and after 1521. In this Introduction, the Jews are described as obstinate, in fact no group is more obstinate. The law was "shadow," a fairly general medieval notion. The law was "imperfect" in contrast to the dawn of the gospel of Christ. Thomas Aquinas had said that the New Testament was "more perfect" than the Old Testament, whereas Nicholas of Lyra gave the contrast as imperfect (Old Testament) and perfect (New Testament).[3] Erasmus lines up with those medievals who emphasized contrast and discontinuity, the two Testaments dividing after the time of Christ. Erasmus can be very critical of the books of the Jews, willing under certain circumstances that the Old Testament "be altogether abolished."[4] The Old Testament was given for a certain period of time and ceases with Christ. The Old Testament saints were virtuous not by the law but by faith.

After Hebrews was accepted as canonical in the West, apparently in the latter half of the 4th century, Erasmus appears to be the first (in 1516) to raise serious doubts about Paul as author.[5] In the 1521 *Paraphrasis* he does not raise the authorship question, in fact he uses the name Paul when introducing the epistle. The medievals generally discussed the authorship question in terms of two problems: *modus scribendi* (no

---

Adeo ut essent inter hos quoque qui Christi doctrinam receperant, qui putarent Legis observationem cum Evangelio miscendam. Hierosolymis igitur qui crediderant variis calamitatibus afficiebantur ab iis, qui resistebant Evangelio, (nam penes hos erat publica auctoritas) conjiciebantur in vincula, caedebantur, diripiebantur illorum bona. Hos itaque consolatur Paulus, partim exemplo veterum sanctorum, quorum plerique similibus, aut gravioribus calamitatibus exerciti sunt, quo virtus illorum esset exploratior spectatiorque, ac praecipue exemplo Christi, partim spe praemii coelestis. Deinde declarat coruscante jam Evangelio Christi, cessasse umbras Legis Mosaicae, multa repetens ex Veteri Testamento, et ad Christum accommodans. Docet non ex observatione Legis ad tempus datae et imperfectae, sperandam esse salutem, sed ex fide, per quam veteres etiam illi probatae sanctimoniae viri, quorum memoria Judaeis erat sacrosancta, Deo potissimum placuissent. In fine tradit praecepta quaedam ad mores Christianos facientia. *Ad Hebraeos paraphrasis* (1521), L 13^{r-v}. This *"argumentum"* appeared in 1519, prior to the Greek and Latin text of the Epistle to the Hebrews: *Novum Testamentum omne, multo quam antehac diligentius ab Erasmo Roterodamo recognitum* (Basel: Johan Froben, 1519), p. 471.

[3] Aquinas, "Super epistolam ad Hebraeos lectura," *Super epistolas s. Pauli lectura,* ed. P. R. Cai, 8th ed. (Rome: Marietti, 1953), II.339. Lyra, "Postilla . . . super epistolam ad Hebraeos," *Biblia cum Glossa ordinaria, Nicolai de Lyra postilla,* 6 Vols. (Basel: Johan Froben, 1506–1508), VI. f. 132^{v}, 133^{v}, cited in Hagen, *A Theology of Testament,* pp. 48–49.

[4] Cited in John W. Aldridge, *The Hermeneutic of Erasmus* (Richmond, Va.: John Knox Press, 1966), p. 48.

[5] *Novum instrumentum cum annotationibus* (Basel: Johan Froben, 1516).

usual Pauline salutation or name of author given in the epistle) and *stilus* (more elegant and different from the known Pauline epistles). The general medieval resolution regarding the first was that Paul purposely left out his usual reference to himself and his credentials because he, the apostle to the Gentiles, did not want to alienate the Jews at the start. It was held, regarding the second, that the style was different because Paul wrote Hebrews in his own tongue and Luke the evangelist translated it into Greek.

A few years before Erasmus's *Annotationes,* Faber Stapulensis rejected the medieval solution regarding the *modus scribendi* question for "who writes a letter without signing his name?" Besides, Paul was writing to believers in Christ.[6] Erasmus held that *modus scribendi* pointed to someone other than Paul. The *stilus* violates the spirit and character of Paul's writing. In his *Annotationes* on Matthew Erasmus says that nobody would have thought that Hebrews was written in Hebrew, and not Greek, except that it was addressed to the Hebrews.[7] Like Luther in 1522 (Preface) Erasmus in 1516 claimed that Hebrews denies repentance after baptism (6.4–6) whereas, Erasmus pointed out, Paul accepted a man into the church who had slept with his father's wife. This text is an example for Erasmus that Hebrews seems to defend certain heretical doctrines.[8] Erasmus raised several other problems: on 2.7, Erasmus

---

[6] "Commentariorum in epistolas beati Pauli apostoli liber quartusdecimus qui est in epistolam ad Hebraeos," *Epistolae Pauli Apostoli* (Paris: Henri Estienne, 1512), f. 230ᵛ.

[7] LB, VI. 47 D.

[8] Erasmus, *Novum instrumentum,* pp. 600–601: Optime lector, nihilo minoris velim esse tibi hanc epistolam, quod a multis dubitatum sit Pauli esset an alterius. Caerte cuiuscumque est, multis nominibus digna est, quae legatur a Christianis. Et ut a stilo Pauli, quod ad phrasim attinet, longe lateque discrepat, ita ad spiritum ac pectus Paulinum vehementer accedit. Verum ut non potest doceri certis argumentis cuius sit, quod nullius habeat inscriptionem, ita compluribus indiciis colligi potest, ab alio quopiam quam a Paulo scriptam fuisse. Primum quod sola omnium Pauli nomen non praeferat. Tametsi non me fugit hoc utcunque dilui ab Hieronymo. Deinde quod tot annis, nempe usque ad aetatem Hieronymi non recepta fuerit a Rhomanis, quemadmodum ipse testatur in epistolis suis. Ad hanc coniecturam facit, quod Ambrosius, cum omnes Paulinas epistolas sit interpretatus, in hanc unam nihil scripserit. Ut ne dicam interim inesse locos aliquot, qui quorundam haereticorum dogmatibus patrocinari videantur. Velut illa, quod velum separans sancta sanctorum, interpretatur coelum, ac multo magis, quod palam adimit spem a baptismo relapsis in peccatum, idque non uno in loco, cum Paulus et eum receperit in communionem sanctorum, qui dormierat cum uxore patris. Adde huc, quod Divus Hieronymus cum aliis aliquot locis ita citat huius epistolae testimonia, ut de autore videatur ambigere, tum edisserens caput Hieremiae tricesimum primum. "Hoc," inquit, "testimonio Paulus apostolus, sive quis alius scripsit epistolam, usus est ad Hebraeos" [*PL* 24.918]. Restat iam argumentum illud, quo non aliud certius, stilus ipse, et orationis character, qui nihil habet affinitatis cum phrasi Paulina. Nam quod adferunt hic quidam

notes that there were doubts in the Latin church, that Ambrose wrote on all the epistles except Hebrews, and that Jerome reported that Hebrews was not received by some;[9] on 9.17, Erasmus argues that the author of Hebrews did not know Hebrew because of the use of "*testamentum*" which comes only from the Septuagint;[10] on 10.33, Erasmus holds that it is ridiculous to argue for Pauline authorship, as did Valla, because of being "publicly exposed to abuse and affliction" – all the disciples were in chains;[11] 12.21 reports that "Moses said": "I suspect that this is the place," said Erasmus, "to which Jerome refers when he says that some do not attribute this epistle to Paul, because it quotes certain things with references to the Old Testament which are not to be found there."[12] In 1517, in his "Apology to Faber Stapulensis" (regarding Hebrews 2.7), Erasmus gives several references to the Fathers, all expressing doubt about Paul as author: cited are Jerome, Origen, Augustine, Eusebius and Ambrose.[13]

Luther will shift his views on authorship. Erasmus seems to have shifted from a very negative discussion (in 1516) about Paul as author to no discussion (in 1521) and the use of Paul's name in his introduction. In other editions of his New Testament *Annotations* and elsewhere Erasmus is critical of Pauline authorship.[14] Erasmus's approach may not be

Paulum ipsum Hebraice scripsisse, caeterum Lucam argumentum epistolae, quam memoria tenebat suis explicuisse verbis quantum valeat, viderint alii. Neque enim in verbis solum aut figuris discrimen est, sed omnibus notis dissidet. Et ut Paulus Graece scribens, multum ex idiomate sermonis hebraici retulit, ita et in hac quam ut volunt isti, scripsit hebraice, non nulla sermonis illius vestigia residerent. Quid quod ne Lucas quidem ipse, in actis apostolorum, hoc est, in argumento, quod facile recipit orationis ornamenta, parum abest ab huius epistolae eloquentia. Equidem haud interponam hoc loco meam sententiam. Caeterum admodum probabile est, quod indicavit Divus Hieronymus in catalogo scriptorum illustrium, Clementem Rhomanum pontificem, a Petro quartum, autorem huius epistolae fuisse. Clementis enim meminit Paulus, et hic Timothei facit mentionem. Sed praestat, opinor, ipsa Hieronymi verba, super hac re asscribere. "Scripsit," inquit, "nempe Clemens, sub persona Rhomanae ecclesiae, ad ecclesiam Corinthiorum, valde utilem epistolam, quae et in nonnullis locis publice legitur, quae mihi videtur characteri epistolae, quae sub Pauli nomine ad Hebraeos fertur [,] convenire. Sed et multis de eadem epistola non solum sensibus, sed iuxta verborum quoque ordinem abutitur. Omnino grandis in utraque similitudo est." Hactenus Divus Hieronymus [*De Viris illustribus* 15, *PL* 23.663]. This discussion of authorship at the end of the 1516 *Annotations* on Hebrews, which begins with "*Optime lector,*" appeared in the 3rd (1522) and 5th (1535) editions of the New Testament *Annotations,* also at the end, with additional arguments and more references to the Fathers.

[9] *Ibid.*, p. 586.

[10] *Ibid.*, p. 593.

[11] *Ibid.*, pp. 594–95.

[12] *Ibid.*, p. 599.

[13] *Apologia ad Jacobum Fabrum Stapulensem,* LB IX, 53B–57F.

[14] Elsewhere Erasmus continues to express and defend negative views on Pauline

unlike Cajetan, who will marshal much evidence against Pauline authorship and then say that he will use the name of Paul.

Martin Luther (1483–1546)[15]

It should be noted in this epistle that Paul exalts grace as opposed to the arrogance of legal and human righteousness. He shows that without Christ, neither the law nor the priesthood nor prophecy nor even finally the ministry of the angels was sufficient for salvation. In fact all these were established and provided in reference to the coming of Christ. Therefore everything considered, he proposes that one should teach Christ alone.[16]

In an earlier study of these lectures of Luther in the light of important medieval commentaries, beginning with Chrysostom, I concluded that Luther's brief introduction differed greatly from the medieval introductions.[17] In medieval *argumenta* the theme of *excellentia Christi* was developed by comparing Christ with the angels, Moses and the priesthood of the Old Testament. The conclusion of the comparison was always that Christ is "more excellent" *(excellentior)* than the old law. Although there was varying emphasis on continuity and discontinuity by the medievals, the common base for comparison or contrast between the Testaments was law. Luther's introduction did not mention the standard theme of *excellentia Christi.* Luther held that Paul in Hebrews emphasizes "grace" and "Christ" as opposed to "law," "priesthood," "prophecy" and "angels." The thrust of Luther's statement was that only Christ alone (no matter what, no matter how you look at it) suffices for salvation in each era or Testament. Christ (alone), who is beyond comparison with anyone or anything, is the common base of both Testaments.

In the seven instances where Luther discusses Pauline authorship in the course of his lectures, he is generally in favor of Pauline authorship.

---

authorship, while endorsing the use of the name of Paul, especially in the title of the epistle (LB IX.865A–866B, 453AB, 542AB, 594D–595E, 1079D–1080A).

[15] *Divi Pauli apostoli ad Hebreos epistola.* Luther's Lectures on Hebrews, given 1517–18, survived as two sets of student lecture notes and were first published in 1929. *Weimarer Ausgabe* 57.III (Weimar: Böhlau, 1939), pp. 1–238.

[16] Notandum in hac epistola, quod Paulus gratiam extollit adversus superbiam legalis et humanae iusticiae, probans, quod sine Christo nec lex nec sacerdotium nec prophecia neque denique angelorum etiam ministerium ad salutem satis fuerit, immo haec omnia in Christum futurum instituta et facta fuerint. Omnino igitur solum Christum docendum proponit. *WA* 57.III. 5.10–16.

[17] *A Theology of Testament in the Young Luther. The Lectures on Hebrews,* pp. 31–61.

Luther is unique among the medieval exegetes in holding that in three cases there are questionable references in Hebrews to the Old Testament and that these three texts raise the authorship question about Hebrews. For example Heb. 9.19–21, referring to Ex. 24, gives many details (wool, hyssop, water, etc.), which are not recorded in the Old Testament. Luther found no Old Testament basis for most of the items mentioned in 9.19–21 and thus concluded that the Pauline authorship of Hebrews is questionable. In the other two instances, Luther tried to harmonize Hebrews and Old Testament. In general Luther in 1517–18 and in 1522 (Preface to the Epistle to the Hebrews) sees Hebrews as a guide to the Old Testament. While Erasmus in 1516 *(Novum instrumentum cum annotationibus)* frequently and sometimes caustically dealt with the authorship question with negative conclusions, in most instances Luther did not raise the question. While Luther saw authorship problems in 1522 with Heb. 2.3 (*vis-à-vis* Gal. 1.1) and 6.4–6 (which "flatly denies" any repentance after baptism), he "still" felt it was "a marvelously fine epistle. It discusses Christ's priesthood masterfully . . . and extensively interprets the Old Testament in a fine way. . . . Who wrote it is not known and will probably not be known for a while; it makes no difference."[18] Also in 1522, in a *Postil* on Heb. 1.1–12 (the epistle text for Christmas Day), Luther praises Hebrews as a "powerful epistle." The author is a "trustworthy man, though he is not St. Paul, because he uses a more refined speech than is St. Paul's custom in other places. Some think he is St. Luke, some St. Apollo. . ." Luther does not opt for any specific alternative to St. Paul (in 1522): "he [the author] is whoever he may be."[19]

John Bugenhagen (1485–1558)[20]

That Paul did not write this epistle is clear from the second chapter, where it says that he heard the gospel of Christ from the preaching of others and the showing of miracles. Paul strongly denies this regarding himself in Gal. 1.

[18] *LW* 35.395; *WA DB* 7.344.20–31.

[19] *WA* 10.I.1.143.13–20. In 1537, in a sermon on I Cor. 1.12 (3, 4 ff.), Luther said, "This Apollos is a highly intelligent man; the epistle of the Hebrews is certainly his" (*WA* 45.389.34–35).

[20] *Annotationes Ioan. Bugenhagii Pomerani in decem Epistolas Pauli, sc. ad Eph., Philipp., Col., Thess. primam et secun., Tim. primam et secun., Tit., Philem., Hebraeos* (Nuremberg: Joannes Petrejus, 1524). Geisenhof ♯54. I have used a 1525 ed., "In epistolam ad Hebraeos Ioannis Pomerani Annotationes," *Annotationes . . . in [XI] epistolas Pauli.* Strasbourg:

The argument and topics of this epistle: Because he [?] is writing to Hebrews, to whom after God nothing is more sacred than Moses and what pertains to the law, therefore those among them who had converted to Christ ought not to defect again from Christ to Moses, which is notorious blasphemy against God, because of persecutions, which they suffered from their own Jews. Let them hear from the holy Scriptures that Christ is by far superior not only to Moses but also to the angels, through whom he (Moses) received the law, although on account of us for a brief time during his passion he (Christ) was made lower than the angels, according to that Psalm, "Thou hast made him [a little lower than the angels]."[21] And therefore this is inferred: If that given through the angels and Moses could not be contemned without God's punishment, how much less will it go unpunished if one contemns the word of Christ, especially after we have been warned by the Psalmist, "Today" he says, "if you shall hear his voice, [do not harden your hearts]," where given the opportunity, he indicates the Christian sabbath (Heb. c. 4). Moreover let them hear that the priesthood of the old law, the sacrifices and other sacred things by no means can be compared with the priesthood and sacrifice of Christ offered once and for all on the cross and with the invisible altar and temple, and to such an extent that the former, as figures, have ceased, yielding to the latter as to truth apparent. And he treats the pontificate of Christ from the Scriptures most worthily, not without great consolation to our consciences (from chapters 7 to 11). In chapter 11 he commends faith exceedingly well, with examples from the Scriptures. Then up to the end he encourages patience and Christian deeds.

The reason why the author of the epistle wrote is clear from his own words. He feared for them lest they be overcome with temptations and afflictions or slide back into infidelity in time of scarcity. Thus he admonishes in c. 10 [.32], "call to mind [the days gone by, in which, after you had been enlightened, you endured a great conflict of suffering]," and c. 12 [.3], "Consider [him who endured such opposition from sinners against himself, so that you may not grow weary and lose heart]." And to this pertain those places where he seems to deny penitence to those who lapsed after acknowledging the truth. The first text is c. 6 [.4–6], "It is impossible [for those who were once enlightened, . . . and then have fallen away, to be renewed again to repentance]." The second place is c. 10 [.26], "For [if we sin] willfully [later receiving the knowledge of the truth, there remains no longer a sacrifice for sins]." The third place is c. 12 [.17] "for he (Esau) found [no opportunity for repentance, although he had sought after it with tears]." These texts we will see in the proper place from the text itself (to see) what they contain.[22]

Johann Knoblouch, 1525; Geisenhof #63), ff. 138^{r}–159^{v}. The 1525 editions added *ad Galatas* which raised the number to 11 epistles. For different editions principally 1524 and 1525, Latin and German, cf. Georg Geisenhof, *Bibliotheca Bugenhagiana* ("Quellen und Darstellungen aus der Geschichte des Reformationsjahrhunderts," Vol. 6; Leipzig, 1908; Nieuwkoop: Graaf. 1963), pp. 77–102.

[21] Psalm 8.5, cited in Heb. 2.7.

[22] Paulum non scripsisse hanc epistolam, vel ex secundo capite palam est, ubi dicit se didicisse ex praedicatione aliorum, et ex ostensione miraculorum Evangelium Christi, id quod fortiter Paulus de se negat Gal. 1.

The title of Bugenhagen's commentary is, "Annotations of John Bugenhagen of Pomerania on [10 or 11] Epistles of Paul, namely . . . Hebrews." Yet he began his prefatory comments on Hebrews by saying, "That Paul did not write this epistle is clear from . . ." Others in the 16th century marshalled evidence against Pauline authorship and still used "Paul" as author, in titles and the body of their texts. Bugenhagen did not slip in the body of his text. For example, on 6.4–6, Bugenhagen said, "the author, whoever he was. . ." Bugenhagen's first (and only) argument against Pauline authorship is the same as Luther's first argument in his Preface to Hebrews (1522). For Bugenhagen Gal. 1 "denies" what Heb. 2.3 says about the author's hearing the gospel from others. This is the only argument against Pauline authorship stated but at the end of his preface Bugenhagen cites two texts (6.4–6 and 12.17) used by Luther (in his 1522 Preface) to deny Pauline authorship. Bugenhagen concludes by saying that these texts (plus a third, 10.26), "where he seems to deny penance after lapsing from the knowledge of the truth," will be explained in their context. The importance of these texts is that they are about what the whole epistle is about.

The principal point of the Epistle to the Hebrews, as stated in Bugenhagen's preface, is, let those Jewish converts beware so as not to

---

Argumentum et loci huius epistolae.

Quia scribit Hebraeis, quibus post Deum nihil sanctius erat Moise, et quicquid Legis erat. Idcirco qui ex eis ad Christum conversi erant, ne ob persecutiones, quae a suis Iudaeis patiebantur, deficerent rursum a Christo ad Moisen, quae esset insignis in Deum blasphemia, audiunt ex scripturis sanctis, Christum, non solum Moise, sed etiam Angelis, per quos ille Legem accepit, longe esse superiorem, licet propter nos ad breve tempus in passione factus sit angelis inferior, secundum illud Psalmi: Minuisti eum, etc. Ideoque hoc infert. Si quae per angelos et Moisen data sunt, non potuerunt sine ultione Dei contemni, multo inultum erit, si quis contempserit Christi sermonem, postquam etiam praemoniti sumus per psalmum: Hodie, inquit, si vocem eius audieritis, etc. ubi data occasione, indicat sabbatum illud Christianorum, capite quarto. Praeterea audiunt Sacerdotium veteris legis et sacrificia et reliqua sacra, sacerdotio Christi et sacrificio semel in cruce oblato et altari et templo invisibili, nequaquam conferenda, atque adeo illa ut figuras in his, ut in veritate iam exhibita cessasse. Atque haec de Christi pontificatu ex scripturis dignissime, non sine magna conscientiarum nostrarum consolatione tractat a cap. 7 usque ad 11. Porro 11 capite fidem egregie commendat ex scripturarum exemplis. Deinde usque in finem ad patientiam et Christianos mores hortatur.

Caussa [*sic*] quare scripserit autor epistolam, ex ipsius verbis deprehenditur. Nam timuit eis, ne superati tentationibus et afflictionibus, sive penuria ad infidelitatem relaberentur. Unde admonet capite decimo: Rememoramini, etc, et 12: Recogitate, etc. Atque huc pertinent illi loci, in quibus videtur negare poenitentiam post agnitam veritatem relapsis. Primus locus cap. 6: Impossibile est eos, etc. Secundus cap. 10: Voluntarie enim, etc. Tertius cap. 12: Non enim invenit, etc. quos locos suo loco videbimus ex ipso textu, quid habeant. "In epistolam ad Hebraeos," (1525), f. 138^{r-v}.

"defect," "be overcome" or "slide back." Lapsing from Christ is "notorious blasphemy against God."

In context Bugenhagen's comments on 6.4–6, which include references to 10.26, are relatively very long.[23] He begins by holding out for Christian penance," because we need forgiveness "not only on account of our temptations but also on account of our sins."[24] "Whoever the author" of Hebrews was, he did not deny this kind of forgiveness. Bugenhagen goes on, citing an epistle of John, to distinguish two kinds of sins, one that is deadly and one that is not. The unforgiveable sin that Heb. 6.4–6 refers to is the deadly sin against the Holy Spirit. Heb. 10.26 means the same, there is no repentance for those who, having "tasted the good word of God," blaspheme Christ.[25]

In medieval exegesis there were generally four avenues of approach to 6.4–6.[26] The dominant interpretation was that 6.4–6 does not deny second repentance, as Novatian had argued, but that it denies second baptism. "Repentance" means "baptism," as the explanation went, since "crucifying the Son of God" (6.6) refers to one's dying with Christ in baptism. Another interpretation mentioned by a few medievals, was that 6.4–6 denies any possibility of repentance after this life. A third interpretation, defended only by Nicholas of Lyra (d. 1349) and vehemently opposed by Luther, was that "impossibility" means "difficult," thus allowing for the possibility of second repentance. Luther's opposition was that one ought not change ("distort") the words of Scripture. A fourth interpretation, identical to Bugenhagen's, was held by Pseudo-Hugh of St. Victor, whose commentary on Hebrews was composed between 1180 and 1230 and probably known to Luther.[27] This commentary held that "those who have fallen away" refers to those who have sinned against the Holy Spirit and, therefore, have no second chance for repentance.

Erasmus in 1516, whose rendering of Heb. 6.4 *("Nam fieri non potest")* Bugenhagen followed,[28] used 6.4–6 in his general argument against Pauline authorship. Luther in 1517–18, not mentioning the authorship question, held that by referring to "those who have fallen away," "The

---

[23] Bugenhagen, f. 146^{v}–149^{r}.

[24] *Ibid.* f. 147^{r}.

[25] *Ibid.* ff. 147^{v}–148^{v}.

[26] For this, Hagen, *Luther's Lectures on Hebrews in the Light of Medieval Commentaries on Hebrew* (Harvard Dissertation, 1966), Vol. I, pp. 252–55.

[27] Hagen, *A Theology of Testament,* p. 18.

[28] Erasmus in 1521, followed the more general rendering of 6.4 as *"Impossible est".*

apostle here is speaking of those who have lapsed from faith to unfaith, that is, to the opinion that they can be saved by their own righteousness, apart from Christ. This is clearly impossible."[29] Erasmus in 1521, not raising the authorship question, followed the general medieval "rebaptism theory" about 6.4–6: it is impossible for those, who have been baptised once and for all into the death of Christ, which was once and for all, and have been raised to the new life, and who then have fallen back to the old life, to be renewed again through baptism; rather "our industry should respond to the kindness of God towards us."[30]

The "whole epistle" for Bugenhagen (on 12.17) is a warning to Jewish converts that "they not forsake the faith and the Christian life because of temporal afflictions."[31] The lament of Esau (12.17), for Bugenhagen, like Luther's rendering of 6.6, is the "repentance of a sinner," one who has lapsed from the righteousness of God, and seeks to be free from sin by way of human righteousness. There is no repentance before God for such.[32]

The Epistle to the Hebrews for Bugenhagen is a warning against backsliding, against defecting "from Christ to Moses, which is a notorious blasphemy against God." The main reason why falling from Christ to Moses is notorious blasphemy is that it is an incomparable comedown. "Christ is by far superior to Moses" and "not only to Moses but also to the angels through whom Moses received the law." Bugenhagen's qualification about Christ's superiority over the angels, namely his interpretation of Heb. 2.7 as referring to "a brief time during Christ's passion," is very similar to Luther's interpretation.[33] Christ is far superior to even Moses' superiors. Christ is so superior that the old (law, sacrifices, etc.) "by no means can be compared with the priesthood and sacrifice of Christ." They are incomparable because Christ's sacrifice was once and for all *(semel)*. The old "ceases" with the coming of Christ, and the Jewish Scriptures (Old Testament cited in Hebrews) are used to prove all this. This is strong language regarding the relation of the old and new. The position is reminiscent of Luther's. The language is extremely clear and to the point that the new is on a completely different level from the old. The contrast is so extreme that the two cannot be compared.

---

29 Luther, *WA* 57.III.182.13–15.

30 Erasmus, *Paraphrasis,* col. 1175.

31 Bugenhagen, f. 157ᵛ.

32 *Ibid.,* ff. 157ᵛ–158ʳ.

33 Hagen, *A Theology of Testament,* pp. 93–96.

Francisci Titelmans (1502–37)[34]

Explanatory Argument About the Epistle of the Blessed Apostle Paul to the Hebrews

Because of the breadth of his charity, the Apostle, not content with having written epistles to his Gentile churches, took the trouble to write this one too to those who had been converted to Christ from among the Jews, with no little depth of meaning and solidity of matter. His principal and most important point is to show how Christ Jesus, the true and highest priest, is the goal of the entire law, which contained only figures to be fulfilled in Christ. And he writes so that, by the forgiveness of sins through Christ and by the perfect unfolding of the Kingdom of heaven, they should no longer pursue carnal observances, but seek salvation by faith in Christ, and so that tribulation or persecution which they sustain for the name of Christ might not break them. Because the message is prepared according to the quality of the hearers, therefore, since he is speaking to Jews, he demonstrates many things from their own histories and ancient legal rites.

In the beginning of this epistle, therefore, the Apostle proposes this directly: how God the Father formerly spoke and appeared ordinarily to the fathers through the prophets; but in this, the fullness of time, he has spoken to us through his Son, co-eternal and co-equal in all things with the Father. He demonstrates the Son's glory, by far above the dignity of the angels, with different testimonies which mention partly the angels, ministers of God, and partly Christ, Son of God; the Son, however, is always more honorable than the angels, administering spirits.

On account of this, in the second chapter, he argues often from the pre-eminent dignity of Christ, that there are those things to be observed by us which now are preached first through Christ and then through the apostles and confirmed with signs and wonders. Lest any one, on account of the weakness of the flesh, should value little him to whom God subjects the future world and all things, he declares consequently how, according to the dispensation, he assumed the infirmity of human nature (according to which also he was seen a little lower than the angels for a while, and was made similar in all things to us his brothers) which results in great exaltation and the highest utility for us, because, on account of the suffering of his death, he was both crowned in glory and made author of salvation for all of us who believe in him. While through

---

[34] b. Hasselt (Belgium), d. Anticoli; 1526 ff. lectured on Scripture at Convent School in Louvain; combined knowledge of biblical languages with the scholastic tradition in opposition to the humanists, Erasmus, Faber Stapulensis, Valla – defended *Vulgata*. *In omnes epistolas apostolicas . . . elucidatio* (Antwerp, 1528, 1529, 1532, 1540; Paris, 1532, 1543, 1551, 1553; Lyons, 1553). I have used the Paris, 1543 ed., "Elucidatio in epistolam ad Hebraeos beati Pauli apostoli," *In omnes epistolas apostolicas Francisci Titelmanni ordinis minoritarum, publici sacrarum literarum apud Lovaniensis quondam Lectoris Elucidatio,* ff. 184^v–215^v.

death the power of death was destroyed, he was made faithful high priest for us, and because he had been tempted, became able to aid our infirmity.[35]

Following is a summary of the remainder of Titelmans' rather long "*Argumentum*": chapter three of Hebrews concerns avoiding apostasy and persevering. The Israelites died and were prohibited from the promised land because of infidelity. Chapter four, emphasizes Titelmans, also concerns incredulity and perseverance. For the Israelites to hear the law without faith was no gain, so for us the announcement of faith is no gain unless the faith works through love. The Psalmist's exhortation, "Today, if you shall hear his voice, do not harden your hearts," concerns the important time when the faithful enter celestial and sabbath rest. The ancients entered the corporeal rest of the promised land. We are admonished to hold fast to the best celestial rest and most perfect sabbath lest we, like them, be deprived through incredulity. The concern is about our celestial rest, because God is a judge discerning all things.

---

[35] Argumentum Elucidatorium in epistolam ad Hebraeos, beati Pauli Apostoli. Propter nimiam charitatis latitudinem, non contentus Apostolus suis Ecclesiis gentium diversas scripsisse epistolas, etiam hanc ad eos qui ex Iudaeis ad christum fuerant conversi, sententiarum profunditate et rerum soliditate non infimam, scribere curavit, in qua hoc tanquam caput et praecipuum quaerit declarare, quemadmodum Christus Iesus verus et summus sacerdos, finis sit universae legis, quae tantum figuras habuit veritatis in Christo adimplendae: Atque ita, ut per Christum peccatorum remissione, caelestisque regni apertione perfecta, non ultra carnalibus insistant observantiis, sed ex fide christi salutem quaerant, neque frangat eos tribulatio aut persecutio, quam pro Christi nomine sustinent. Et quoniam iuxta auditorum qualitatem sermo aptandus venit, iccirco apud Iudaeos loquens, ex ipsorum historiis et antiquis legalibus ritibus, plurima demonstrat. In ipso itaque epistolae huius exordio, mox illud proponit Apostolus, quemadmodum Deus pater olim per Prophetas patribus loqui et apparere solitus, in hac temporis plenitudine per filium nobis sit eloquutus, sibi coaeterum et per omnia coaequalem. Cuius gloriam longe super angelorum dignitatem eminere, ex testimoniis diversis demonstrat, quae partim de angelis ministris Dei partim de Christo Dei filio faciunt mentionem, semper tamen de filio honorificentiorem, quam de angelis administratoriis spiritibus. Propter quod secundo capitulo, ex Christi praecellenti dignitate, arguit multum nobis esse observanda, quae modo sunt per Christum primum, deinde et per Apostolos praedicata, signisque et prodigiis confirmata. Et ne quis propter carnis fragilitatem illum parvipendat, cui Deus futurum saeculum et omnia subiecit: consequenter declarat, quomodo secundum dispensationem, assumpta humanae naturae infirmitas (iuxta quam etiam angelis ad tempus minor visus, nobisque fratribus suis per omnia fuit assimilatus) illi ad maximam exaltationem, nobisque ad summam provenerit utilitatem: quoniam propter passionem mortis, et ipse gloria fuit coronatus, et nobis omnibus qui credimus in eum, author salutis est effectus: dum per mortem destructo mortis imperio, nobis factus est pontifex fidelis, potens in eo quod tentatus fuit, nostrae quoque infirmitati auxiliari. "Elucidatio in epistolam ad Hebraeos," (1543), ff. 184ᵛ–185ʳ.

Chapter five declares that Christ fulfilled the office of priesthood (which is to offer gifts and sacrifices for the sins of the people) for us. Christ offered prayers to the Father for us. His obedience unto death is the cause of our salvation. The apostle writes extensively about the pontificate of Christ in the following chapters starting with chapter six. Also in chapter six the good people are forewarned to have caution, the unfaithful to have fear. It is dangerous for one who once was a participant of celestial benefits through the acceptance of faith and the Holy Spirit to reject the same through apostasy. The message is to persevere in works of love to the end, according to the example of patience of the Fathers (Abraham). Chapter seven, pursuing the priesthood of Christ compares Christ with Melchisedec, as truth with figures, and shows the consummation and perfection of the priesthood of Christ. In chapter eight, the apostle praises the priesthood of Christ, which the prophets foretold would be more excellent in the fullness of time compared to the antiquated old law. In chapter nine, the priesthood of the former tabernacle, entering through the blood of a corporeal host, has a mystical referent. He compares this with the tabernacle of Christ, into which he entered with his own blood once and for all, as more excellent.

Chapter ten declares the infirmity of the old law which was not sufficient for the cleansing of sin. Certainly the holy body of the immaculate lamb, who died once and for all and was made host for us, is sufficient for us in perpetuity. The apostle exhorts the faithful to true and sincere perseverance lest they fall into damnation. In chapter eleven he first describes faith, then praises the faith of the faithful fathers. He offers examples in the following chapter. Also in chapter twelve he explicates the dignity of the new testament and the new church. In chapter thirteen, he exhorts to love, hospitality, legitimate marriage, confidence in God and obedience. End of the argument.[36]

Titelmans did not raise the authorship question, either in his "*argumentum*" or in the body of the "*elucidatio.*" The body of the "*elucidatio*" consists of rather short paraphrases of the text printed in the margin. There is an occasional comment, of 6–12 lines, often regarding the contrast of old und new (e.g., *ad* 5.12, 6.1, 7-introduction) and other themes discussed in the "*argumentum.*"

---

[36] Titelmans, ff. 185^r–187^r.

Of note first in Titelmans' *"argumentum"* is the explicit reference to Paul's strategy – the language *(sermo)* is adapted to the Jewish audience, hence the references to "their own histories and ancient legal rites." The strategic and polemical purpose of Old Testament citations in Hebrews was assumed among the medievals and only really explicitated by Chrysostom. For Chrysostom and Titelmans the purpose of the use of the Jewish Scriptures by Paul was to meet the Jews on their own ground and to show the superiority of the new over the old. Titelmans is on the side of Chrysostom and the majority of the medievals who emphasized the contrast or discontinuity between the Testaments.[37]

Dominant in Titelmans is the theme of the dignity of Christ. Often derivatives of *praecellere* (excell, distinguish) are used. The frequent medieval phrase, *"excellentia Christi,"* is used.[38] For Titelmans "the Son's glory [is] by far above the dignity of the angels." Parenthetically, regarding Heb. 2.7, Titelmans says that it was "seen" or perceived *("visus")* that Christ was "a little lower than the angels for a while." The incarnation and suffering of Christ's death are cast in terms of his "distinguished dignity," "great exaltation" and "highest utility for us." The suffering led to being "crowned in glory."

Also dominant in Titelmans is the warning to avoid apostasy and to persevere in the faith. To fall into incredulity is to be like those (early) Israelites who died not seeing the promised land because of unfaithfulness. Perseverance in the Old Testament was inferior to the New Testament. Those Israelites who made the promised land entered only "the corporeal rest." "We are admonished to hold fast to the best celestial rest." God is judge. Persevere to the end. Good people are forewarned.

The superiority theme permeates the theme of perseverance as it does in Titelmans' explanation on the priesthood of Christ – its excellence and perfection. Christ persevered in his priesthood to the end. Even the prophets foretold that his priesthood would be more excellent than the old. The old law was weak and insufficient. The immaculate lamb "is sufficient for us in perpetuity." The dignity of the new testament is based on the perfect priest who is the author of salvation. "Hold fast" to it.

---

[37] Hagen, *A Theology of Testament*, p. 54.

[38] Titelmans, f. 189^r.

Cajetan (Tommaso de Vio; 1469–1534)[39]

There are two prefatory items about this Epistle to the Hebrews: 1. whether this epistle was written in the Hebrew language, as is commonly supposed, and 2. whether it is certain that Paul is the author of this epistle. As to the first question the text itself, in chapter seven, gives evidence that it was not written in Hebrew. For there it speaks about Melchisedec. It is first interpreted to mean "king of justice." If the epistle were written in Hebrew, in what language, I ask, is Melchisedec interpreted as "king of justice"? For Melchisedec in Hebrew is a compound word from "king" and "justice." Thus in Hebrew he would have had to say, Melchisedec means Melchisedec. And all the more because in Hebrew *Melchi* and *Sedec* are written separately. Because this reason convinces me (as it is also convincing about Matthew), I believe, therefore, without a doubt that this epistle was not written in the Hebrew language. A sign of this is that neither is the Hebrew epistle extant nor is its translator from Hebrew to Greek known for certain.

Concerning the author of this epistle, it is certainly a common custom for the church and the theologians to name Paul as author. Jerome, however, in his *Epistola ad Paulinum de omnibus divinae historiae libris,* does not dare to affirm that this epistle is Paul's, for he says, "The apostle Paul wrote to seven churches, the eighth to the Hebrews, is placed by many outside that number." Thus Jerome affirms that there are only seven epistles to churches. And in his *Epistola ad Evagrium de Melchisedec* he explains who these many are by whom it is not accepted, saying concerning this Epistle to the Hebrews, "which all of the Greeks receive and some of the Latins." Concerning this he says *(In lib. de viris illust.)*, "The epistle which is called to the Hebrews is not believed to be his," namely Paul's, "because of the difference of style and language, but Barnabas', according to Tertullian, or Luke the Evangelist's, according to some, or Clement's, bishop of the church of Rome," etc. Regarding Jeremiah chapter 31 (commenting on, "Behold the days are coming and I will place a new covenant"), Jerome says, "with this testimony the apostle Paul, or whoever else wrote the Epistle uses [the name] to the Hebrews." Again *(In libro de viris illust. in Caio)* concerning this epistle he says, "but also among the Romans up to today it is not regarded as Paul's." Commenting on Is. 6 ("The Seraphim stood"), Jerome says, "Thus also the apostle Paul in the Epistle to the Hebrews, which the Latin custom does not receive," etc. Again, commenting on Is. 8 ("I and my sons," etc.), Jerome says, "Again the blessed apostle in the epistle

---

[39] *Epistolae Pauli, et aliorum apostolorum ad Graecam veritatem castigatae, et per. . . Thomam de Vio. . . juxta sensum literalem enarratae* (Paris, 1532, 1537, 1540, 1542). I have used, "In epistolam ad Hebraeos commentarii," *Opera Omnia* 5 Vols. (Lyons: Prost, 1639), V. 329–61. The end of the *ad Hebraeos* is dated 1 June 1529, after which, reflecting Cajetan's serious doubts about the Pauline authorship of Hebrews – even though it is classified under the commentaries of Paul, it reads, "The end of the commentaries of Thomas de Vio . . . on all the genuine epistles of Paul and that which was written to the Hebrews." Cajetan used the Greek text of Erasmus, feeling the *Vulgata* was insufficient.

written to the Hebrews (although the Latin custom does not receive it among the canonical Scriptures) teaches," etc.

I have cited all these [references], so that from these and other words of Jerome a prudent reader will observe that Jerome was not at all certain about the author of this epistle. And because we have chosen Jerome's rule lest we err in the discernment of canonical books (for we hold as canonical those he handed down as canonical, and we hold as extra canonical those he separated from the canonical books) and with doubt existing with Jerome about the author of this epistle, the epistle itself is rendered doubtful, for it is not clear that it is canonical if it is not Paul's. And therefore if any doubt occurs in matters of faith, it cannot be resolved on the sole authority of this epistle. Behold how much harm a book without the title of the author causes.

There are two places in this epistle which evoke some conjecture that this epistle is not Paul's. The first is in the beginning of the epistle [1.5] where, to prove that Christ is superior to the angels, it says, "To what angel did God ever say, 'Thou art my son, today I have begotten thee'?" It adds, "Or again, 'I will be to him a father, and he shall be to me a son'?" These words of 2 Kings (2 Sam.) 7 and 1 Par. (1 Chron.) 28 are written literally [*ad literam*] with reference to Solomon. Thus he [the Lord] says explicitly to David, " 'Solomon your son will build my house and my court, I have chosen him to be my son and I will be to him a father' ", etc. [I Par. 28.6] And in 2 Kings (2 Sam.) it is added [to v. 14 of c. 7], " 'if he commits iniquity, I will chasten him with the rod of men,' " etc. It would be very unsuitable in such a thing for the apostle to use such an argument, since the Hebrews could easily respond to him that these words were said by God through Nathan to David, not with reference to the Son of God, but with reference to a plain man, who both was able to sin and in fact did sin later. Thus from such sonship, superiority over the angels is not proven. Use of these words in a mystical sense lessens the authority of the one offering the proof, especially in the beginning of the epistle, and among Hebrews.

The second place is in chapter nine where "testament" is most properly spoken of in contradistinction to "covenant." A covenant is between the living while a testament is only validated with the death of the testator. And thus speaking about a testament properly made, it says, "For where there is a testament, the death of the testator must intervene, for a testament is valid only when men are dead, otherwise it has as yet no force as long as the testator is alive" [9.16–17]. And he adds, "Hence, not even the first was inaugurated without blood; for when every commandment of the law had been read by Moses to all the people, he took the blood of the calves and of the goats, with water and scarlet wool and hyssop, and sprinkled both the book itself and all the people, saying, 'This is the blood of the testament which God has commanded for you' " [9.18–20]. This is taken from Ex 24 [.6–8], where there is no word about "testament" but about "covenant." Thus one can respond to the author of this epistle that he changes from "testament" properly so called to "covenant," or that he errs in thinking that in Exodus there is talk of "testament." Each is highly unbecoming to the apostle, especially [writing] to the Hebrews who know the peculiar quality of the words of the Hebrew text.

But for what purpose do I engage in conjectures? In the second chapter of this epistle, its author includes himself among those to whom evangelical salvation was confirmed through those who heard from the Lord Jesus. Paul, however, declares that he learned neither from men nor through men, but through a revelation of Jesus Christ, and that the apostles conveyed nothing to him. We, however, like others in commenting will use the name of Paul as author; for this is also what Jerome did when writing about this epistle.[40]

---

[40] Multifariam. Circa hanc Epistolam ad Hebraeos, duo occurunt praetractanda. Alterum, an haec Epistola fuerit condita Hebraico sermone: ut communiter supponitur: alterum an certum sit Paulum fuisse authorem huius Epistolae. Et quoad primam quaestionem, textus ipse cap. 7, testatur non esse conditam Hebraice. Nam ibidem de Melchisedec dicitur: Primum quidem interpretatur rex iustitiae. Si Hebraice scripta est epistola, in quo, quaeso, idiomate interpretatur Melchisedec rex iustitiae? Melchisedec enim apud Hebraeos dictio composita est, ex rex et iustitiae. Unde in Hebraeo debuisset dicere, Melchidec [*sic*] interpretatur Melchisedec. Et tanto magis quanto scribitur apud Hebraeos divisim: primo "Melchi" et deinde "Sedec." Et quoniam haec ratio me convincit (sicut convincit et de Matthaeo) ideo hanc epistolam non esse conditam Hebraico idiomate indubie credo. In cuius signum nec Hebraea invenitur epistola, nec scitur certus eius interpres ex Hebraeo in Graecum.

De authore vero huius epistolae, certum est communem usum Ecclesiae et doctorum nominare Paulum. Hieronymus tamen in epistola ad Paulinum de omnibus divinae historiae libris, non audet affirmare illam esse Pauli ait enim: "Paulus Apostolus ad septem scribit Ecclesias, octava enim ad Hebraeos, a plerisque extra numerum ponitur." [*Epist. ad. Paulinum* 8, *PL* 22.548]. Septem itaque tantum affirmat Hieronymus epistolas ad Ecclesias. Et in Epistola ad Evagrium de Melchisedec, explicat qui sunt isti plerique a quibus non acceptatur: dicendo de hac epistola ad Hebraeos: "Quam omnes Graeci recipiunt et nonnulli Latinorum." [Epist. ad Evang. 4, *PL* 22.678]. De qua in lib. de viris illust. dicit: "Epistola autem quae fertur ad Hebraeos, non eius" (scilicet Pauli) "creditur propter styli sermonisque distantiam: sed vel Barnabae iuxta Tertullianum, vel Lucae Evangelistae iuxta quosdam, vel Clementis Romanae Ecclesiae episcopi," etc. [*De Vir. illust.* 5, *PL* 23.647–50]. Super Hieremiae autem 31. cap. (tractando illud: "Ecce dies venient et feriam pactum novum") ait: "Hoc testimonio Apostolus Paulus, sive quisquis alius scripsit Epistolam, usus est ad Hebraeos." [*Commentar. in Jer.* XXXI. 31, *PL* 24.918]. Rursus in libro de viris illust. in Caio, de hac epistola loquens dicit: "Sed et apud Romanos usque hodie quasi Pauli non habetur." [*De Vir. illust. in Gaio* 59, *PL* 23.706]. Et Esa. 6. exponens textum, "Seraphim stabant," ait: "Unde et Paulus Apostolus in Epistola ad Hebraeos, quam Latina consuetudo non recipit," etc. [*Commentar. in Is.* VI. 2, *PL* 24.96]. Item Esa. 8. exponens textum, "Ego et pueri mei," etc. "Ceterum, inquit beatus Apostolus in epistola quae ad Hebraeos scribitur (licet eam Latina consuetudo inter Canonicas scripturas non recipiat) docet," etc. [*Commentar. in Is.* VIII. 18, *PL* 24.124].

Quae omnia ideo attulerim, ut ex his et aliis Hieronymi verbis alibi prudens lector advertat Hieronymum non fuisse omnino certum de authore huius epistolae. Et quoniam Hieronymum sortiti sumus regulam ne erremus in discretione librorum canonicorum (nam quos ille canonicos tradidit, canonicos habemus: et quos ille a canonicis discrevit, extra canonem habemus) ideo dubio apud Hieronymum authore huius Epistolae existente, dubia quoque redditur epistola: quoniam nisi sit Pauli, non perspicuum est canonicam esse. Quo fit ut ex sola huius Epistolae authoritate non possit, si quod dubium in fide accideret, determinari. Ecce quantum parit malum liber sine authoris titulo.

Coniecturam quoque nonnullam efficiunt duo in hac epistola contenta, quod non sit Pauli. Alterum est in principio Epistolae: ubi ad probandum Christum esse superiorem

There are several different and unique aspects to Cajetan's discussion about the language the epistle was written in and the authorship question. At the outset Cajetan's argument about the language (regarding Melchisedec) is unique among medieval exegetes and Faber, Luther, Erasmus (1516 and 1521) and Bugenhagen. Following the *Glossa ordinaria* the medievals, without any argumentation, held that Hebrews was written in Hebrew which accounted for the different linguistic style of the epistle. Faber Stapulensis (1512) held that the salutation problem developed in the translation from Hebrew to Greek – the translator either worked from a defective copy or omitted the salutation.[41] Luther and Bugenhagen did not raise the language question. Cajetan raised the question (about a Hebrew original), came up with a different answer (negative) and used a unique argument (about Melchisedec). The argument is that it makes no sense to say, in Hebrew or any language, "king

---

Angelis, cum dixisset: "Cui aliquando dixit Angelorum, filius meus es tu, ego hodie genui te:" addidit, "et rursus: Ego ero illi in patrem, et ipse erit mihi in filium." Quae verba scripta sunt 2 Reg. 7. et 1. Paralip. 28. ad literam de Salomone. Unde Davidi dicit expresse, "Salomon filius tuus aedificabit domum meam et atria mea: ipsum enim elegi mihi in filium, et ego ero illi in patrem," etc. Et in 2 Reg. subiungitur: "Quod si inique aliquid gesserit, arguam eum in virga virorum," etc. Minus siquidem decet in tanta re tantum Apostolum uti tali argumento: cum potuissent Hebraei facile respondere quod non de filio Dei, sed puro homine, et qui potuit peccare, et de facto postea peccavit, dicta sunt haec verba a Deo per Nathan ad Davidem. Unde ex tali filiatione non probatur superioritas ad Angelos. Uti autem his verbis in sensu mystico, minorem reddit authoritatem probantis: in principio praesertim Epistolae et apud Hebraeos.

Alterum est in cap. 9. ubi de testamento propriisime loquitur ut distinguitur contra pactum: nam pactum est inter vivos, testamentum autem nisi mors intercedat testatoris, nondum valet. Et de testamento sic proprie sumpto loquens, dicit: "ubi enim testamentum est, mors necesse est intercedat testatoris: testamentum enim in mortuis confirmatum est: alioquin nondum valet dum vivit qui testatus est." Et subiungit: "unde nec primum quidem sine sanguine dedicatum est: lecto enim omni mandato legis a Moyse universo populo, accipiens sanguinem vitulorum et hircorum cum aqua et lana coccinea et hysopo, ipsum quoque librum et omnem populum aspersit, dicens: Hic sanguis testamenti quod mandavit ad vos Deus." Ex Exo. 24. haec afferuntur: ubi non est sermo de testamento sed de pacto. Unde responderi potest authori huius epistolae quod de testamento proprie sumpto, migrat ad ad [*sic*] pactum: aut quod errat, putando in Exodo esse sermonem de testamento. Quorum utrumque dedecet tantum Apostolum: ad Hebraeos praesertim, verborum textus Hebraici proprietatem scientes.

Sed quid per coniecturas vagor? In secundo huius Epistolae capitulo author huius Epistolae numerat se inter illos, in quos Evangelica salus confirmata est per illos, qui audierunt a Domino Jesu. Paulus autem clamat quod non ab homine, neque per hominem didicit: sed per revelationem Jesu Christi: et quod Apostoli nihil sibi contulerunt, etc. Nos tamen loquentes ut plures, Paulum authorem nominabimus: nam et sic quoque Hieronymus fecit, utendo scriptis in hac Epistola. "In epistolam ad Hebraeos commentarii," pp. 329–30.

[41] Hagen, *A Theology of Testament*, pp. 21–33.

of justice" means "king of justice," which is in effect what the epistle would read if it were written in Hebrew. In his preface and in his commentary on 7.2, Cajetan reasoned that the translation of Melchisedec (Hebrew compound) into "king of justice" was due to the fact that the epistle was written in Greek, and Melchisedec was not a proper name of a king but a general Hebrew term for king like the terms Caesar (Roman) and Pharoh (Egyptian).[42] Obviously (for Cajetan only) the Hebrews would know their own word for king. And, without saying so, Cajetan has pulled the rug out from under a major argument for Pauline authorship, and he did so not from "conjecture" but from "the text itself."

In the body of his commentary Cajetan makes the connection between language and authorship. In Heb. 8.10, 9.18, 20, citing the Old Testament, the author uses testament *(testamentum)* rather than covenant *(pactum)*, which means he was following the LXX rather than the Hebrew. "On this account (as we have said before) not a small argument is made, both that this epistle was written in Greek and that Paul never saw it."[43]

Cajetan begins his authorship discussion by observing that it is a "common custom" in the church to use the name of Paul for the author of Hebrews. Then Cajetan develops some arguments of his own against Pauline authorship. But he concludes his prefatory discussion by saying that he will follow the "common custom" of using "the name of Paul as author," which he does except in those places where the authorship question is raised. The reason given for following the common custom is, "that is what Jerome did."

The first argument against Pauline authorship is the uncertainty expressed by St. Jerome, who reflected the uncertainty of the (early) "Latin custom." Although Erasmus (1516 and 1517) pointed to and cited the uncertainty of Jerome and others, only Cajetan provided so many quotations from Jerome. The conclusion of this argument is uncertainty and "doubt" about Paul as author. The epistle itself also occasions doubt about Pauline authorship (1.5, 9.16–20 as well as 2.3).

Cajetan is unique in being the first to comment on 1.5 in terms of a problem for Pauline authorship, and this is because his interpretation is different. The interpretations of earlier 16th century exegetes and Lyra provide some historical context for understanding Cajetan's prefatory

---

[42] Cajetan, p. 342.

[43] *Ibid.*, pp. 348 (on 9.20), 346 (on 8.10).

remarks. Luther first conjectured about 1.5 ("I will be to him a father, and he shall be to me a son"), "We do not want to reject out of hand that this text can be interpreted literally to refer both to Solomon and to Christ at the same time."[44] Is this Lyra's (supposed) double literal interpretation? No. For Lyra the Old Testament text refers literally to Christ.[45] It is the same for Luther: "Nevertheless, it can be amply established that it is both said and understood to refer to Christ alone."[46] Erasmus (1521; he did not comment on it in 1516) said that 1.5, 6, 7 are to be interpreted "mystically." In the Psalm, (Heb. 1.5), it is said "mystically" of Christ.[47] Bugenhagen[48] refers to Luther's *Postilla* (1522, on 1.1–12), where again for Luther, Heb. 1.5 (as well as 2 Sam 7.14) refers to Christ alone, otherwise Scripture would not have one, simple sense.[49] For Titelmans the text is the "voice of the Father to Christ."[50] For Lyra, Luther, Bugenhagen, and Titelmans the text itself refers to Christ, for Erasmus the text mystically interpreted refers to Christ.

For Cajetan, in his Preface, in contrast to these (and others), the text literally refers to Solomon *(ad literam de Salomone)*.[51] This is clear from the text cited in Heb. 1.5, and from the addition in 2. Sam. 7.14, not cited in Hebrews. The fuller Old Testament text shows that the "son" could sin "and in fact did sin later." Since especially the Hebrews would know all this, Heb. 1.5 is very unpauline. In his commentary on 1.5 Cajetan repeats that the Old Testament texts were said literally about Solomon, as David himself witnesses and the fuller text convinces: "the author of this epistle appropriates this authority [text] in a mystical sense for his own argument, so that he shows the argument not only from a literal sense but also from a mystical sense."[52] A mystical interpretation, especially so early in the epistle, carries little weight. Since 1.5 raises the authorship question Cajetan said, "author of this epistle," rather than "Paul."

Heb. 9.16–20 also raises questions about Pauline authorship because, referring to the Old Testament where the equivalent of "covenant" is used, it uses the word "testament." Since the Hebrews especially knew

---

[44] Luther, *WA* 57.III.103.10–11.

[45] Lyra, "Postilla . . . super epistolam ad Hebraeos," f. 134v.

[46] Luther, *WA* 57.III.103.13–14.

[47] Erasmus, pp. 1166–67.

[48] Bugenhagen, f. 140v.

[49] Luther, *WA* 10.I.1.168–71.

[50] Titelmans, f. 188r.

[51] Cajetan, p. 330.

[52] *Ibid.*, p. 332.

the "peculiar quality" of covenant, this is very unpauline. Faber (1512), noting the different words, held that covenant, pact and testament were often used in sacred declarations for the same thing, but here (9.16 ff) the word testament was more appropriate.[53] Erasmus held that 9.17 shows that whoever wrote the epistle did not know Hebrew since the Hebrew behind this text is the word for covenant or pact. The author was following the Septuagint. Cajetan's reasoning was similar to Erasmus'.

At the end of his Preface, Cajetan simply and strongly states that apart from whatever "conjectures" he has engaged in, Heb. 2.3 conflicts with Paul's claim in Gal. 1.[54] On balance, Cajetan, to date, raised more questions, cited more references and gave more (and different) textual analyses, all about and against Pauline authorship.

Heinrich Bullinger (1504–75)[55]

The Argument of the Epistle[56]

There are three things which are treated in this epistle. In the first place, he advises the Jews not to reject Christ and despise the import of the gospel through disbelief, since he is more powerful than the angels and greater than Moses, even Lord of angels and God the creator. For his human nature, which he derives from the race of Abraham, adds nothing to his majesty. Let them consider, moreover, the poor example of their ancestors, whose murmuring, faithlessness and disbelief was strongly punished in the desert. Hence it would be fitting that things would go very badly with them, if they should continue to contemn the Word himself and the Son of God himself. These things are treated

---

[53] Faber, ". . .in epistolam ad Hebraeos," f. 249ʳ.

[54] Cf. also Cajetan's commentary on 2.3–4 (p. 333).

[55] *In piam et eruditam Pauli ad Hebreaeos epistolam, Heinrychi Bullingeri commentarius.* Zürich: Christoph Froschouer, 1532. Staedtke #38. Then it was printed in *In Omnes apostolicas epistolas . . . commentarii* (Zürich: Christoph Froschouer, 1537, 1539, 1544, 1549, 1558; Staedtke #84–88). The 1582 printing I have used, and compared with the 1532 printing. The title distinguishes between the epistle to the Hebrews and the epistles of Paul, however, the title of the commentary on Hebrews, dated 17 August 1532, Zürich, reflects Bullinger's position on Pauline authorship: "In piam et eruditam Pauli ad Hebraeos epistolam Heinrychi Bullingeri," *Commentarii in omnes Pauli apostoli epistolas, atque etiam in epistolam ad Hebraeos* (Zürich: Christoph Froschouer, 1582; Staedtke #89), pp. 490–562. Joachim Staedtke, *Beschreibendes Verzeichnis der gedruckten Werke von Heinrich Bullinger* ("Heinrich Bullinger Bibliographie," Vol. I; Zürich: Theologischer Verlag, 1972).

[56] The "*Argumentum*" will be translated first. It is preceded by a lengthy discussion of authorship, which we will paraphrase and interpret after the "*Argumentum.*" The "*Argumentum*" helps clarify Bullinger's discussion of authorship.

throughout the whole first four chapters. Certainly he speaks against those who rejecting Christ make the following objections: we are disciples of Moses, to whom God has spoken through the angels; but this Jesus, whence he is and who he is, we do not know; and so we continue in the ways of our fathers. By these objections they turn aside both the weak (and primarily those converted to Christ from Judaism) and the unlettered from evangelical truth. With this letter Paul attempts to strengthen them and retain these in true religion and discipline.

Then he places before their eyes by way of example, that the Aaronic priesthood was completely a shadow, but that Christ is the true priest, created by God by an oath, and not ordained according to the order of Aaron but according to the order of Melchisedec, greater and better than the Levites, seeing that his priesthood is unchangeable and eternal. And so the shadows are antiquated, both the priesthood and the sacrifice. For the sacrifices of the ancients, no less than the priesthood, were ineffectual and types of Christ, who is the true, unique and eternal victim for the sins of the whole world. These things he treats most learnedly and at the same time most copiously through the early part of chapter 5 (for at the end of 5 and through the whole of chapter 6 he digresses) and again through the whole of chapters 7, 8, 9, to the middle of 10. Clearly [he writes] against those who depend on ceremonies, priesthood and sacrifices who were claiming that by the Christian religion all divine cult is destroyed, together with all antiquities and the glory of the race. To these, therefore, he points out distinctly that in Christ there is every fullness and perfection of the law, so that he who possesses Christ through faith, possesses the glory of God, the priesthood and the victim most absolutely.

Finally, using the spur, he urges them to have confidence in Christ's unique priesthood and perpetual victimhood. For it is that faith of all the just men, from the beginning of the world, which is true religion, by which they might serve God and in which they might persevere in much patience. Patience then is also a work here as well as perseverance, to which he exhorts them with many examples, judgments and the like. For those who had left Moses for Christ were considerably tormented. At the end of the epistle, namely through all of chapter 13, by way of an appendix, he adds certain brief aphorisms, sayings, and principles. This indeed is the argument of the whole epistle.

The style indeed is pure, serious, clear, plain and proper. But the literary form is mixed. For the middle part of the epistle belongs to the didactic form. For the apostle teaches with demonstrative arguments that the old shadows, namely the priesthood and sacrifice, were entirely abolished, and that Christ indeed is the true priest and eternal victim. But the beginning and the end of the epistle belong to the deliberative form. In both parts he exhorts, in the former not to reject Christ, in the latter so that they believe in Christ and persist in truth through patience.[57]

Argumentum epistolae

[57] Tria sunt quae tractantur hac epistola. Principio enim monet ne reiiciant Christum Iudaei, neque aspernentur evangelii negotium per incredulitatem: quando quidem angelis potentior sit, et Mose maior, angelorum etiam dominus, et deus conditor: nihil interim elevante eius maiestatem humana natura, quam sibi ex Abrahae traxerit prosapia. Con-

Bullinger's description of the contents of the epistle is rather standard: 1) rigorous warning about rejecting Christ, 2) teaching that Christ is the perfection of the law, 3) admonition to persevere in the faith. What is different about Bullinger's *"Argumentum"* is the tripartite breakdown of the epistle and the discussion about the form of the language in these parts. The usual medieval approach to a summary was by chapter. Erasmus (1521) at the beginning of each chapter gave a one sentence paraphrase. Bullinger's literary division has parts one and three (basically chapters 1–4 and 10.19 ff) characterized as *"Deliberativum,"* a determined admonition to the Jews 1) not to reject Christ, and 3) to hold

---

siderent autem miserum maiorum suorum exemplum, quorum murmur, perfidia et incredulitas misere sit mulctata in deserto: unde consentaneum sit ipsos pessime nunc quoque habituros, si ipsum verbum, ipsumque dei filium perrexerint contemnere. Et haec agit per integra prima quatuor capita. Nimirum adversum eos perorans, qui Christum aspernantes objiciebant, Nos Mosi discipuli sumus, cui per angelos loquutus est deus, hunc vero Iesum unde sit aut quis sit nescimus, pergemus ergo in viis patrum nostrorum. Quo simul et infirmos, primumque Christo ex Iudaismo initiatos et rudes, a veritate avertebant evangelica: quos interim Paulus istis suis et firmare et in vera religione officioque retinere contendit.

Deinde vero velut hypotyposi quadam ob oculos ponit, sacerdotium Aharonicum prorsus fuisse umbram, Christum autem verum esse sacerdotem, ab ipso deo iureiurando creatum, neque secundum ordinem Aharon, sed secundum ordinem Melchizedeck ordinatum, Levitis maiorem et meliorem: utpote cuius sacerdotium sit et ἀπαράβατον et sempiternum. Antiquatas igitur esse umbras, cum sacerdotii tum sacrificii. Quippe cum veterum sacrificia, non minus quam sacerdotium, fuerint inefficacia et typi Christi, qui sit vera hostia unica et sempiterna pro peccatis totius mundi. Haec autem doctissime simul et copiosissime tractat per initium capitis quinti, (nam in fine, et per integrum caput sextum digreditur) item per integrum caput. 7. 8. 9. et decimi mediam partem. Plane adversus eos qui nitebantur ceremoniis, sacerdotio et sacrificiis: qui clamitabant Christiana religione omnem semel tolli divinum cultum, omnem vetustatem et gentis gloriam. His igitur commonstrat, in Christo omnem esse plenitudinem et legis perfectionem, ut qui Christum per fidem possideat, is dei gloriam, et sacerdotem et hostiam absolutissime possideat.

Postremo adhibitis calcaribus urget eos ad fidendum Christo sacerdoti unico et hostiae perpetuae. Esse enim fidem illam omnium ab exordio mundi iustorum veterum, veram religionem, qua illi deo servierint, et in qua multa perstiterint patientia. Patientia ergo hic quoque opus esse et constantia: adquam deinde multis hortatur exemplis, iudiciis, similibus. Nam mire torquebantur qui a Mose desciverant ad Christum.

Ad finem autem epistolae, per integrum videlicet cap. 13. appendicis loco, subdit breves quosdam velutis Aphorismos, sententias et institutiones. Hoc vero totius epistolae argumentum est. Dictio vero pura est, gravis, dilucida, evidens et propria. Genus autem orationis mixtum est. Nam epistolae meditum, genus agnoscit didacticum. Docet enim Apostolus veluti demonstrativa contentione, veterum umbras, quoad sacerdotium et sacrificium, prorsus abolitas, Christum vero esse verum sacerdotem et aeternam hostiam. At initium epistolae et finis, sub genus referunter Deliberativum. Nam utraque parte hortatur, illic ne Christum reiiciant, hic autem ut Christo fidant, et per patientiam in veritate persistant. "In piam et eruditam Pauli ad Hebraeos epistolam" (1582), p. 495.

on to him, because 2) teaches *("didacticum")* that Christ is the true priest, *maior et melior,* and his priesthood is eternal. These themes are not unlike the emphases of Bugenhagen and Titelmans. In his preface Bullinger claims that in this commentary on Hebrews all the main elements of "our religion" are clearly presented and that he teaches sound orthodoxy.[58]

Bullinger's rather lengthy discussion about authorship is structured in terms of responses to four (traditional) arguments against Pauline authorship. He begins by saying that, "Those who take this epistle away from Paul seem to depend on these" arguments: 1) Novatian heresy is found in c. 6, 2) for a long time it was not received by the Latins, 3) the name of Paul is lacking after the beginning; the style is unpauline, 4) c. 2 says the author learned the gospel from the apostles which is contrary to Galatians.

Bullinger's response to the first argument is that the apostle (Paul) does nothing in c. 6 to aid the Novatians, as he will show in his commentary on c. 6.[59] In his comments on 6.4–6 he says that Paul does not there nor anywhere else deny penance to the lapsed, in fact, the opposite is affirmed in Hebrews. The emphasis of Hebrews is that Christ, in his unique offering, takes away all sins, not just some sins once – Christ is our intercessor, we come to him in time of need, and so on. In 6.4–6 (the digression from the didactic to the deliberative, mentioned in the *"Argumentum"*) Paul is vigorously warning the Hebrews to avoid inconstancy and laziness.[60] This is similar to Titelmans' summary of c. 6.

Bullinger's response to the second argument that the Latins did not accept Hebrews (into the canon) for a long time is along traditional lines. He cites the fact that it was always accepted by the Greeks. He cites references from Clement, Origen, Eusebius and Jerome in favor of Pauline authorship. He uses an argument that is used often in the 16th century: the Greeks did not receive the Apocalypse with the same liberty as they received Hebrews, "and yet we receive both." The conclusion of all this is that it is clear that the ancients regarded this epistle as Paul's.[61]

The response to the lack of Pauline superscription (third argument) is very traditional: Paul did not want to offend the Jews with his name at

---

58 *Ibid.*, pp. 490–91.

59 *Ibid.*, pp. 492–93.

60 *Ibid.*, p. 522.

61 *Ibid.*, 493–94.

the beginning. The response to the difference of style begins with a review of the traditional position that it was written first in Hebrew, but then a different twist to the argument is given. Paul used different secretaries ("I do not know if Paul wrote any one or other epistle himself"), who colored the eloquence or character of the language. There is no single style for all of Paul's epistles ("Certainly the style of Ephesians is very different from the other epistles of Paul"). Thus Hebrews, while it differs "from the style of Paul" [sic], strongly agrees with the spirit and heart of Paul.

The key to c. 2, and the (fourth) argument *vis-à-vis* Gal. 1, is the order: the gospel was first preached by the Lord, then by the apostles and then it was brought to Paul. Whereas most previous exegetes had argued against such a three step order, Bullinger argues that c. 2 presents the same order as I Cor. 15: 1) Peter, 2) the 12, 3) the 500, 4) "to me." "Unto us" (Heb. 2.3) can refer not only to Paul but to the person of the whole church.[62]

Bullinger's conclusion mentions the references in the later chapters of Hebrews to persecution and prison and to Timothy. Really, the value and status of the epistle is confirmed by Scripture and by itself. "Christ is more purely and better taught here than elsewhere; . . . the genius of the epistle will prove itself; . . . nothing more worthily conforms to Paul."[63]

Johannes Oecolampadius (1482–1531)[64]

The Preface of Johannes Oecolampadius concerning the Inscription and Authority of the Epistle to the Hebrews

While some, both ancient and more recent, objecting to this inscription, deny that Paul is the author of this epistle, its authority, however, seeing it is worthy

---

[62] *Ibid.*, 494. [63] *Ibid.*, pp. 494–95.

[64] *In epistolam ad Hebraeos, Ioannis Oecolampadii, explanationes, ut ex ore praelegentis exceptae, per quosdam ex auditoribus digestae sunt.* Strasbourg: Matthias Apiarius, 1534. Staehelin # 175: *Oekolampad Bibliographie*, 2nd ed. (Basel, 1918; Nieuwkoop: Graaf, 1963). It appears to Staehelin that Oecolampadius lectured on Hebrews between early 1529 and the Fall of 1530. The lectures were printed in 1534: Oecolampadius dictated the commentary up to and including Heb. 2.5; the remaining "very reliable" text was prepared, from notes of both the Latin and German parts of the lectures, by Johann Gast and Konrad Hubert (Ernst Staehelin, *Das theologische Lebenswerk Johannes Oekolampads* ["Quellen und Forschungen zur Reformationsgeschichte," Vol. 21; Leipzig, 1939; New York: Johnson Reprint, 1971], pp. 571–74.

of Paul's spirit, has remained and will remain secure. It is considered to have been received more slowly among the Latins than among the Greeks. We acknowledge that it is properly Paul's. Therefore, we do not want to fight with anyone about who put it into Greek, and when, whether it was Luke, or Barnabas, or Clement. It is certainly acknowledged that it was first written in Hebrew. Therefore it will not be permissible for us to deny that it is Paul's, that it was written in Greek by another. Otherwise we will deny that the gospel of Matthew is Matthew's who wrote in Hebrew beyond question, and it is not known who his translator was. The arguments by which certain Latins shy away from this seem too frivolous to detain such distinguished men. Their opinion takes its origin from the fact that a certain Gaius of Rome, a most distinguished man, while arguing with a Cataphrygian [Montanist], who was publishing certain new Scriptures, asserted among other things that there are thirteen epistles of the apostle Paul, not mentioning that which was written to the Hebrews. Thus Eusebius, bk. 6, c. 16 [cf. cc. 20, 25], said that among the Latins it is not thought to be the apostle Paul's, while others, enumerating the canonical books of the New Testament, count fourteen epistles of Paul, and Hebrews among them. It is possible moreover that Gaius did not outright deny that it is Paul's, but since it came to the Greeks by way of translation, he thought it to be someone else's. If anyone consults the most ancient Latins about this, he will find that Clement is more ancient that Gaius, and that Irenaeus mentions this epistle. They [Clement and Irenaeus] flourished among the Latins, although they wrote in Greek. Who is more ancient of the writers than Clement, who was the third pontiff of Rome after Peter? In his Epistle to the Corinthians, he mentions the epistle of Paul to the Hebrews and uses its witness. Concerning this see Eusebius bk. 3, c. 38, who adds that the apostle, since he is writing to the Hebrews, wrote it in his ancestral language, and (as some say) Luke the Evangelist or (for others) Clement translated it; Eusebius prefers the latter, because both the style of Clement's epistle is in accordance with Hebrews and there is much similarity in the thought of both writings.

Another, Clement of Alexandria, asserts concerning this epistle that it is clearly the apostle Paul's written, however, in the Hebrew tongue for Hebrews, and translated into Greek by Luke, who was a disciple of Paul. Whence, also style seems similar to that little book which Luke wrote about the Acts of the Apostles. See Eusebius bk. 6, c. 11 [14].

Let us destroy certain weak conjectures which some have held in order to deny that Hebrews is Paul's. There are those who are offended that the usual salutation, "Paul, the Apostle," does not come first, as in the other epistles. Clement of Alexandria responds to this in these words: "The reason there is no usual superscription, namely Paul, the Apostle, is this, that the name of Paul would have prejudiced the Hebrews not to accept his words, and so he prudently avoided it, lest right from the beginning, seeing the name of Paul, they would not have read it. As the blessed presbyter says, because the Lord, the apostle of the Almighty, was sent, it is said, to the Hebrews, Paul, out of humility, since he had been sent to the Gentiles, did not inscribe himself as an apostle of the Hebrews, either because of honor due the Lord, who was sent to the sheep of Israel, or else because he was seen as an apostle of the Gentiles." [Eus. bk. 6, c. 14.]

Origen refutes another conjecture which has it that this epistle is too eloquent to be considered Paul's. The same Eusebius, bk. 6 c. 18 [25], cites these words of Origen: "But he who was made worthy to become a minister of the new testament, not of the letter but of the spirit, Paul I say, who fully preached the gospel from Jerusalem and all the way to Illyricum, did not write to all the churches he taught, but only 14 epistles and some very brief. There are some who have doubts about that which was written to the Hebrews – because Paul's assertion about himself, namely that his language is unskilled, does not seem to hold true. But I say, as it has been handed down to me by the men of old, it is clearly Paul's and all our most ancient men of old have always received it as Paul's. If you ask me who wrote the epistle, in truth God knows. Yet I say that the account which has reached us is this: by some it is said that Clement, disciple of the apostles and bishop of Rome, put it in the Greek language; he did not embellish the meaning, however; others, that it was Luke, who wrote the Gospel and the Acts of the Apostles."

Jerome indicates that certain writers have rejected this epistle, because, contrary to the practice of Paul, texts are cited not according to the Hebrew original but according to the LXX. See Jerome on Isaiah c. 6 [.2]. Indeed it is not surprising if a translator cites texts to Greeks in their familiar Greek. The translator, moreover, is thought to be Luke who also used the LXX translation elsewhere for texts. And to be sure, Jerome, knowing this, freely acknowledged and cited this epistle as Paul's, and perhaps also moved Theophylactus, who audaciously asserts that to deny that this epistle is Paul's, is to deny that God spoke through the mouth of Paul.

Faber Stapulensis together with Erasmus, who, following Jerome, showed that this epistle was received late by the Latins, wrote argumentatively. For Erasmus deemed Hebrews almost worthy of the name Paul; although in his annotations συναϑροισμὸν he calls that conjectural by which he seems to prejudice its authority no little. For he says that the Greeks received this epistle more freely in their hatred of the Arians. But in truth, Clement and Origen, who preceded Arius, sufficiently indicate that it was was well accepted also before the time of Arius. Likewise others relate that it was despised by the Romans on account of the Novatians who deny penance, because from it Novatus either thought up his heresy or attempted to establish it. Remember, moreover, that they say it was received late by the Romans, and in this they are not consistent. By such reasoning everything in Scripture becomes worthless: for no text is so sound, that the impious cannot seek in it support for their errors.

Erasmus adds that Ambrose did not write a commentary on Hebrews, even though he wrote on all the other [epistles of Paul]. Let us add that by citing quotations from Hebrews, he moderates himself even in commenting on places in Genesis, where there was occasion. It is apparent that among certain Latin bishops he was more neglected. For contrary to their custom they cited by name, Paul to the Hebrews, in books on faith. The same occurs in *A Book on*

Penance and if they are Ambrose's in *On Those Initiated*. Let us grant that this is the case. Nonetheless the contemporaries of Ambrose, Augustine and Jerome make use of Hebrews freely. Should the silence of a few, prejudice the wisdom of many? And the slight hesitations of some outweigh the certain judgment of the Spirit? Luther with his [Prologues] acknowledges that it [Hebrews] is by a most learned man of above moderate learning, teaching about the priesthood of Christ and the Old Testament properly and extensively. But Luther does not allow that it is the Apostle's, establishing this with somewhat more erudite arguments from chapters 2, 6, 10 and 12, which we will refute in their respective places. Let this suffice concerning the inscription and authority of the epistle. For us nothing occurs in it for which Paul ought to be even slightly ashamed.[65]

Ioannis Oecolampadii de inscriptione et autoritate epistolae ad Hebraeos Praefatio

[65] Inscriptioni huic contradixere nonulli, tum prisci, tum recentiores, negantes Paulum huius Epistolae autorem, mansit tamen, et manebit salva eius, utpote Paulino spiritu digna, autoritas. Apud Latinos tardius quam apud Graecos recepta haec existimatur. Nos eam, ut Pauli propriam agnoscimus. Tametsi propterea cum nemine digladiari velimus, per quem cumque tandem graecitate donata sit, sive is Lucas, sive Barnabas, sive Clemens sit. Ex confesso quidem est, quod principio Hebraice scripta sit. Non autem idcirco licebit nobis negare eam esse Pauli, quod ab alio graece scripta. Nam alioqui et Matthaei Evangelium, negabimus esse Matthaei, qui citra controversiam Haebraice scripsit, ignoraturque quis nam fuerit eius interpres.

Quare autem Latini quidam ab hac abhorruerint, argumenta magis frivola videntur, quam quae tam eximios viros morari debuerint; Opinio sane illorum inde sumpsit originem, quod Romae Gaius quidam, vir disertissimus Cataphrygam arguens, novas quasdam scripturas obtrudentem, inter cetera tredecim Pauli Apostoli Epistolas esse asservit, eam quae ad Hebraeos scripta est non commemorando. Inde Eusebius lib. 6. cap. 16. inquit: Apud latinos illa non putatur esse Pauli Apostoli, cum reliqui, canonicos libros novi instrumenti enumerantes, quatuordecim Pauli Epistolas supputent, et in illis etiam hanc. Fieri autem potest, quod Gaius non negarit simpliciter eam esse Pauli, sed quia per interpretem ad Graecos venit, alterius cuiuspiam esse censuerit. Et enim si de hac re quis consulat Latinos antiquissimos inveniet Clementem antiquiorem Gaio, et Irenaeum meminisse epistolae huius, qui quidem apud Latinos floruerunt, et scripserunt, licet Graece. Quis enim antiquior ex scriptoribus Clemente, qui tertius post Petrum Romae Pontifex? Et is in epistola ad Corinthios memenit epistolae Pauli ad Hebraeos, et utitur eius testimoniis. De quo, vide Eusebium lib. 3. ca. 38. Qui subdit, quod Apostolus, tanquam Hebraeis mittendam, patrio eam sermone conscripserit, et (ut quidam tradunt) Lucam Evangelistam, alii autem hunc ipsum Clementem interpretatum esse, quod magis placet Eusebio, quia et stylus ipse epistolae Clementis, cum hac concordat, et sensus utriusque scripturae plurimam similitudinem ferunt.

Alius item Clemens Alexandrinus ita disserit de hac epistola, quod manifeste sit Pauli Apostoli, scripta autem Hebraeo sermone, tanquam Hebraeis, a Luca vero, qui erat Pauli discipulus, interpretata in Graecum: Unde et stylus eius assimilis videtur libello illi, quem Lucas de Actis Apostolorum scripsit. Vide Eusebium lib. 6. cap. 11.

Iam tenues quasdam coniecturas diluamus, quae moverunt nonullos, ut negarent eam esse Pauli. Sunt enim qui offenduntur quod non praemittitur solita salutatio: Paulus apostolus, sicut in caeteris epistolis. His respondet Clemens Alexandrinus in haec verba: Quod autem superscriptionem solitam non habet, nempe Paulus Apostolus, haec ratio est, quia praeiudicasset Hebraeis Pauli nomen, ne eius dicta susciperent et idcirco prudenter

Oecolampadius includes several items in his "Preface": "Concerning the inscription and authority of the Epistle to the Hebrews," "Concerning the name Hebrews," "Argument," "Concerning the order of this

---

declinavit, ne statim a principio, inspecto nomine Pauli, lectio eius repudiaretur. Et sicut Beatus presbyter dicebat: Quia Dominus, Apostolus omnipotentis, dicitur missus ad Hebraeos. Pro humilitate ergo Paulus, qui ad gentes fuerat destinatus, non scripsit semetipsum Hebraeorum Apostolum, vel propter honorem Domini, qui se missum dixerat ad oves Israel, vel quia gentium videbatur Apostolus. Haec ille.

Origenes aliam coniecturam refutat, quae habet, quod epistola haec disertior sit quam ut Pauli putetur. Et enim idem Eusebius lib. 6. cap. 18. haec Origenis verba citat: Is vero qui idoneus factus est minister novi testamenti, non literae sed spiritus, Paulum dico, qui replevit Evangelium a Hierusalem usque Illyricum, nec ad omnes ecclesias, quas docuerat, scripsit, sed quatuordecim epistolas solas et in illis plures brevissimas. Quamvis et nonnulli de ea, quae ad Hebraeos scripta est dubitarint, eo quod non videatur servari eius illa sententia quam de seipso pronunciat, dicens, se imperitum esse sermone. Sed ego dico, sicut mihi a maioribus traditum est, quia manifestissime Pauli est et semper omnes vetustissimi maiores nostri, eam ut Pauli epistolam susceperunt. Si vero requiras a me per quem sermo eius compositus, pro certo quidem deus viderit. Hoc dico tamen, opinio quae ad nos usque pervenit, haec est. A quibusdam dicebatur quod Clemens Apostolorum discipulus, et Episcopus urbis Romae, Graeco sermone, non tamen sensibus expoliverit. Alii quod Lucas, qui Evangelium scripsit et actus apostolorum.

Hieronymus vero indicat quosdam huic Epistolae, ideo contradixisse, quod praeter morem Pauli testimonia citentur, non iuxta hebraicam veritatem, sed iuxta LXX. Vide eundem super 6 cap. Esaiae. Verum non est mirum si interpres, Graecis testimonia citarit, quemadmodum apud illos legebantur. Interpres autem fuisse putatur Lucas, qui etiam alias LXX interpretum testimoniis usus est. Haec nimirum sciens Hieronymus, hanc ut Pauli libenter agnovit et citavit, et fortassis etiam movit Theophylactum, quod tam audacter asserit, negantem hanc epistolam esse Pauli etiam negare deum per os Pauli locutum.

Faber Stapulensis cum Erasmo, qui, post Hieronymum, hanc epistolam sero a latinis receptam ostendit, contentiosius egit. Nam eam Erasmus, Pauli nomenclatura fere dignatur quamvis in annotationibus συναθροισμὸυ coniecturalem ponat, quo non nihil autoritati eius praeiudicare videtur. Dicit enim Graecos epistolam hanc libentius recepisse in odium Arrianorum, Verum Clementes et Origenis qui Arrium praecesserunt, satis indicant etiam ante Arrii tempora fuisse receptissimam, Simile est quod alii referunt eam sorduisse Romanis propter Novacianos poenitentiam negantes, quia Novatus inde suam haeresim vel excogitavit, vel firmare studuit. Memor autem tu esto, quod illi sero receptam a Romanis dicant, et sic sibi non constant. Praeterea hac ratione, omnes nobis scripture vilescent: Nullae enim tam sincerae sunt, e quibus impii suffragium erroribus suis non petant.

Addit Erasmus, in hanc Ambrosium non scripsisse, cum tamen in omnes alias commentatus sit. Addamus nos quod et a testimoniis huius epistolae citandis, sibi temperarit, etiam in enarrandis locis Geneseos, ubi tamen erat occasio, Unde apparet, quod apud quosdam Latinos Episcopos neglectior fuerit. Nam praeter consuetudinem suam citant nominatim Paulum ad Hebraeos in libris de fide. Item in In libro de paenitentia et si sunt Ambrosii: De his qui initiantur etc. Demus autem ita esse, σύγχρονοι tamen Ambrosii, Augustinus et Hieronymus, hac libenter usi sunt. Nunquid paucorum silentium, sapientiae plurimorum praeiudicabit? Et quorundam hesitatiuncula, certo iudicio spiritus praevalebit?

Lutherus cum suis, fatetur eam esse doctissimi viri, et supra modum eruditam, sacerdotium christi, et vetus testamentum, apposite et copiose docentem. Sed non sinit

Epistle." The first item, translated here in its entirety, will be interpreted shortly. The very short etymological discussion of the word "Hebrews" is the first such discussion among medieval and earlier 16th century commentaries: "Hebrews" (עברים) means "those who pass over" from Abraham (עברי) who left Mesopotamia, "passing over" the river, for the land of Canaan.[66] The section of "Argument" is not translated here because it includes some lengthy quotations from Scripture and because it is an extension of the authorship discussion raised by Luther, which we will treat in connection with "the inscription and authority."[67] The section on "the order of this epistle" is short and traditional: Christ is "more excellent" than the angels and Moses, the unworthy are frightened, and every good work is praised.[68]

The entire section on "the inscription and authority of the epistle" is concerned with the authorship question. It begins the way it ends, reflecting the tone of the entire section: the arguments against Pauline authorship are frivolous and Paul is the author for sure, no matter what anybody has said or will say – its authority is assured.

Previously, in the 16th century, Luther and Bugenhagen were quite negative on Pauline authorship, Erasmus (1516) and Cajetan were very negative, Erasmus (1521) and Titelmans were silent, and Bullinger was very positive on Pauline authorship as is Oecolampadius. For example, in the beginning Oecolampadius simply assumes that Paul wrote it in Hebrew – there is no doubt about it. The identity of the translator is uncertain and unimportant, uncertain because Eusebius, whom Oecolampadius cites, is uncertain. The use of Eusebius by Bullinger[69] and Oecolampadius is new, in relation to these other exegetes and their authorship discussions.

The use of Eusebius opens up new questions from the Fathers about the authorship and language of Hebrews. The question about Hebrews stemming from Gaius, as reported in Eusebius, has not been exposed before, nor was it cited by Bullinger. Oecolampadius (and Bullinger) do not always cite Eusebius' *Ecclesiastical History* accurately. In c. 20 (not 16, of bk. 6) Eusebius reports the Gaius enumeration of 13 Pauline

---

eam esse Apostoli, hoc aliquanto eruditioribus argumentis confirmans ex ca. 2. 6. 10. et 12. quae nos suis locis refutabimus. Haec de inscriptione et autoritate epistolae dicta sufficiant: Nobis enim in ea nihil occurret, cuius Paulum vel suppudere debeat. *In epistolam ad Hebraeos, Ioannis Oecolampadii, explanationes,* ff. 1ʳ–3ᵛ.

66 *Ibid.*, f. 3ᵛ.

67 *Ibid.*, ff. 3ᵛ–4ʳ.

68 *Ibid.*, f. 4ᵛ.

69 Bullinger, p. 393.

epistles (Hebrews would be the 14th) and says "even to this day among the Romans there are some who do not consider it [Hebrews] to be the Apostle's."[70] Oecolampadius adds at this point that "others" enumerate 14 epistles of Paul. There is no basis at this point in Eusebius for the claim about "others" counting Hebrews. Oecolampadius' response to Gaius is the claim about "others," the explanation that perhaps Gaius was confused by the Greek translator and Eusebius' reference to Clement, more ancient than Gaius who quotes from the epistle ("of Paul," add Oecolampadius and Bullinger) to the Hebrews.[71] Eusebius does clearly say that Paul wrote Hebrews in Hebrew,[72] as does Clement of Alexandria, cited by Eusebius, Oecolampadius and Bullinger. More citations then, via Eusebius, are brought to light.

Oecolampadius cites Origen, via Eusebius, both of whom are positive on Pauline authorship. Clement of Alexandria was a clear authority for Oecolampadius and Bullinger for Pauline authorship and he provided an explanation, accepted throughout the Middle Ages, for the lack of a Pauline superscription. Origen, however, was clearer to Oecolampadius and Bullinger than he was to Eusebius. In Eusebius, at least in a 20th century edition, Origen says, "If any church, therefore, holds this epistle as Paul's, let it be commended for this also. For not without reason have the men of old time handed it down as Paul's."[73] In Oecolampadius and Bullinger, Origen in Eusebius reads, "I say that it has been handed down to me by the men of old because it is clearly Paul's and all our most ancient men of old have always received it as Paul's." Similarly, in Oecolampadius it reads, "Paul did not write to all the churches he taught, but only 14 epistles." In our edition, "only 14 epistles" is lacking.[74]

The same type of thing holds true with regard to the reading of Jerome: Jerome is a clear authority for Pauline authorship for Oecolampadius and Bullinger, whereas the opposite was the case for Erasmus (1516) and Cajetan. We have seen that for both Erasmus and Cajetan, especially for Cajetan with all his citations from Jerome, Jerome's "uncertainty" was a major reason for their "doubt" about Pauline authorship.

Finally, Oecolampadius knows of, and is opposed to Erasmus' *Annotationes* (1516), for which he assisted as proofreader, and Luther's

---

[70] Loeb, Vol. II, p. 67.

[71] Loeb I. 289 (bk. 3, c. 38).

[72] *Ibid.*

[73] Loeb II. 79 (bk. 6, c. 25).

[74] Loeb II. 75–77 (bk. 6, c. 25).

Preface (1522). In his *"Argumentum,"* Oecolampadius opposes Luther's statement in his Preface that the Epistle to the Hebrew is made of many pieces and that it does not lay the foundation of faith. For Oecolampadius, Hebrews is a whole piece: Paul admonishes the Hebrews to hear Christ with faith and to press on in the good fruit of faith. Oecolampadius' use and interpretation of the Fathers is very similar to Bullinger's. It is clear that the fight for the Fathers is on.

François Bonade[75]

The Argument

In this epistle Paul does not follow his normal custom, and omits mention of his name and the dignity of his office, in order to demonstrate his humility to those who were believers from the circumcision, being himself an Apostle of Gentiles and not of the Hebrews whose pride he knew. For the same reason John also in his epistle did not put down his name. The tradition is that the apostle sent this epistle to Hebrews written in the Hebrew language. After the death of the apostle Paul, Luke the evangelist, retaining its meaning and order, composed it in the Greek tongue.[76]

While this *"Argumentum"* is the *"Argumentum"* or prologue of the 12th century Gloss, which in turn is a collection of earlier material, Bonade did preface his paraphrase with it. It does bring out what was "common

[75] There is little biographical and bibliographical information on Bonade. The *Dictionnaire des lettres françaises* [xvi^e^s.] notes that Bonade was 16th century, a priest from Augers, a historian and theologian, and that he wrote commentaries on Scripture and the Kings of France. The catalogue of the Bibliothèque Nationale lists nine works, ranging from 1531 to 1544. "In epistolam ad Hebraeos," *Divi Pauli Apostoli gentium, ac Christi Jesu ecclesiae doctoris evangelici, epistolae divinae ad Orphicam lyram traductae Francisco Bonado Angeriae Presbytero Paraphraste* (Basel: Bartholomaeus Westhemer, 1537), pp. 210–39, which is the edition I have used. There is also an edition from Paris of the same year (In-8°, 100 ff.). In Bonade's work on the saints and martyrs, in verse, Paris, 1538, the title reads, in part, *"a sacris musis, Angeriae presbytero."* The work on Hebrews, given among the epistles of Paul, "is transposed into Orphic poetry." It contains an *"Argumentum,"* which is the *Argumentum in epistolam ad Hebraeos* of the *Glossa ordinaria,* sometimes printed in Middle Ages as the Prologue of Jerome. It also contains chapter summaries placed at the beginning of each chapter.

[76] Argumentum: Hac in epistola morem suum Paulus minime servavit nominis sui vocabulum vel ordinis dignitatem omittens ea de causa ut [ad eos] qui ex circuncisione crediderant, quasi gentium Apostolus, et non Hebraeorum quorum suberbiam sciret suam humilitatem demonstraret. Quod et Ioannes pari ratione in epistola sua nomen suum non praetulit. Hanc ergo epistolam fertur Apostolus ad Hebraeos conscriptam hebraica lingua misisse, cuius sensum et ordinem retinens Lucas evangelista post excessum apostoli Pauli Graeco sermone composuit. "In epistolam ad Hebraeos," (Basel, 1537), pp. 210–11.

property" in 16th century exegesis, the *Biblia cum glossa ordinaria*. The first and third arguments of the prologue have been widely restated (and argued or disputed) in the 16th century: Paul omitted his name because of his wisdom and humility, and the epistle was written in Hebrew by Paul and translated into Greek by Luke. The second point, building on the first, has not received the same discussion: Paul was not alone in omitting his name; for the same reasons of wisdom and humility, John did not give his name "in his epistle."

Le Grand (Nicolas) (d. 1560), Richard du Maine (d. 1552)[77]

The *"Argumentum"* as well as the *"enarratio"* are something of an anthology of the authorities. Cited (in order) in the *"Argumentum"* are Jerome, Augustine, Chrysostom, Eusebius, Dionysius, Ambrose, Origen, Cyprian, John Damascene, Theophylactus, and the Councils of Laodicea and Carthage III. Cited as the opposition are Erasmus and Cajetan. The subject of the *"Argumentum"* is the authority of the Epistle; it is discussed in terms of Pauline authorship. The *"Argumentum"* is unusual because of the many and various references, including lengthy quotations, from the authorities, and because Erasmus and Cajetan received extensive coverage. The result for this study is that because of its character and length the *"Argumentum"* will not be translated. The structure, character and thesis of the *"Argumentum"* will be explained. Some of the texts of the authorities will be listed, with the texts, as they appear in the *"Argumentum,"* cited in the footnotes. The importance of the *"Argumentum"* seems to be in the selection of sources and the abundant testimonies for Pauline authorship.

The overall structure, character and thesis could be outlined as follows: I. It begins with lengthy quotations from the authorities for Pauline authorship and Scriptural canonicity; II. Citation of Erasmus' objections, followed by short, often elliptical and mixed references and citations from many authorities presented as attacks on the Erasmus

---

[77] According to Hurter *(Nomenclator)*, and there is little else to go on, Richardus Cenomanus completed and edited the commentaries of Nicolas Grandis *in epistolas ad Rom. et Heb.* The commentaries can be found listed under either Le Grand or Richard of Le Mans (du Maine). Richard was connected with the Sorbonne, the Paris OFM, Obs., convent, the Paris Province and the Council of Trent. Le Grand was a fellow Franciscan. *In divi Pauli Epistolam ad Hebraeos enarratio a fratre Nicolao Grandis* (Paris: Ponset le Preux, 1537, 1552). The 1537 edition, which I have used is, in-fol., 82 ff. The *ad Rom. aeditio* was published in Paris, 1546.

citation; III. Citations (three) of Cajetan's objections, each followed by mixture of proofs against Cajetan from Scripture and principally Jerome and Theophylactus; IV. Ending, with the assertion that Paul wrote Hebrews in Hebrew. The citations and references are strung together with minimal editorial connections provided.

I. The *"Argumentum"* begins with a catena of citations from Jerome[78], Augustine[79], Chrysostom[80] and Eusebius[81]:

A. Jerome, *In epistola ad Dardanum* [*De terra promissionis, 3*].
–, *Ad Matt. 26* [.8].
–, *Ad Titum 1* [.5].

---

[78] (Hieronymus) in epistola ad Dardanum inquit, Hanc epistolam quae inscribitur ad Hebraeos, non solum ab ecclesiis orientis, sed ab omnibus retro ecclesiis graeci sermonis scriptoribus, quasi Pauli apostoli suscipi nostris dicendum est: licet plerique eam vel Barnabae vel Clementis arbitrentur: et nihil interesse cuius sit cum ecclesiastici viri sit, et quotidie ecclesiarum lectione celebretur. Quod si eam Latinorum consuetudo non recipit inter scripturas canonicas, nec Graecorum quidem ecclesiae Apocalypsim Ioannis suscipiunt, et tamen nos utraque suscipimus: nequaquam huius temporis consuetudinem, sed veterum scriptorum autoritatem sequentes, qui plerunque utriusque abutuntur testimoniis. Haec Hieronymus [*PL* 22.1103]. Qui rursus in Matth. cap. 26 ait, Paulus in sua epistola quae scribitur ad Hebraeos (licet de ea multi Latinorum dubitent) sanctorum merita descripsit [*PL* 26.199]. Et ad Titum primo, Si quis vult recipere eam epistolam, quae sub nomine Pauli ad Hebraeos scripta est [*PL* 26.597].

[79] Augustinus lib. 6 de civitate dei, cap. 26, Epistolam quae ad Hebraeos inscribitur, plures eam Pauli apostoli esse dicunt, quidam vero negant, [*CCSL* 48 (*De civ. dei* XVI.22), 524.10–12], hac (ut coniicio) ratione adducti, quod in morem aliarum Paulus eam non auspicatur, nec nominis sui vocabulum, nec ordinis dignitatem describit. Ast haec ratio facile diluitur, cum eo iure eam quae ad Philippenses, utranque ad Thessalonicenses, et ad Philemonem, Pauli non esse comprobari posset: in quarum nulla officii sui praerogativam expressit. Haec autem huius causa extitit, quod ad eos qui ex circumcisione crediderent scriberet, quorum Petrus apostolus erat, ipse vero gentilium, Galat. 2, Qui operatus est Petro in apostolatu circuncisionis, operatus est mihi inter gentes. Ideo Hebraeis scribens, apostolatus dignitatem subticuit, ne Petri autoritatem sibi arroganter vendicare videretur: sciens etiam eorum superbiam, qui se ex genere Abrahae progenitos gloriabantur, Iohan. 8, Nos filii Abrahae sumus, et nemini servivimus unquam. Quos idcirco taxat Paulus Rom. 2, Si autem tu Iudaeus cognominaris, inquit, et requiescis in lege, et gloriaris in deo. Et ut humilia de se sentiens acceptior haberetur, sui officii simul et nominis meritum praeponere noluit.

[80] Chrysostomus homil. 1 in hanc epistolam, Quare prophetas nominans, semetipsum contra non posuit: siquidem tanto eis maior extabat, quanto ei fuerat dispensatio praeclarior credita. Sed non hoc fecit, quid ita? Quia de se dicere maiora recusavit [*PG* 63.237].

[81] Ratio Eusebii Caesariensis lib. 6 ecclesiasticae historiae cap. 10, Pauli quippe, ait, Iudaeis *nomen* infensum erat, eiusque doctrina ingrata: audierant enim de illo quod discessionem doceret a lege Act. 21. Ideo nomen suum prudenter declinavit, ne statim Pauli nomine inspecto, lectio epistolae repudiaretur, et ante displiceret quam legeretur. Dignitatem similiter subticuit, propter domini honorem, quem omnium apostolum dicturus erat: ne se temere Christo componere videretur, et pari ordine se illi coniungere [Loeb II.47; bk. 6, c. 14].

B. Augustine, *De civitate dei,* VI. 26 [XVI.22].
C. Chrysostom, *Homiliae in epistola ad Hebraeos,* I.
D. Eusebius, *Historia Ecclesiastica,* VI. 10 [14].

We have seen that in 16th century commentaries Jerome is usually cited in reference to the problem of Pauline authorship and as a witness to the uncertainties about Hebrews in the early church. Here with three initial citations and three more references to Jerome before the Erasmus discussion, Jerome is the lead – off authority in favor of Paul as author and Hebrews as canonical.

The actual Augustine citation is only a part of what seems to be cited as Augustine's position on the topic. It is possible that the additional material found its way into the literature on Augustine's opinion. The text had not been cited before in medieval or previous 16th century commentaries on Hebrews. The general argument of the text is traditional, however parallel references to Philippians, both Thessalonians and Philemon were not generally made, the parallel being that Paul did not parade the credentials of his office in those epistles either. Augustine is known to have changed his mind about Pauline authorship, not, however, about the canonicity of Hebrews; after 409 he no longer cites Hebrews as a work of Paul. Here Augustine reports that "most" say it is Paul's, although "some" deny this.

The Chrysostom text, not cited before, is typical of the citations in response to Erasmus: the text is not about authorship, but it relates to, and carries on, some motif in the previous reference. In this case, the Chrysostom text carries the motif that Paul kept a low profile over against the Jews and their prophets.[82]

The Eusebius citation (from Clement of Alexandria), cited before, continues the (generally held) motif that Paul because of modesty withheld his name.

II. The next concern of the "*Argumentum*" is, would that Erasmus would have seen it this way. The Erasmus quotation is from his *Annotationes* (1516, pp. 600–601, cited above under the Erasmus section). The part cited includes Erasmus' observations about the lack of Pauline inscription, Jerome's negative witness, Ambrose's lack of a commentary, heretical doctrines in Hebrews and the unpauline style of Hebrews. There are two omissions. The important one is Erasmus'

[82] Cassiodorus, writing in 560 (*Institutes* I.8.3), knew of no Latin commentary on Hebrews, and had thirty-four Homilies of John Chrysostom translated for his works (in *PG* 63.237–456).

example of heretical doctrines namely, that Hebrews denies repentance after baptism, whereas Paul accepted a man into the church who had slept with his father's wife.

The response to Erasmus consists of an amalgamation of twenty-three references to the various fathers and councils listed above, as an anthology of the authorities. This mixture of short references is supposed to blunt Erasmus' arguments.

III. The next citation from the opposition is Cajetan's argument about Hebrew 1.5 (" 'Thou art my Son,' " cited above in the Cajetan section – pp. 329–30 of Cajetan). The response consists of New Testament references to prove that an allegorical interpretation of the Old Testament is not limited to Heb. 1.5.

The next "no less rancid and defective" text of Cajetan cited is his argument about the words testament (Heb. 9) and covenant (Ex. 24, in Hebrew). The response via Scripture citations is that the two words are used interchangeably.

The next Cajetan citation concerns his argument about the interpretation of Melchisedec (in Hebrews). The response is that Paul is following the Septuagint.

IV. The ending of the *"Argumentum"* places the writing of Hebrews before I Tim. (Theophylactus) and after Rom. and the two Corinthians (Origen). Paul wrote Hebrews from Rome.

Huldrych Zwingli (1484–1531)[83]

The Argument

Since, with the preaching of the gospel, all observations of ceremony and Mosaic law were gradually made obsolete in all respects, the Jews who held fast

[83] *In evangelicam historiam de domino nostro Iesu Christo, per Matthaeum, Marcum, Lucam, et Joannem conscriptam, Epistolasque aliquot Pauli, Annotationes D. Huldrychi Zwinglii per Leonem Judae exceptae et aeditae. Adjecta est epistola Pauli ad Hebraeos, et Joannis Apostoli Epistola per Gasparem Megandrum* (Zürich: Christoph Froschouer, 1539; Finsler #104). In *Opera Zwinglii*, Vol. 4, (Zürich: Christoph Froschouer, 1545 and 1581; Finsler #105). "In epistolam beati Pauli ad Hebraeos expositio brevis Huldrychi Zwinglii. Per Megandrum ab ore eius excepta et edita," *Zwingli Opera*, ed. Schuler-Schultess, abb. SS (Zürich, 1838), VI. 2.291–319. Caspar Megander (1495–1545), who returned to Zürich in 1537 and became *dekan* of the Grossmünster, in his preface "To the Reader," explains something of the situation surrounding Zwingli's commentary: "Since I owe not only my understanding of the Epistle to the Hebrews but also the beginning and foundation of my sacred faith and religion to Huldrych Zwingli –, a man of learning, piety . . ., how fitting that I repay

to the Mosaic law, even those who were initiated into Christ from Moses, not only took it ill but it brought them no little or ordinary controversy and trouble. Paul writes this epistle therefore to refute and to remove the excessive love of ceremonies from the minds of the wavering. Accordingly he teaches that all these were a figure and type of Christ and that Christ is the end and consummation of all these things. And he teaches that we today have another temple, namely heaven, other purifications, another priest and sacrifice, namely Christ whom he proves to be the true son of God, and existing as God himself from eternity. He admonishes them solicitously not to reject Christ but receive him, and he clearly shows with what evil and danger they would contemn him. He shows distinctly how everything of the Old Testament was a type and figure of the New Testament as was said above. In the New Testament Christ expiates the sins of the world by the unique offering of his own death; and those coming to him by faith, he leads to the heavenly tabernacle, perpetually sanctifying and perfecting them. He is much concerned about exhortation to faith in Christ and to patience, and he does this with several appropriate examples. Finally, as is his custom, he adds on moral exhortations and strong admonitions.[84]

---

him. It is pleasing to the prayers of some that the things which I also received from his mouth about this Epistle I was able to edit with summaries and publish for others. It seems unnecessary to expand on these things since all things, not only copiously, but also piously, eruditely and learnedly, are found in the edited commentaries of Bullinger, my beloved brother and fellow priest. Since all the remaining things have not been edited at some time by Leo, that is the reason that I alone have received them, especially since Leo is occupied with the more difficult task of translating the Bible. Farewell. . ." (SS. p. 291). Critical textual problems regarding Zwingli's New Testament exegesis have yet to be thoroughly researched: for example, questions of time, place and sources (Ulrich Gäbler, *Huldrych Zwingli im 20. Jahrhundert. Forschungsbericht und annotierte Bibliographie 1897–1972* [Zürich: Theologischer Verlag, 1975], pp. 21–22). Georg Finsler, *Zwingli-Bibliographie. Verzeichnis der gedruckten Schriften von und über Ulrich Zwingli* (Zürich, 1897; Nieuwkoop: Graaf, 1962).

Argumentum

[84] Quum praedicatione evangelii, ceremoniae, legisque Mosaicae observationes omnes paulatim undique antiquarentur, Iudaei qui legis Mosaicae tenaces, etiam qui ex Mose Christo initiati iam erant, non modo moleste illud ferebant, sed et controversiam, negotiumque illis peperit non modicum, aut vulgare. Quo ergo ista, ac ceremoniarum affectum nimium e nutantium animis refelleret, et eximeret, hanc scribit Paulus epistolam. Qua docet omnia ista figuram fuisse, et typum Christi, Christumque harum rerum finem et consummationem esse. Atque ita nos hodie aliud habere templum, coelum scilicet, alia purificantia, alium sacerdotem, et sacrificium, videlicet Christum; quem probat verum dei esse filium, et deum ipsum ab aeterno exstitisse. Ne quem aspernentur, sed recipiant, sollicite monet, quantoque malo et periculo contemnant, manifeste indicat. Omnia veteris testamenti, typum et figuram fuisse novi, ut dictum est, commonstrat. In quo Christus, unica oblatione suae mortis mundi peccata expiavit; fideque ad ipsum accedentes, perpetuo sanctificans, et perficiens, in coeleste deducit tabernaculum. Multus etiam est in fidei Christi, et patientiae adhortatione, et hoc multis et aptis facit exemplis. Postremo suo more, paraeneses morum, et admonitiones annectit validissimas. *"In Epistolam Beati Pauli ad Hebraeos Expositio Brevis,"* (SS), VI.2.291.

While there are source problems regarding the *Sitz-im-Leben* of Zwingli's New Testament commentaries, the theology of the relationship between the Old Testament and New Testament in the *"Argumentum"* and the *"Summa"* of each chapter of Hebrews is similar to the views Zwingli held before late 1525.[85] In the *"Argumentum"* Christ is presented as the end of the Mosaic law "and all these things." As was common in the tradition the Old Testament was seen as a *"figura"* and *"typus,"* to be "gradually" ended with the preaching of the gospel. The epistle to the Hebrews addresses itself to those who mixed Moses with Christ. It is clear that "we" have a different temple, purification, priesthood and sacrifice.

The tone of Zwingli's exegesis of Hebrews is set in his summary of chapter one: Christ is not a prophet or angel, he is "more excellent" than all.[86] Chapters two and three show that Christ is "more excellent" than the angels, the New Testament is "superior" to the Old Testament, and the ministry of Christ is "much superior" to the ministry of Moses.[87] In other summaries "type and figure" are repeated[88], as is the "superiority" of Christ.[89] The constant emphasis is that the New Testament is "more excellent" than the Old Testament.[90]

Zwingli's view of the Old Testament (before late 1525) was similar to Erasmus'. We have seen for Erasmus that the Old Testament was considered to be a "shadow" and "imperfect," given for a certain period which ended with Christ. An early indication of Zwingli's understanding of the Old Testament is found in his treatise "On the Clarity and Certainty of the Word of God" (1522). The discussion is hermeneutical and differences between the two Testaments are presupposed. The treatment of the Old Testament is considerably shorter and more negative. The Old Testament is used as an example of disobedience. The Old Testament brought toil and death. In his "Commentary on the Sixty-two Articles" (1523), the contrast between the Old Testament and New Testament highlighted the contrast, for example, between the blood of animals and the blood of Christ. In his work "On Baptism" (May, 1525) Zwingli remains critical of the Old Testament – its sacraments are carnal and external. Later in 1525 (*"Antwort über Balthasar*

---

[85] Hagen, "From Testament to Covenant in the Early Sixteenth Century." *The Sixteenth Century Journal* 3 (1972), 15–20.

[86] SS p. 292.

[87] SS pp. 294, 296.

[88] SS p. 297.

[89] SS pp. 299, 303, 306.

[90] SS p. 307.

Hubmaiers Taufbüchlein," 5 Nov. 1525), there is a positive treatment of the Old Testament and the continuity of the two Testaments is emphasized. Abraham's covenant is the Christian's covenant or new testament. In his "Answer to Hubmaier" and treatises after 1525, Zwingli emphasized the unity of the two Testaments. For example, "Against the Anabaptists" (1527) Zwingli argued that the two Testaments are not different testaments, because then there would have to be two different peoples and two different gods. The testament from the beginning to the end of the world is "one and the same."[91] In 1525 Zwingli shifted his attack from Rome to the Anabaptists and, thus, his emphasis from the differences to the unity of the Testaments. Zwingli's "Brief Exposition of the Epistle of Blessed Paul to the Hebrews," as edited by Megander (1539), is similar in its Old Testament hermeneutic to Erasmus, and would seem to antedate his "Answer to Hubmaier." Pauline authorship is not discussed.

The major emphasis of the "Exposition" is the contrast between the two Testaments. There is also "much (in the epistle) about faith in Christ . . . and the admonition of morals."[92] The later chapters of Hebrews concern faith and example, and exhort "to the solidity of faith and innocence of life."[93]

Konrad Pellikan (1478–1556)[94]

The Argument

Many dispute the authorship and authority of this most holy, learned and useful epistle to the Hebrews; we, with a care for brevity, will introduce the judgment of others about this, especially of the men of authority from among both the Greeks and the Latins. Eusebius of Caesaria (in bk. 6, c.18 [25], telling about the canon which Origen reckons with regard to the sacred books) cites the position of the most learned and religious doctor, Origen: "Origen counts fourteen canonical epistles of Paul, and then adds, 'although some have doubts about the one written to the Hebrews, because that position which Paul himself makes

[91] Hagen, "From Testament to Covenant," pp. 16–20.

[92] SS p. 291.

[93] SS p. 310.

[94] "Commentarium in epistolam D. Pauli ad Hebraeos," *Commentaria Bibliorum,* 7 Volumes (Zürich: Christoph Froschouer, 1532–39), VII. 608–80. The commentary on Hebrews was 1539. Pellikan came to Zürich in 1525 on Zwingli's invitation, and worked there as Prof. of Greek and Hebrew until his death. Also: *In omnes apostolicas epistolas commentaria* (Zürich, 1582).

known about himself, saying that he is rude in speech, does not seem to be observed in the epistle, nevertheless, I [Origen] say that it is clearly Paul's just as it has been handed down to me by my predecessors, and all our ancient authorities have always thus received it as Paul's." Concerning this Clement of Alexandria also argues that it is clearly the apostle Paul's, written, however, in the Hebrew tongue as to Hebrews, translated into Greek by Luke, who was a disciple of Paul; thus the style seems rather similar to that little book which Luke wrote about the Acts of the Apostles. The opinion of blessed Jerome, a most celebrated doctor among the Latins agrees with these. In his book, *De terra promissionis,* explaining to Dardanus, he says, ["] what I have to say to you is this, that this epistle inscribed to the Hebrews was received as the apostle Paul's, not only by Eastern churches but by all churches of the past, by writers of the Greek language, although many think it to be Barnabas' or Clement's, this is of no interest, because it is by a man of the church and is daily celebrated in the lection of the churches. But if the custom of the Latins does not receive it among the canonical Scriptures, neither do some of the Greek churches receive the Apocalypse of John with the same liberty. We, however, receive both, by no means following the custom of this time but, the authority of the ancient writers, who frequently used testimonies of both, not as from time to time they were accustomed to do with the Apocrypha and even frequently used examples of Gentile writings, but precisely as canonical and ecclesiastical. ["] Such judgment of so many men abundantly suffices for us. The reason why Paul, contrary to his custom, does not give his name or the dignity of his apostolic rank is that he was writing, as the apostle of the Gentiles, to those from circumcision who were believers; knowing, therefore, their pride and demonstrating his humility, he was unwilling to set before them the merit of his office. The argument of this epistle, moreover, does not differ from all the others. For he writes to the churches of the Hebrews concerning the eminence of Christ according to both natures, concerning the abrogation of legal ceremonies; moreover, since the temple of Jerusalem was standing and things of the law were held fast by the Jews, even those converted to Christ. He adds in many ways that faith in Jesus Christ without things of the law suffices for salvation and justice, that after the passion of Christ and the sacrifice consummated, things of the law not only do not help but they hinder. He excludes the superstitious tradition of certain Hebrews, who, confessing Christ, thought that legal observances are to be held on to. And they led some, who were converted to Christ from the Gentiles, into this error by their authority. This he does in a most noble way; from the beginning with various reasons and testimonies of Scripture he beautifully explains the dignity of him who has spoken to us, Christ, showing that he is equal to God the Father, that he is superior to the highest and most worthy creatures, namely the angels and Moses. He threatens them if they should refuse to hear so great an apostle and teacher. He invites and draws them by the goodness and mercy of Christ the Lord, also the highest and best priest; and with this he continues to c. 10. Then he teaches the duties of the disciples, lest with so great a preceptor they are found wanting, and lose or do not show the faith. Thus he praises patience, peace, mercy towards strangers, the imprisoned and poor, obedience, chastity, prudence and prayer, so that being thus perfect, they are rendered faithful in every good work.[95]

Argumentum

[95] Cuius authoris et authoritatis sit haec ad Hebraeos sacrosancta, erudita et utilissima epistola, disputant multi, nos brevitati studentes, aliorum iudicium super hac re inducamus, maxime authoritatis virorum, apud tum Graecos tum Latinos. De Origenis sententia doctissimi et religiosissimi doctoris, sic scribit Eusebius Caesariensis libro 6. cap. 18. canonem edisserens, quem in sacris libris posuerit Origenes, XIIII. numerat canonicas Pauli epistolas, mox adiiciens, Quamvis et nonnulli de ea quae ad Hebraeos scripta est dubitaverint, pro eo quod non videatur in ea servari eius illa sententia, quam de se ipse pronunciat, dicens se imperitum esse sermone: sed ego dico, sicut mihi a majoribus traditum est, quia manifestissime Pauli est, et semper omnes antiqui majores nostri ita eam ut Pauli epistolam susceperunt. De ea quoque Clemens Alexandrinus sic disseruit, quod manifeste Pauli sit apostoli, scripta autem Hebraeo sermone tanquam Hebraeis, a Luca vero, qui erat Pauli discipulus, interpretata in Graecum, unde et stilus eius magis similis videtur libello illius, quem Lucas de Apostolorum actibus scripsit. His astipulatur sententia divi Hieronymi, apud Latinos doctoris celeberrimi, in libro De terra promissionis, qui ad Dardanum disserens, inquit, Illud vestris dicendum est, hanc epistolam quae inscribitur ad Hebraeos, non solum ab ecclesiis Orientis, sed ab omnibus retro ecclesiis, Graeci sermonis scriptoribus, quasi Pauli apostoli suscipi, licet plaerique eam vel Barnabae vel Clementis arbitrentur, et nihil interesse cuius sit, quum ecclesiastici viri sit, et quotidie ecclesiarum lectione celebretur. Quod si eam Latinorum consuetudo non recipit inter scripturas canonicas, nec Graecorum quidem ecclesiae Apocalypsim Ioannis eadem libertate suscipiunt. Et tamen nos utraque suscipimus, nequaquam huius temporis consuetudinem, sed veterum scriptorum authoritatem sequentes, qui plaerunque utriusque utuntur testimoniis: non ut interdum de apocryphis facere solent, quippe qui et gentilium literarum non raro utuntur exemplis, sed quasi canonicis et ecclesiasticis. [*Epist. ad Dardanum* 3, *PL* 22. 1103–1104]. Tale huiusmodi tantorum virorum iudicium nobis abunde sufficit. Cur vero praeter morem Paulus in hac epistola non adscripserit nominis sui vocabulum, vel ordinis apostolici dignitatem, haec causa est, quod ad eos scribens qui ex ciruncisione crediderant, quasi gentium apostolus habebatur, sciens quoque eorum superbiam, suamque humilitatem ipse demonstrans, meritum officii sui noluit anteferre. Argumentum autem huius epistolae non abhorret a caeteris omnibus. Scribit enim ecclesiis Hebraeorum, de eminentia Christi secundum utranque naturam, de abrogatione legalium ceremoniarum, utcunque adhuc tunc quoque templum staret Hierosolymis, et a Iudaeis mordicus legalia urgerentur, etiam conversis ad Christum, astruitque multis modis fidem Iesu Christi absque legalibus sufficere ad salutem et iustitiam, post Christi passionem, et consummatum sacrificium, legalia non modo non proficere, verumetiam officere: quorundam Hebraeorum superstitiosam traditionem excludens, qui Christum confitentes, legales observantias tenendas putabant. Et in hunc errorem quosdam etiam, qui de gentilitate convertebantur ad Christum, sua authoritate induxerant. Id autem agit honestissimo ordine, dum ab initio variis rationibus et scripturae testimoniis, pulchre explanat dignitatem eius qui nobis loquitur Christi, ostendens illum deo patri aequalem, creaturis summis et dignissimis, utpote angelis et Mose superiorem. Terret quoque minis, si audire dedignati fuerint tantum apostolum et magistrum. Invitat et alicit beneficentia ac misericordia Christi domini, et sacerdotis summi et optimi, et in ea pergit usque ad caput decimum. Docet deinde officium discipulorum, ne tanto praeceptore indigni inveniantur, et fidem amittant vel non ostendant. Commendat itaque patientiam, pacem, misericordiam erga hospites vinctos et pauperes, obedientiam, castitatem, prudentiam ac orationem, ut sic absoluti reddantur fideles in omni opere bono. "Commentarium in epistolam D. Pauli apostoli ad Hebraeos," (1539), pp. 608–609.

Pellikan's introductory discussion of authorship is very similar to the arguments of Bullinger and Oecolampadius. Both Bullinger and Oecolampadius cited the ancient authorities of Origen and Clement of Alexandria, via Eusebius. Eusebius supposedly cited Origen's count of fourteen Pauline epistles, and Eusebius cited Clement's assertion that the epistle to the Hebrews was written in Hebrew, translated by Luke which accounts for the similarity of style between Hebrews and the Acts. Oecolampadius also noted that the Greeks were late in accepting the Apocalypse.

Pellikan continues the "fight" for Jerome. Among the medievals only Thomas Aquinas cited Jerome as being in favor of Pauline authorship, and that was only by way of mentioning Jerome's name along with Dionysius'. In the 16th century Jerome was referred to in terms of the problem of authorship and generally on the negative side of the argument. Erasmus and Cajetan gave Jerome's report that Hebrews was not received by some, and Cajetan and Oecolampadius noted that Jerome indicated that certain things in Hebrews contradicted the practice of Paul. It has been pointed out that Cajetan gave many quotes from Jerome, all of which concluded uncertainty and doubt about Paul as author. Bullinger and Oecolampadius in a general way claimed Jerome as being in favor of Pauline authorship. The *"Argumentum"* of Le Grand/Richard provided several Jerome citations, including the one cited by Pellikan, in favor of Pauline authorship and against Cajetan (as well against Erasmus' views of 1516). Pellikan's citation of Jerome's *Epist. ad Dardanum* is more complete, including Jerome's statement that Hebrews (and the Apocalypse) are "canonical and ecclesiastical."

Pellikan also gives the "Argument" of the *Glossa ordinaria* on why Paul did not give his name: "his humility and their pride."

While Pellikan's handling of Jerome is similar to Le Grand/Richard, his use of other authorities is quite similar to Bullinger and Oecolampadius. In commenting on 6.6 (*"Impossibile est"* and the question of second repentance) Pellikan cites Bullinger and others (including Chrysostom) in favor of the "rebaptism theory." Authorship is not mentioned.[96] On 2.3 (*"in nos confirmata est"* in relation to Gal. 1), the "conjecture" of some that Hebrews is not Paul's, is discussed. Pellikan gives the traditional observation, as did Bullinger, that "us" does not only mean Paul, but he also has his own twist on the verse: those giving

---

[96] *Ibid.*, pp. 627–28.

the conjecture "do not note that the word is confirmation, not revelation."[97]

Pellikan begins his summary of the "Argument" by finishing up his authorship discussion, namely, that the argument of Hebrews is no different from the other, presumably Pauline, epistles. Pellikan's overall view of Hebrews is rather basic and standard: *"eminentia Christi"* and the abrogation of legal ceremonies *(legalia)*. The *dignitas Christi* is *superior* and does not mix with *legalia*, wh. hinder and lead to error. Pellikan speaks about the end of Jewish ceremonies as did Zwingli, who also spoke about the end of Mosaic laws. Pellikan, perhaps being the Hebraist he was, did not extend h comments, as did Zwingli, into a discussion of the contrast between the Old Testament and New Testament.

Robert Estienne (1503–59)[98]

Isidorus Clarius (1495–1555)[99]

Gasparo Contarini (1483–1542)[100]

Paul wrote this epistle from Italy to those Hebrews who had believed. Because they depended on the law and were addicted to legal observances, as if faith in Christ did not justify believing men, but the shadow of the old law did, he

[97] *Ibid.*, p. 614.

[98] In 1526, he became head of the family press (Stephanus) near the Sorbonne; in 1539 he was appointed the King's printer (for Hebrew and Latin works, in 1540 for Greek works). In 1541, he published a small 2 volume (in-8°), annotated New Testament: "Epistola Pauli Apostoli ad Hebraeos." *Pauli Apostoli Epistolae ad Rom. . . . ad Heb. . . . Breves variarum tralationum annotationes* (Paris, 1541), II, ff. 97ᵛ–111ʳ. Other editions (attacked by the Sorbonne in 1547) were 1542, 1543, and 1545, which incorporated the notes of François Vatable (d. 1547). The "Annotations," consist of very brief *marginalia*, and lack an *Argumentum*.

[99] b. as Taddeo Cucchi in Chiari, entered the Benedictine Order (1517) and took the name Isidorus, hence Isidoro Chiari: d. in Foligno, where he was made bishop (1547). "Epistola Beati Pauli Apostoli ad Hebraeos," *Novi Testamenti Vulgata quidem aeditio, sed quae ad vetustissimorum utriusque linguae exemplarium fidem, nunc demum emendata est diligentissime, ut nova non desideretur, adiectis scholiis, et doctis et piis. . .* 2 Vols (Venice: Petrus Schoeffer, 1541), II. 327–80. *Vulgata aeditio veteris ac Novi Testamenti* (Venice: Petrus Schoeffer, 1542). A New Testament *Vulgata* (Antwerp, 1544). *Biblia sacrosancta Veteris ac Novi Testamenti . . . ex secunda eius recognitione* (Venice: Iunta, 1557, 1564). His fairly short and selective notes are also in the very useful, "Annotata in epistolam ad Hebraeos," *Critici sacri*, ed. John Pearson, 9 Vols (Amsterdam: Boom, 1698), VII, 883–1190. There is no *Argumentum*.

[100] "Epistola ad Hebraeos," *Scholia in epistolas divi Pauli, Opera* (Paris: Sebastian

therefore first established the dignity of Christ, pertaining both to the divine nature and also the human nature which he assumed. He prefers Christ first over the angels, then Moses and lastly the Levitical priests. Finally, he concludes with faith, which he defines, and the power of faith, declaring that all the saints have been justified purely from faith and through faith. Thus the summary. "In multifarious and many ways, God spoke formerly to the fathers by the prophets, but in these last days he has spoken to us in the Son." Some have doubted whether this epistle is Paul's, relying on some arguments among which is this: in the beginning no mention is made of his name, as is Paul's custom in all his other epistles. We will follow the authority of the church, which recognizes and reads it as an epistle of Paul. One true reason, among others, why his name is not given in the beginning I think is this: Paul was an apostle of the Gentiles, not of the circumcision, as is clear in the epistle to the Galatians. Therefore, in writing to the Gentiles, he was not forgetful of his authority, and mentioned his name; writing, however, to the Hebrews, whose apostle he was not, he followed the way of humility.[101]

Contarini's *"summa"* stands out, in the context of previous 16th century exegetes, in terms of his emphasis on faith without mixture, the faith in Christ that justifies. Luther, Titelmans, and Bullinger, in their opening summaries, stressed the importance of Christ in Hebrews. Contarini gives the standard account of Hebrews, namely, that Paul is writing to Jewish converts who wanted to mix law and Christ, "as if faith in Christ did not justify." Because of his audience Paul stresses the dignity of Christ. And then, in his rather short summary, the emphasis on faith reappears: Paul zeroes in on faith by defining it [11.1] and

---

Nivelle, 1571), pp. 515–29. The *Scholia* on Paul was written near the end of his life in Bologne, 1542 (Friedrich Lauchert, *Die italienischen literarischen Gegner Luthers* ["Erläuterungen und Ergänzungen zu Jansssens Geschichte des deutschen Volkes," Vol. 8; Freiburg i. B.: Herder, 1912], p. 374.)

[101] Hanc Epistolam ab Italia scripsit Apostolus ad eos qui crediderant, Hebraeos; qui, quoniam pendebant a lege, et observantiis legis erant addicti, quasi fides in Christum non iustificaret homines credentes, sed umbra veteris legis: idcirco primum statuit dignitatem Christi, tum pertinentem ad divinam naturam, tum etiam pertinentem ad naturam humanam quam assumpsit: ac primo praefert eum angelis, deinde Moysi, postremo sacerdotibus Leviticis; demum desinit in fidem quam definit, et fidei vim, declarans sanctos omnes mere iustificatos fuisse, ex fide et per fidem. Haec summa. "Multifariam multisque modis olim loquens Deus patribus in prophetis, novissime diebus istis locutus est nobis in filio." Quidam dubitarunt an haec Pauli sit Epistola, nixi nonnullis argumentis, inter quae est hoc, quod in exordio nulla eius nominis facta sit mentio, quemadmodum mos eius est in omnibus aliis suis Epistolis. Nos sequemur auctoritatem Ecclesiae, quae hanc Epistolam recognoscit, et legit ut Pauli Epistolam; quod nomen eius non sit positum in exordio, praeter alias causas, puto hanc veram. Erat gentium Apostolus Paulus, non circumcisionis, ut in Epistola ad Galatas patet: idcirco scribens gentibus, suae auctoritatis non obliviscitur, et nominis sui meminit, scribens autem Hebraeis, quorum non erat Apostolus, humilitatem secutus est. "Epistola ad Hebraeos," p. 515.

explaining [cc. 11–13] that the Old Testament "saints were justified purely *("mere")* from faith and through faith."

Contarini's handling of the authorship question is traditional. His statement that, "We will follow the authority of the church" turns out to mean the *Glossa ordinaria*. The only authorship problem raised is the lack of Pauline salutation. The response is that Paul, being an apostle to the Gentiles, took the path of humility in writing to the Hebrews by omitting his name. The use of authority in this case is the use of the *Glossa ordinaria*. Likewise in his comment on 2.3, a *textus classicus* for raising the authorship question, Contarini appeals to Paul's humility: Paul identified himself with the Hebrews ("confirmed unto us") out of humility.[102]

Jean de Gagny (d. 1549)[103]

The Argument of the Epistle to the Hebrews

Although the apostle was sent to be an apostle especially to the Gentiles, nevertheless how greatly he desired the salvation of the Jews he testifies in Rom. 9 [.3], "I could wish to be anathema myself from Christ for the sake of my brethren," and 11 [.13–14]. "As long, indeed, as I am an apostle of the Gentiles, I will honor my ministry, in the hope that I may provoke to jealousy those who are my flesh, and may save some of them." Indeed, of all the apostles, Paul and Barnabas were chosen for ministring alms to them. He wrote this consolatory epistle, therefore, to Jews and converted Hebrews, living in Palestine and Jerusalem, who were afflicted in various ways by infidels. He admonishes them to bear afflictions patiently and to hope in Christ the remunerator. He teaches to lay every trust in Christ, leaving behind the law, inasmuch as, the priesthood of the law being abrogated, the eternal priest intercedes for them before God. It is fitting that they are saved by faith in him (concerning faith and its power he explains much). Intentionally, moreover, he omitted his name because he was

---

[102] *Ibid.*, p. 516.

[103] Also Gaigny, Ganay, Gannay, Gagne, Gagni, Gagnée, Guigni, Gagney, Ganney. Born in Paris, Gagny became rector of the University in 1531; he lectured on the epistles of Paul at the College of Navarre; in 1533 his work on Romans was published. In 1539, he annotated, *Divi Pauli apostoli epistolae brevissimis . . . scholiis . . . illustratae* (Paris: Simon Colinaeus, 1539). In 1540, he translated the 6th century African bishop Primasius, *Briefve et fructueuse exposition sus les épistres sainct Paul aux Rom. et Hebreux par Primasius* (Paris: Roffet, 1540). In 1543 there was the first printing of the work I will use, *Brevissima et facillima in omnes D. Pauli epistolas scholia, ultra priores editiones ex antiquiisimis Graecorum authoribus, abunde locupletata.* (Paris: Simon Colinaeus, 1543; Paris: Vivant Gaultherot, 1547, 1550), I will use, "Epistola divi Pauli ad Hebraeos," *Ibid.* (Paris: Sebastian Nivelle, 1563), ff. 149r–188v.

odious to them on account of the circumcision which he made ineffective and also (as we read in Acts), leaving them aside, he went over to the Gentiles. Therefore, useless is the argument of those who deny that this epistle is Paul's because of the silence of his name, and, what is no more useful, because of the difference of style. Paul was not greatly skilled in the Greek tongue (except in so far as the necessity of preaching demanded). But he was most learned in Hebrew. Thus this epistle is more eloquent than the others and, so to say, more lofty in style. They say it was written in Hebrew and translated into Greek by the most learned Luke, as Eusebius of Caesaria asserts (Ecclesiastical History bk. 6, c. 11 [cf. c. 14]). Also worthless is the argument where chapter two says, regarding evangelical doctrine, "it was confirmed unto us by those who heard," while Galatian says that he was not helped by the apostles. In that place [scholia on c. 2] we will say that by "us," he understands "us" to be not himself but those to whom he is writing. Other inane arguments and similar worthless and perverse opinions, with which Cajetan sprinkles his farrago about holy Scripture, brother Lancilotus Dominicanus, a pious and learned man, abundantly blunts. Against all who deny that this epistle is Paul's, I will ascribe to the judgment of Theophylactus, who, in his explication of this text [1.3], "carrying all things by the word of his power," says: 'I am not able for my part not to be astonished at the impudence of many men who, while they understand from the beginning of this epistle that so many heresies have been refuted, nevertheless they do not at all cease to claim that this epistle is not consistent with Paul, or that it is different from the other epistles. I do not wish them to be ignorant of the fact that the sense and the profundities of this epistle, and its irresistable force cannot be anyone else's but Paul's, who had Christ speaking in him. But if the manner of speaking offends them, let them understand that Paul dictated this epistle in the Hebrew tongue, as a sermon to the Hebrews, and one of his companions translated it into Greek. And many assert that Luke or Clement translated it. Nor do those who deny that this is Paul's letter, err less than if they were denying Christ was with [*adesse*] Paul.'[104]

---

[104] Argumentum epistolae Ad Hebraeos:

Etsi ad gentes potissimum apostolus delegatus esset Paulus, quatopere tamen Iudaeorum salutem cuperet testatur ad Rom 9. dicens, Optabam ego anathema esse a Christo pro fratribus meis: et 11. Quandiu quidem ego sum gentium apostolus, ministerium meum honorificabo: si quo modo ad aemulandum provocem carnem meam, et salvos faciam aliquos ex illis. Quinimo ex omnibus apostolis, Paulus et Barnabas ad ministrandas illis eleemosynas delecti sunt. Ad Iudaeos ergo et conversos Hebraeos in Palaestina et Hierosolymis habitantes, qui ab infidelibus varie affligebantur, consolatoriam hanc scribit epistolam, patienter afflictiones ferre, et in Christum remuneratorem sperare admonens, in quem omnem fiduciam, relicta lege, collocare docet: quippe qui abrogato legis sacerdotio aeternus apud deum pontifex pro illis interpellat, cuius fide (de qua et de potentia multis disserit) saluari illos oporteat. De industria autem nomen suum omittit, quod ob circumcisionem, quam enervaret, odiosus illis esset, tum etiam (sicut in Actis legimus) quod illis neglectis ad gentes transisset. Quare inutile est argumentum eorum, qui ob tacitum nomen hanc esse Pauli epistolam negant: neque magis validum ob styli differentiam. Paulus enim graecae linguae non ad modum peritus, nisi (quatenus praedicandi necessitas exigebat) Hebraicae doctissimus fuit: unde et haec epistola caeteris

Gagny began his "*Argumentum*" on a traditional note: the apostle to the Gentiles was zealous for the conversion of the Jews. In the exegetical tradition on Hebrews this goes back to Chrysostom. Lyra used the point as one of six arguments for Pauline authorship – many of these are echoed in Gagny. Lyra's six points were as follows: 1) the authority of the church (also in Contarini and Gagny), 2) the ancient *doctores* (also in Gagny), 3) Chrysostom, 4) the reference to Timothy, 5) Paul's being zealous for the conversion of the Jews (in Gagny), and 6) his being zealous for evangelical truth (echoed in Gagny). These add up for Lyra to the assertion that Paul indubitably is author.[105] Also in Lyra and

---

est eloquentior, et ut ita dicam magniloquentior: Hebraice scriptam Lucas grece doctissimus vertisse fertur: ut ecclesiasticae historiae lib. 6, cap. 11, asserit Eusebius, Caesariensis. Subfrigidum est quoque argumentum quod 2 cap. de evangelica doctrina dicat: Ab eis qui audierunt in nos confirmata est, quum ad Gal. dicat nihil se ab apostolis adiutum. Nam sicut eo loco dicemus, per "nos" non se sed eos ad quos scribit intelligit. Inania autem alia argumenta, et similes nugas perversasque opiniones, quibus suas in scripturam sanctam farragines inspersit Caietanus, abunde retudit frater Lancilotus Dominicanus, homo pius et doctus. Adversus autem omnes qui Pauli negant hanc esse epistolam, Theophylacti sententiam adscribam in explicatione huius loci, "portans omnia verbo virtutis suae," ita dicentis: "Non possum equidem non admirari multorum hominum impudentiam qui quum intelligant per epistolae huius exordium tot fuisse haereses confutatas, haud tamen desinant asserere epistolam hanc Paulo non convenire, ceu a caeteris epistolis alienam. Velim tamen hos non esse nescios epistolae huius et sensum et profunditates, et vim illam inconfutabilem, nullius alterius esse posse nisi Pauli, qui Christum haberet in se loquentem. Quod si dicendi modus illos offendit, intelligant Paulum Hebraica lingua hanc ipsam dictitasse epistolam, ut qui ad Hebraeos haberet sermonem, et unum aliquem e suis contubernalibus in Graecum vertisse. Et plerique Lucam hanc transtulisse ferunt, aut Clementem. Nec secus hi peccant qui hanc esse Pauli epistolam negant, quam si Paulo abesse [sic] Christum negarent." [Cited by Lancilotus (Ambrosius Catharinus), which I located in "Ambr. Catherini Dissertatio de epistola ad Hebraeos," *Commentaria et disputationes in Epistolam D. Pauli ad Hebraeos, auctore D. Ludovico Tena. . . Quibus adduntur ob argumenti similitudinem hi tractatus: Fr. Spanhemii Exertationes de autore et epistola ad Hebraeos; Ambr. Catharini Dissertatio de epist. ad Heb., Christ. Schlegelii Quaestiones. . .*, ed. Luis de Tena (London: Scott, 1661), p. 803]. "Epistola divi Pauli ad Hebraeos," (1563), f. 149^r.

105 Lyra *(Proemium)*, f. 133^r: Ad maiorem autem sequentium et predictorum evidentiam queritur, utrum hec epistola sit Pauli apostoli. Et arguitur primo quod non, quia in hac epistola non tenetur modus scribendi qui in aliis epistolis Pauli, preponendo nomen suum et sui apostolatus officium ut patet, ergo etc. Item quia elegantior est stilus in hac epistola quam in aliis. Ad contrarium est usus et consuetudo ecclesie in qua allegatur ista epistola tanquam ab apostolo scripta. Respondeo dicendo quod propter rationes predictas ab aliquibus fuit opinatum, quod hec epistola non esset Pauli, propter quod aliqui dicebant quod erat epistola Clementis pape et martyris. Et movebantur ad hoc quia ipse scripsit Atheniensibus epistolam per omnia consimilem. Alii autem dicebant quod erat Luce evangeliste et movebantur ad hoc quia ipse eam primo scripsit Grece, ut dicitur in prologo. Alii autem dicebant quod erat Tertulliani qui fuit propinquus apostolorum tempori. Sed modo indubitanter tenetur quod est epistola Pauli. Quod probatur multiplici ratione. Primo auctoritate ecclesie, cuius est talia dubia determinare. In synodo autem

Dionysius the Carthusian (1402–71), and echoed in Gagny (citing Theophylactus), is the assertion that the difference in the linguistic style

---

Niceno recepit ecclesia istam epistolam tanquam ab apostolo scriptam. Secundo hoc idem probatur per auctoritatem antiquorum doctorum, et potissime beati Dionysii qui fuit discipulus beati Pauli. Iste autem in scriptis suis allegat dicta huius epistole tanquam dicta Pauli magistri sui. Tertio hoc probatur ex auctoritate Chrysostomi super epistolam istam dicentis quod Paulus eam scripsit Rome existens. Postquam enim biennio Rome fuerat propter appellationem factam ad Cesarem, de qua habetur in Actibus Apostolorum. Habuit licentiam transeundi in Hispaniam, et Iudeos ibi vidit, et postea Romam rediens de illo loco hanc epistolam eis scripsit, ut dicit Chrysostomus. Quarto patet propositum ex his que dicuntur ultimo capitulo huius epistole, videlicet quod missa fuit hec epistola per Timotheum qui fuit filius spiritualis Pauli apostoli. Quinto hoc idem arguitur ex zelo apostoli ad salutem Iudeorum, de quo zelo dicit ad Rom. ix: Optabam anathema esse pro fratribus meis qui sunt cognati mei, ex quibus Christus secundum carnem. Ad Roma. xi, b.: Quamdiu quidem ego sum gentium apostolus ministerium meum honorificabo, si quo modo ad emulandum provocem carnem meam, id est Iudeos, et salvos faciam aliquos ex illis. Ideo non est aliquo modo probabile quin Paulus scripsit Iudeis ad eorum salutem, qui tot alia scripsit aliis gentibus pro salutem earundem. Nulla autem alia epistola Pauli dicitur scripta Hebreis nisi ista, ergo etc. Sexto probatur propositum ex zelo Pauli apostoli ad evangelicam veritatem, ex quo zelo reprehendit Petrum manifeste, ut habetur ad Gal. ii. Nunc autem ita est quod sicut necessarium fuit ecclesiasticam veritatem predicari ad conversionem fidelium, sic necessarium fuit eam scribi ad confutationem heresum insurgentium. Propter quod Iohannes evangelium suum incipit a nativitate Christi eterna, quia videbat heresim Hebionitarum insurgere, qui dicunt Christum ante Mariam non fuisse. Paulus autem apostolus vidit tempore suo heresim Nazareorum insurgere, qui dicunt esse necessarium ad salutem servare legem veterem, et nimium invalvit hoc dictum. Ita quod etiam Petrus aliquo modo offendit in observatione legalium, propter quod apostolus ei restitit in facie, ut dictum est. Ideo non est verisimile quin Paulus apostolus aliquid scriberet conversis de Iudaismo ad confutationem huius erroris. Hoc autem fit in hac epistola, ut patebit Domino concedente. Et ideo tenendum est indiscusse quod ista epistola fuit a Paulo apostolo scripta. Ad primum argumentum patet solutio in prologo. Non enim erat apostolus Iudeorum, sed gentium, secundum quod dicit ad Gal. ii, b.: Creditum est mihi evangelium preputii, sicut et Petro circumcisionis etc. Et ideo non scripsit in hac epistola que dirigebatur Iudeis nomen sui officii; similiter nec nomen persone, quia ipse erat odiosus Iudeis, ut patet in Actibus Apostolorum in multis locis. Propter quod epistola fuisset minus recepta a Iudeis si nomen Pauli esset ibi prepositum. Ad secundum dicendum quod stilus est elegantior quia quilibet elegantius loquitur linguam propriam quam alienam. Ipse autem Paulus scripsit hanc epistolam solum Hebraice, et ideo loquitur magis ornate. Sed contra hoc insurgit unum dubium, quia per infusionem Spiritus Sancti habuit donum linguarum, secundum quod habetur I Corinth. xiiii, d.: Gratias ago Deo meo quod omnium vestrum lingua loquor. Dona autem Spiritus Sancti perfecta sunt, ergo ita perfecte loquebatur alia idiomata sicut Hebraicum. Dicendum quod donum linguarum datum est apostolis ad predicandum fidem Christi omnibus populis, et ideo est hoc donum apostolis prout faciebat ad efficaciam predicationis. Ad hoc autem non multum facit ornatus verborum, sed aliquando magis impedit, ut patet per apostolum I Corinth. ii, a.: Sermo meus et predicatio mea non in persuasibilibus humane sapientie verbis etc. Et ideo non est mirum si Paulus apostolus habuit aliquem ornatum verborum in Hebraica lingua ex humane acquisitione quem non habuit in aliis. Habuit tamen omnia idiomata inquantum valent ad efficaciam predicandi.

of Hebrews is due to Paul's gift of languages.[106] For Nicolas and Dionysius the gift is from the Holy Spirit, for Gagny (Theophylactus) it is "Christ speaking in him." In his opening point, "Paul greatly desired the salvation of the Jews," Gagny cited Rom. 9 and 11. The text from Rom. 11 was cited in the introduction of the *Glossa ordinaria.*[107]

Other traditional notes in Gagny's introduction to the "consolatory epistle" include the following: with regard to the omission of Paul's name, Gagny holds that Paul's name was odious to the Jews. This point was made by Ps. Hugh of St. Victor and several others including St. Thomas,[108] and generally in the Middle Ages it was held that, given

---

[106] Dionysius the Carthusian, "Enarratio in epistolam beati Pauli ad Hebraeos," *Opera Omnia* (Monstrolii: Typis Cartusiae S. M. de Pratis, 1901), XIII, 469–70: Porro, nonnulli opinati sunt epistolam hanc non esse Pauli, sed Lucae, vel Clementis Papae, Apostolorum discipuli, vel Barnabae, vel Tertulliani, qui erat propinquus Apostolorum temporibus. Quorum motivum duplex fuit. Primum, quoniam in aliarum epistolarum exordiis ponit Apostolus nomen suum, non autem in ista epistola; secundum, quoniam stilus huius epistolae multo venustior est quam stilus ceterarum. Sed ad haec facile est respondere. Apostolus quippe suspectus et odiosus erat Iudaeis, tanquam legis destructor, ideo nomen suum subticuit, ne eo audito vel lecto, abhorrerent epistolam, eamque legere aspernarentur. Ad secundum dicitur, mirum non esse si Paulus in proprio idiomate, puta Hebraeo, quo scripta est praesens epistola, eloquentior fuit quam in peregrino, videlicet Graeco, quo ceteras scripsit. Nec obstat quod a Spiritu Sancto accepit donum linguarum. Accepit enim hoc donum quantum ad sufficientem praedicandi facultatem, non eloquentiae venustatem, ne fides putaretur humanae inniti facundiae. Denique gratia perficit naturam secundum suam dispositionem et capacitatem, ideo non est mirandum quod per gratiam doni linguarum potentior fuit in lingua propria quam aliena. Firmiter ergo tenendum est, hanc esse Pauli epistolam, maxime propter determinationem Ecclesiae; et etiam quia B. Dionysius in suis libris passim allegat scripturam huius epistolae, Paulo magistro suo eam adscribens.

[107] *Biblia cum Glossa ordinaria,* ff. 131^r–131^v: Non est ergo mirum si in hac tanto doctrine fulget eloquio; propulsatis ergo calumniis adversantium veritati nullatenus ambigendum est, et hanc Pauli fore epistolam. In qua intendit Christi eminentiam et fidei sufficientiam necnon et legis insufficientiam et inutilititatem ostendere. Paulus doctor egregius gentium apostolus ministerium suum colens honorificare iuxta quod in epistola ad Romanos [11:13–14] ait: Quamdiu quidem sum apostolus gentium honorificabo ministerium meum, temptans si quomodo ad emulandum provocem carnem meam. Ecclesiis Hebreorum scripsit de eminentia Christi secundum utramque naturam et inutilitate legis Mosaice, astruens multis modis fidem Iesu Christi absque legalibus sufficientie ad iustitiam et salutem. Legalia vero post passionem Christi non modo non perficere, verum etiam officere quorumdam Hebreorum superstitiosam traditionem excludens, qui Christum confidentes legales observantias tenendas putabant. Et in hunc errorem quosdam etiam qui de gentilitate venerant ad Christum sua auctoritate induxerant. Ideo apostolus providens gentibus ne deinceps in hunc errorem Hebreorum auctoritate trahantur; Iudeos quoque ad emulandum provocans: quod est honor ministerii sui, gratiam Dei hic commendat per Christum verum pontificem hoc tempore fidelibus factam legem ostendens reprobatam; ad ultimum etiam de moribus instruit.

[108] Hagen (Dissertation), I. 57–64.

Paul's stand on the law, he omitted his name for reasons of humility and strategy. With regard to the "more elegant" and "more lofty" style of Hebrews, Gagny repeats the widely held argument, from Clement of Alexandria (Eusebius), *Glossa ordinaria* and the following exegetical tradition,[109] that it was written in Hebrew and translated into Greek by Luke. With regard to the problem of Heb. 2.3, Gagny reiterates the rather general notion that "us" does not only refer to Paul, but, as Contarini had said, it also includes those to whom Paul was writing.

Gagny ended his *"Argumentum"* with a long citation from Theophylactus, preceded by a reference to "Lancilotus Dominicanus," who gave the Theophylactus citation. Lancelloto, a Dominican from 1517 on, is Ambrosius Catharinus Politus (born in the noble family of Lancelottus Politi) who wrote his *Annotationes* against Cajetan in 1535.[110] Gagny is going to use this to attack Cajetan's "inane," "worthless and perverse opinions."

Gagny cites Theophylactus to end on a very strong note: it is outright wrong *("peccant")* to deny Pauline authorship. While Aquinas, Lyra and others in the Middle Ages, Contarini and others in the 16th century held that the tradition and authorities were very definite on Pauline authorship, none has claimed that it is a *peccatum* to deny Pauline authorship. Gagny uses the strong stance of Theophylactus to hold that the epistle simply cannot be by anyone other than Paul. To deny this is to deny that Christ was with Paul.

Jean Benoît (ca. 1484–1573)[111]

Claude Guilliaud (1493–1551)[112]

The Status of Paul's Epistle to the Hebrews

Christ is God, King and Priest; and therefore undoubting faith is to be had in him in all things

Concerning the author of this epistle

It is the opinion of some that this epistle is not Paul's in that it is more ornate in words than the other epistles of this apostle. There are those who attribute it to

[109] *Ibid.*

[110] Politus, *Annotationes . . . in excerpta quaedam de Commentariis . . . Cardinalis Caietani S. Xisti Dogmata* (Paris: Simon Colinaeus, 1535; Lyon: Joannes Bonhomme, 1542).

[111] Along with Gagny he was Prof. of Scripture at Collège de Navarre; b. Vernevil, d.

Luke; some make its author Apollo, whom Luke in Acts praises for having been powerful in the use of Scripture in confuting the Jews, Acts 8 [.18]. Against these the Censure of the faculty of sacred theology of Paris will do sufficiently. Their words are as follows: "These two propositions" (Concerning the author of the epistle to the Hebrews there has always been doubt, and I myself still doubt as I may frankly admit) "are arrogantly and schismatically asserted contrary to the use and determination of the church in many councils, Nicean, Laodicean, Carthaginian III, at which Augustine was present, and in the council of 70 bishops with Gelasius as president. Moreover this is clear because the author of this epistle says that he sent it through Timothy his brother, whose legation Paul was accustomed to use in certain other epistles. Blessed Peter also demonstrates the same: at the end of his second Canonical epistle, sent to the Hebrews, to whom also he had sent the first, he says that his beloved brother Paul had written to the same [Hebrews]. Likewise Dionysius the Greek cites certain things from this epistle to the Hebrews, as though drawn from Paul his teacher. Similarly Clement the first, Innocent the first, Ambrose, Chrysostom, Gregory of Nazianzus, Damascene, Isidore, and many other Catholic doctors confirm the same. It is not true that there has always been doubt about the author of this epistle to the Hebrews, since Origen wrote that before his time the ancients and predecessors accepted and received it as the Apostle Paul's. Moreover the arrogance and stubbornness of this author is extraordinary because where catholic doctors, popes, councils, all declare that this epistle is Paul's and the use and consent of the universal church confirms the same, this writer still doubts as being more prudent than the whole world." Thus far the faculty [of Paris] . . .[113]

Paris. He edited Gagny on the Gospels and Acts (Paris, 1552). *Novum testamentum, haud poenitendis sacrorum Doctorum scholiis, . . . illustratum* (Paris, 1543, 1551, 1554², 1564). The scholia consist of very brief *marginalia.*

[112] b. Beaujeu; of the Sorbonne (1523), doctor (1532); commentaries on Paul (1543), John (1550), Matt. (1562). "Epistola beati Pauli ad Hebraeos." *Collatio in omnes divi Pauli apostoli epistolas* (Lyon: Sebastian Gryphius, 1543), pp. 441–527.

[113] STATUS EPISTOLAE PAULI AD HEBRAEOS.

Christus Deus rex & Pontifex, eoque habenda illi in omnibus indubitata fides.

De Autore Huius Epistolae.

Est opinio quorundam hanc epistolam non esse Pauli, eo quod ornatior est verbis, quam caeterae huius Apostoli. Sunt qui Lucae ipsam tribuunt: nonnulli autorem eius faciunt Apollo, quem Lucas in Actis praedicat potentem fuisse in Scripturis ad revincendos Iudaeos, Act. 8. Adversus hos faciet satis Censura sacrae facultatis theologiae Parisiensis, cuius verba adscribam. Hae duae propositiones, (de epistolae ad Hebraeos autore semper est dubitatem, & ipse, ut ingenue fatear, adhuc dubito) arroganter et schismatice asseruntur, contra usum et determinationem Ecclesiae in multis conciliis, Niceno, Laudicensi, Carthaginiensi tertio, cui adfuit Augustinus, et in concilio septuaginta episcoporum praeside Gelasio. Hoc insuper liquet: quia autor huius epistolae dicit illam se misisse per Timotheum fratrem suum, cuius legatione in quibusdam aliis epistolis solebat uti Paulus. Idem etiam demonstrat beatus Petrus, qui in fine secundae Canonicae ad Hebraeos destinatae, quibus et primam miserat, eisdem dicit scripsisse charissimum fratrem suum Paulum. Magnus item Dionysius quaedam ex hac epistola ad Hebraeos citat, tanquam a

Guilliaud's introduction is a report on the "status of the epistle." It consists basically of two long citations, one a "Censure" by the Paris faculty against Erasmus (*ca.* 1526) and the Theophylactus quote which was also cited by Gagny (and translated above). With these two citations Guilliaud's introduction is as strong as any to date in favor of Pauline authorship. With the "Censure" citation it is stronger than Gagny's.

Guilliaud's report of the Paris Censure is not quite accurate, at least according to the "Determinatio Facultatis super quamplurimis Assertionibus Desiderii Erasmi Roterodami," given in the *Collectio judiciorum de novis erroribus,* edited by d'Argentre (Paris, 1728).[114] There "Proposition I," allegedly from Erasmus, is, "He who has doubts about the author of a book is not immediately doubting in faith." Then a "Censure" follows. "Proposition II" under censure is, "It can be contended with many arguments that the epistle which is sent to the Hebrews is not Paul's, since it was written more truly in a rhetorical style than in an apostolic style." "Proposition III," the only one cited by Guilliaud, is, "Concerning the author of the epistle to the Hebrews there has always been doubt, and I myself still doubt as I may frankly

---

Paulo praeceptore suo deprompta. Idem similiter comprobant Clemens primus, Innocentius primus, Ambrosius, Chrysostomus, Gregorius Nazianzenus, Damascenus, Isidorus, et alij multi catholici doctores. Nec verum est, semper dubitatum esse de autore huius epistolae ad Hebraeos: cum scribat Origenes quod ante tempora sua antiqui et maiores eam, ut Pauli Apostoli, suscipiebant. Mira autem arrogantia atque pertinacia est huius scriptoris, quod ubi tot catholici doctores, Pontifices, concilia, declarant hanc epistolam esse Pauli, et idem universalis ecclesiae usus ac consensus comprobat, hic scriptor adhuc dubitat tanquam toto orbe prudentior. Hactenus facultas. Cui admodum conformis est Theophylactus: cuius verba et sententiam adponam. Non possum equidem (inquit ille) non admirari multorum hominum impudentiam, qui cum intelligant per epistolae huius exordium fuisse tot haereses confutatas, haud tamen desistant, asserere epistolam hanc Paulo non convenire, ceu a caeteris epistolis alienam. Velim tamen hos non esse nescios epistolae huius et sensuum profunditates, et vim illam inconfutabilem, nullius alterius esse posse nisi Pauli, qui Christum haberet in se loquentem. Quod si dicendi modus illos offendit: intelligant Paulum Hebraica lingua hanc ipsam dictitasse epistolam, ut qui ad Hebraeos haberet sermonem, et unum aliquem e suis contubernalibus in Graecum vertisse: et plerique Lucam hanc transtulisse ferunt, aut Clementem, cuius etiam in ea vel stylus servetur. Nec secus hi peccant qui hanc esse Pauli epistolam negant, quam si a Paulo abesse Christum negarent. Hactenus ille. Tacuit in praefatione Paulus nomen suum, nimirum cui praeter caeteros, incredibili odio Iudaei succenserent, quod tam subita et insperata conversione ostenderet Christi potentiam inexpugnabilem, ex Saulo factus Paulus, lege antiquata Christum unicum amplexatus, eundem ferventissimo zelo praedicaret, et ceremoniis legis, modis omnibus adversaretur. "Epistola beati Pauli ad Hebraeos," pp. 441–42.

[114] Tome II, pp. 59–60.

admit." The "Censure," then, of both propositions II and III, begins, "These two propositions. . ."[115]

The Paris "Censure" compacts *"Doctores, Pontifices et Concilia"* in such a way that the consent of the church is conclusive – the church has received fourteen epistles under the name of Paul. The one argument from II Peter 3.15 is developed, seemingly so because it has not been so developed before. The key to the argument is the Censure's assertion that the epistles of Peter were directed to the Hebrews, so that when II Peter 3.15 says that "Paul wrote to you," the "you" becomes Hebrews.

Guilliaud concludes his account of the "status of the epistle" with the

---

[115] De autoribus librorum novi Testamenti.

PROPOSITIO I. in Elencho.

Non statim dubius est in fide, qui de auctore libri dubitat.

CENSURA.

Haec propositio, temerarie et erronee asseritur, loquendo, ut scriptor loquitur de dubio autorum sanctorum librorum novi Testamenti ab Ecclesia sub nomine talium autorum receptorum, cujusmodi sunt autores quatuor librorum Evangeliorum, septem Epistolarum Canonicarum, quatuordecim epistolarum Pauli, actuum Apostolorum et Apocalypsis: nam cum Deus viros illos sanctos organa sua constituerit in editione talium librorum, honori eorum detrahit quisquis ab hujusmodi libris nomina eorum aufert, vel in dubium vertit, nec non et a frequenti abducit et fructuosa eorum lectione. Praeterea quamvis de autoribus aliquorum huiusmodi librorum a nonnullis olim dubitatum sit, nihilominus postquam Ecclesia sub nomine talium autorum suo usu universali illos recepit et sua probavit definitione, jam non fas est Christiano dubitare, aut in dubium revocare.

PROPOSITIO II.

Epistola quae fertur ad Hebraeos multis argumentis coniici potest non esse Pauli, cum stylo rhetorico verius, quam Apostolico sit scripta.

PROPOSITIO III.

De Epistolae ad Hebraeos autore semper est dubitatum, et ipse ut ingenue fatear, adhuc dubito.

CENSURA.

Haec duae propositiones arroganter et schismatice asseruntur contra usum et determinationem Ecclesiae in multis Conciliis, Nicoeno, Laodicensi, Carthaginensi tertio cui affuit Augustinus et in Concilio septuaginta Episcoporum praeside Gelasio. Hoc insuper liquet, quia autor hujus Epistolae dicit illam se misisse per Timotheum fratrem suum, cujus legatione in quibusdam aliis epistolis solebat uti Paulus. Idem etiam demonstrat B. Petrus qui in fine secundae Canonicae ad Hebraeos destinatae, quibus et primam miserat eisdem dicit scripsisse charissimum fratrem suum Paulum. Magnus item Dionysius quaedam ex hac epistola ad Hebraeos citat tanquam a Paulo praeceptore suo deprompta. Idem similiter comprobant, Clemens primus, Innocentius primus, Ambrosius, Chrysostomus, Gregorius, Nazianzenus, Damascenus, Isidorus et alii multi Catholici Doctores. Nec verum est semper dubitatum esse de autore hujus epistolae ad Hebraeos, cum scribat Origenes quod ante tempora sua omnes antiqui & majores eam, ut Pauli Apostoli, suscipiebant. Mira autem arrogantia atque pertinacia hujus scriptoris, quod ubi tot Catholici Doctores, Pontifices et Concilia declarant hanc epistolam esse Pauli, et idem universalis Ecclesiae usus, ac consensus comprobat, hic scriptor adhuc dubitat toto orbe prudentior.

traditional notion, in very strong language, that Paul kept his name silent because it was odious to the Jews: "the Jews were inflamed with anger and incredible hatred of Paul's name, because by his so sudden and unexpected conversion he showed the impregnable power of Christ."

Rudolf Gualter (Walter) (1519–86)[116]

Wenzeslaus Linck (1483–1547)[117]

François Vatable (d. 1547)[118]

Veit Dietrich (1506–49)[119]

This epistle, written to the Hebrews or the Jews, revolves particularly around this [theme]: let them receive the gospel and both recognize and hold Christ as the true Messiah. He is truly high priest; he offered his own body on the cross for our sins, and thus fulfilled everything that was signified in the Old Testament through the priesthood, temple and sacrifice. Therefore, the Jews

---

[116] "In epistolam D. Pauli Apostoli ad Hebraeos D. Rodulphi Gualtheri Pastoris Ecclesiae Tigurinae Homiliarum archetypi," *In Divi Pauli Apostoli epistolas omnes . . . Homiliarum archetypi,* ed. H. Vuolphius (Zürich: Christoph Froschouer, 1589), ff. 318–52. The *explicit* is dated, 26 Iunii, 1543. The date after the first homily on Hebrews is 6 Nov. 1542. Under the text of Heb. 1.1, some short introductory comments are made, including a three sentence *"argumentum."* The argument is that Paul both admonishes those who had erred badly and consoles those who were afflicted by these errors. Paul shows that *legalia,* weak under the law, were not abrogated under the gospel, but completed and confirmed (f. 318ʳ). Gualterus also says that there is no need to say much about the authorship of Hebrews, "since it has always retained apostolic authority" (f. 318ʳ).

[117] *Das zwölfft Capitel der Epistel an die Ebreer, mit kurzer einfeltiger ausslegung* (1544), *ca.* 32 ff.

[118] Watebled (old spelling), who died in Paris, was Prof. of Hebrew at Collège de France from 1531 on. Estienne printed his *Biblia sacra cum . . . annotationibus* in 1545. Other 16th century editions of Vatable's Latin Bibles were printed in Geneva (1557), Basel (1564), Salamanca (1584), and Leiden (1599). Vatable's very short notes are also in the *Critici Sacri* (ed. Pearson, 1698).

[119] In 1530 Dietrich became Luther's *amanuensis,* in 1535, preacher in Nuremberg where he died. "Summaria in epistolam sancti Pauli ad Hebraeos," *Annotationes compendiariae in novum testamentum. Quibus summatim in singula Capita praecipui Loci et selectiores Sententiae explicantur, annotanturque . . . Per M. Vitum Theodorum* (Frankfurt: Christian Egenolph, 1545), ff. 249ʳ–259ᵛ. A German version appeared in Nuremberg, 1553: *Summaria über die gantze Bibel, das Alte unnd Newe Testament.* The "Summary" is general. The introductory summary is very general and standard. It will be given without further comment.

ought to relinquish all these things and believe in Christ in true faith, just as all the saints have had this faith in this blessed seed and through this were saved. After this admonition to faith, true religion, and Christian doctrine, he also exhorts them to holy and pious living.[120]

John Calvin (1509–64)[121]

The Argument of the Epistle to the Hebrews. Various opinions were formerly entertained as to the author of this epistle, and it was only at a later period that it was received by the Latin Churches. They suspected that it favoured Novatus in denying pardon to the fallen; but various passages will show that this was a groundless opinion. I class it without hesitation among the apostolical writings; I do not doubt that it has been through the craft of Satan that any have been led to dispute its authority. There is, indeed, no book in Holy Scripture which speaks so clearly of the priesthood of Christ, which so highly exalts the virtue and dignity of that only true sacrifice which He offered by His death, which so abundantly deals with the use of ceremonies as well as their abrogation, and, in a word, so fully explains that Christ is the end of the Law. Let us therefore not allow the Church of God or ourselves to be deprived of so great a benefit, but firmly defend the possession of it.

As to its author, we need not be greatly worried. Some think that the author was Paul, others Luke, others Barnabas, and others Clement, as Jerome says; yet Eusebius, in the sixth book of his *Church History*, mentions only Luke and Clement. I well know that in the time of Chrysostom it was received everywhere by the Greeks as among the Pauline epistles; but the Latins thought otherwise, especially those who were nearest to the apostolic times.

I can adduce no reason to show that Paul was its author; for those who say that he designedly suppressed his name because it was hateful to the Jews, make no relevant case. Why, then, did he mention the name of Timothy? By this he betrayed himself. The manner of teaching and the style sufficiently show that Paul was not the author, and the writer himself confesses in the second chapter that he was one of the disciples of the apostles, which is wholly different from the way in which Paul spoke of himself.

---

[120] Haec epistola ad Hebraeos, sive Iudaeos scripta, circa hoc potissimum versatur, ut Evangelium suscipiant, et Christum pro vero Messia et cognoscant et habeant, qui vere pontifex summus sit, et proprium suum corpus in cruce pro peccatis nostris obtulerit, et sic omne id impleverit, quod in veteri testamento, per sacerdotium, templum, et sacrificium significatum fuit. Ideoque Iudaei haec omnia relinquere debebant, et in Christum vera fide credere, ut omnes sancti semper hanc fidem in hoc benedictum semen habuerunt, et per hoc servati sunt. Post hanc admonitionem ad fidem, rectam religionem et doctrinam Christianam, adhortatur etiam ad sanctam ac piam conversationem. "Summaria in epistolam sancti Pauli ad Hebraeos," f. 249[r].

[121] *Ioannis Calvini Commentarii in Epistolam ad Hebraeos* (Geneva: Joannes Girardus, 1549). The work was also printed in Calvin's commentary "on all of Paul's epistles and also on the epistle to the Hebrews" in 1551 by Girard, 1556 by Estienne, 1557/63 by Crispin, and in 1896 in the *Corpus Reformatorum* (Vol 83, cols 1–198).

I know the excuse that is usually made as to the style, namely that no opinion can be formed therefrom, because the Greek is a translation made from the Hebrew by Luke or someone else. This conjecture can be easily refuted. I pass by other places quoted from Scripture; but if the Epistle was written in Hebrew, there would have been no allusion to the word Testament, on which the writer so much dwells. What he says of a *Testament,* in the ninth chapter, could not have been drawn from any other source than from the Greek word, for διαθήκη has two meanings in Greek, while *berith* in Hebrew means only a covenant. This reason alone is enough to convince men of sound judgment of what I have said that the epistle was written in the Greek language. The objection on the other hand, that it is more probable that the apostle wrote to the Jews in their own language, has no weight in it; how few then understood their ancestral language? Each had learned the language of the country where he dwelt. Besides, the Greek was then more widely known than all other languages. We shall proceed now to the Theme.

The object at the beginning is not to show to the Jews that Jesus, the Son of Mary, was the Christ, the Redeemer promised to them. Because he was writing to those who had already made a profession of Christ, that point is taken as granted. The concern of the writer is to prove what the office of Christ is. From this it appears evident, that by His coming an end was put to ceremonies. It is necessary to draw this distinction. As it would have been a superfluous task for the apostle to prove to those who were already convinced that He who had appeared was the Christ, so it was necessary for him to show what He was, because they did not as yet clearly understand the end, the effect, and the advantages of His coming, but being taken up with a false view of the Law, they laid hold on the shadow instead of the substance. Our business with the papists is the same today, for they confess with us that Christ is the Son of God, the Redeemer who had been promised to the world, but when we come to the reality, we find that they rob Him of more than one-half of His power.

He begins from the dignity of Christ; because it seemed strange to the Jews that the Gospel should be preferred to the Law. First he settles that point which was in dispute, that the doctrine brought by Christ had the pre-eminence, because it was the fulfilment [*clausula*] of all the prophecies. Since the reverence in which they held Moses might have been a hindrance to them, he shows that Christ was far superior to all others. After he has briefly referred to those things in which He excelled others, he mentions by name the angels, so as to include all the others with them in their proper order. Thus he advances prudently in his course. If he had begun with Moses, his comparison would have been more disliked, but when it is made clear from Scripture that celestial powers are subordinate to Christ, there is no reason why Moses or any mortal being should refuse to be classed with them, so that the Son of God may appear eminent above angels as well as men.

After he has thus brought the angels under the power and dominion of Christ, the apostle having, as it were, gained their confidence, declares that Moses was inferior to Him as a servant is to his master.

In thus setting Christ in the three first chapters in the supreme step of power, he indicates that when He speaks all ought to be silent, and that nothing should prevent us from seriously attending to His doctrine. At the same time he sets Him forth in the second chapter as our Brother in our flesh, and he thus allures us to devote ourselves more willingly to Him. He also blends exhortations and threatenings in order to lead to obedience those who are tardy or who perversely resist; and he continues in this strain nearly to the end of the fourth chapter.

Then he turns to explain the priesthood of Christ, the true, pure understanding of which abolishes all the ceremonies of the Law. After he has briefly showed how welcome that priesthood ought to be to us, and how gladly we ought to acquiesce in it, he turns aside for a bit to reprove the Jews, because they stopped at the first elements of religion like children – and he also terrifies them with a grievous and severe denunciation, because there was danger that if they were slothful to make progress, they might at length be rejected by the Lord. Presently he softens this asperity by saying that he hoped better things of them, in order to encourage those, whom he had depressed, to make progress.

Then he returns to the priesthood, and first shows that it differed from the ancient priesthood under the Law; secondly, that it was more excellent, because it took its place, and was sanctioned by an oath, because it is eternal, and remains for ever efficacious and because he who performs its duties is superior in honour and dignity to Aaron and all the rest of the Levitical tribe, of all of which the type was shadowed forth in the person of Melchizedek.

In order to prove more fully that the ceremonies of the Law were abrogated, he mentions that the ceremonies were appointed, along with the tabernacle, for a particular end, namely to set forth the heavenly prototype. Hence it follows, that they were not to be rested in unless we wish to stop in the middle of our course, and have no regard to the goal. On this subject he quotes a passage from Jeremiah, in which a new covenant is promised, which was simply an improvement on the old. Hence it follows that the old was weak and fading.

Having spoken of the likeness and similitude between the shadows and the reality exhibited in Christ, he then concludes that all the rituals appointed by Moses have been abrogated by the one only true sacrifice of Christ, because the efficacy of this sacrifice is perpetual, and that not only is the sanction of the New Testament made by it complete, but that it is also a true and a spiritual accomplishment [*complementum*] of that external priesthood which was in force under the Law.

To this doctrine he again connects an exhortation like a goad that they put aside all impediments and receive Christ with due reverence.

With regard to the many examples he mentions in the eleventh chapter concerning the fathers, they seem to me to have been brought forward for this purpose – that the Jews might understand, that if they were led from Moses to Christ they would not be departing from the fathers, but would be especially connected with them. If the chief thing in them was faith, and the root of all other virtues, it follows that this is especially that by which they could be counted the children of Abraham and the Prophets. On the other hand all those who do not follow the faith of the fathers are illegitimate. This is no small commendation of the Gospel, that by it we have union and fellowship with the universal Church, which has been from the beginning of the world.

The last two chapters contain various precepts as to the way in which we ought to live. They speak of hope, of bearing the cross, of perseverance, of gratitude towards God, of obedience, of mercy, of the duties of love, of chastity, and of such like things. Lastly, he concludes with a prayer, and at the same time gives them a hope of his coming to see them.[122]

---

[122] "The Epistle of Paul the Apostle to the Hebrews," *Calvin's Commentaries,* tr. Wm. Johnston (London: Oliver and Boyd, 1963), pp. 1–4. ARGUMENTUM in Epistolam ad Hebraeos. Non tantum de authore huius Epistolae varie olim disputatum fuit: sed ipsa quoque vix sero recepta fuit in Latinis Ecclesiis. Suspectam habebant quasi Novato suffragaretur, in neganda lapsis venia: sed quam vana fuerit illa suspicio, suis locis tractabitur. Ego vero eam inter Apostolicas, sine controversia, amplector: nec dubito Satanae artificio fuisse quondam factum, ut illi authoritatem quidam detraherent. Nullus enim est ex sacris libris, qui de Christi sacerdotio tam luculente disserat, unici, quod morte sua obtulit sacrificii, vim dignitatemque tam magnifice extollat, de caeremoniarum tam usu quam abrogatione uberius tractet: qui denique plenius explicet, Christum esse finem Legis. Quare ne patiamur Dei Ecclesiam et nos ipsos tanto bono spoliari: sed eius possessionem constanter nobis asseramus. Quis porro eam composuerit, non magnopere curandum est. Putarunt alii Paulum esse, alii Lucam, alii Barnabam, alii Clementem: ut refert Hieronymus. Quamquam Lucae tantum et Clementis Eusebius meminit, libro sexto Ecclesiasticae Historiae. Scio Chrysostomi tempore passim inter Paulinas a Graecis fuisse receptam. Sed Latini aliter senserunt: praesertim qui propriores fuerunt Apostolorum temporibus. Ego ut Paulum agnoscam authorem, adduci nequeo. Nam qui dicunt nomen fuisse de industria suppressum, quod odiosum esset Iudaeis, nihil afferunt. Cur enim mentionem fecisset Timothei si ita esset. Hoc enim indicio se prodebat. Sed ipsa docendi ratio et stylus alium quam Paulum esse satis testantur: et scriptor ipse unum se ex apostolorum discipulis profitetur, capite secundo: quod est a Paulina consuetudine longe alienum. Scio qualis de stylo excusatio adduci soleat: non posse scilicet iudicium inde fieri, eo quod Epistolam hanc ex Hebraica lingua in Graecam, vel Lucas, vel alius quispiam transtulerit. Atqui ea coniectura nullo negocio refellitur. Ut enim alios locos, qui ex Scriptura citantur, praeteream: si Hebraice scripta fuisset Epistola, nulla in nomine Testamenti fuisset allusio, in qua scriptor immoratur. Non potuit, inquam, ex alio fonte hauriri quod de iure testamenti capite nono disputat, quam ex Graeca voce. Nam διαθήκη ambiguam apud Graecos significationem habet. Berith autem Hebraeis non nisi foedus significat. Haec una ratio sani iudicii hominibus sufficiet ad probandum quod dixi, Graeco sermone scriptam fuisse Epistolam. Quod autem obiicitur ex adverso, probabilius esse, Iudaeis nonnisi sua lingua Apostolum scripsisse, nihilo plus habet ponderis. Quotus enim quisque tunc fuit, qui avitam linguam intelligeret? Quam quisque regionem incolebat, eius idioma didicerat. Porro lingua Graeca latius patebat, quam aliae omnes. Iam venio ad argumentum. Principio, non hic est status causae, ut Iesum filium Mariae Iudaeis persuadeat esse Christum et Redemptorem illis promissum. Quia enim ad eos scribit, qui iam Christo nomen dederant, caput illud pro confesso sumit. Sed in hoc cardine versatur, ut probet quale sit officium Christi: unde pateat, eius adventu finem esse caeremoniis impositum. Hanc distinctionem notare operae precium est. Nam sicuti Apostolo supervacuus fuisset labor, hunc esse Christum qui exhibitus fuerat, apud eos probare, qui iam ita persuasi erant: sic eos doceri qualis esset, oportuit: quia finem, vim, et fructum adventus eius nondum tenebant: sed falsa Legis interpretatione occupati, umbram prehensabant pro corpore. Eiusmodi hodie negocium nobis est cum papistis. Nobiscum enim

In his "*Argumentum*" on the authorship and authority of Hebrews, Calvin is confident about two things. One, there is no proof for Pauline authorship. Two, there is no doubt about its apostolic authority. In the

---

fatentur, Christum esse Filium Dei, qui redemptor mundo promissus fuerat. Sed quum ad rem ventum est, eum plusquam dimidia virtutis suae parte nudant. Orditur autem a Christi dignitate: quia Iudaeis absurdum videbatur, Legem Evangelio posthaberi. Ac primum quidem illud statuit, de quo erat disceptatio: allatam a Christo doctrinam primas tenere, quia sit omnium prophetiarum clausula. Sed quoniam reverentia, quam Moisi deferebant, obstare poterat: docet Christum longe omnibus praecellere. Ac postquam summatim attigit, quibus nominibus praecellat: nominatim Angelos illi submittit, ut cum illis reliquos omnes cogat in ordinem. Prudenter autem hac ratione progreditur. Nam si a Moise coepisset, magis odiosa fuisset comparatio. Ubi autem ex Scripturis constat, coelestes quoque principatus subsidere infra Christum: non est cur recuset Moises, vel ullus quispiam mortalium, illis aggregari: ut supra omnes, tam homines quam Angelos, Filius Dei emineat. Itaque postquam Angelos Apostolus sub Christi dominium et potestatem redigit, mox quasi sumpta fiducia, quanto inferior sit Moises, pronunciat. Nempe quantum differt servus a domino. Quod ergo tribus primis capitibus Christum in summo gradu principatus collocat, huc tendit, ut eo loquente, omnes sileant: nec quicquam nos impediat, quominus eius doctrinae solidam audientiam praestemus. Quanquam secundo capite eum nobis fratris loco in carne nostra proponens, hoc modo nos allicit, ut libentius nos totos illi devoveamus ac tradamus. Et simul exhortationes minasque admiscet: si quis vel ad obsequendum sit tardior, vel contumaciter repugnet. Idque agit prope ad finem usque quarti capitis. Inde transit ad explicandum Christi sacerdotium: cuius vera et pura cognitio omnes Legis caeremonias abolet. Sed ubi breviter tantum indicavit, quam debeat nobis illud esse amabile, et quam suaviter acquiescere in eo liceat, paulisper ad increpandos Iudaeos digreditur, eo quod in primis elementis, tanquam pueri, haesitarent. Ubi etiam gravi et severa denunciatione eos terret. Periculum enim esse, ne si ad proficiendum adeo sint segnes, tandem abbiiciantur a Domino. Verum hanc asperitatem mox temperat, cum dicit meliora se sperare: ut eorum potius animos erigat ad studium profectus, quam deiiciat. Postea ad sacerdotii tractationem redit: in qua docet primo, differre ipsum a veteri sacerdotio, quod sub Lege fuit: deinde esse praestantius, quod in eius locum succedat, et iureiurando sanciatur, quod aeternum sit, semperque vigeat, quod qui eo fungitur Aaronem et reliquos omnes ex genere Levitico honore superet. Quorum omnium adumbratam fuisse imaginem in persona Melchizedec ostendit. Quo autem certius abrogatas esse Legis caeremonias probet, in alium finem institutas una cum tabernaculo fuisse commemorat: nempe ut coelesti prototypo servirent. Unde sequitur, non esse in illis manendum: nisi velimus contempta meta, in medio viae desidere. Ad hoc Ieremiae locum adducit, ubi promittitur novum Testamentum, quod nihil aliud est, quam veteris correctio. Unde sequitur, infirmum illud fuisse et caducum. Postea de similitudine congruentiaque umbrarum et veritatis in Christo exhibitae disputans, concludit unico Christi sacrificio abrogatos fuisse ritus omnes a Moise institutos: quia perpetua sit huius sacrificii efficacia: et in eo non modo absoluta sit novi Testamenti sanctio, sed verum et spirituale complementum externi illius sacerdotii, quod sub Lege viguit. Doctrinae rursus exhortationem annectit instar stimuli: ut impedimentis omnibus valere iussis, Christum qua decet reverentia, excipiant. Tot patrum exempla, quae recenset capite undecimo, mihi videntur in hunc finem esse adducta, ut agnoscerent Iudaei, si a Moise traducti essent ad Christum, adeo se a sanctis patribus non discedere, ut hac maxime in re illis coniuncti forent. Nam si praecipua in illis virtus fuit fides, radixque omnium virtutum: sequitur hanc esse praecipue, qua censeantur Abrahae et Prophetarum filii. Contra, degeneres esse

medieval period and continuing in the 16th century, authorship and authority were seen as interrelated. Generally, Pauline authorship was considered necessary in order to maintain the authority of the epistle. Luther, with his hermeneutic of a canon (Christ) within the canon (Scripture), could distinguish (in 1522) between the author as a "trustworthy man, though he is not St. Paul," and the authority as "a marvelously fine" and "powerful epistle." Erasmus moved in a different direction: holding, like Luther, that Heb. 6.4–6 is unpauline, Erasmus concludes that the status of Hebrews is heretical. Cajetan moved in a direction similar to Erasmus': from non-Pauline to non-canonical. In reaction to these distinctions and directions, Oecolampadius and Gagny moved in the direction that it is heresy to deny Pauline authorship: the authority of Hebrews, under Pauline authorship, will remain secure. Calvin's distinction between "no" on Paul and "yes" on apostolic authority is different from all these positions.

Calvin's distinction is clear and strong. To "dispute its authority" is to be under the employment of Satan; and, "I can adduce no reason to show that Paul was its author."

Calvin then proceeds to dispute the (traditional) reasons offered for Pauline authorship. The "odious-argument," that Paul omitted his name because the Jews would not have read his letter if his hated name was given, makes no sense to Calvin, because the mention of Timothy would give Paul away. In other words, the "odious-argument" is inconsistent: if Paul were the author and wanted to keep his identity secret, he would not have mentioned Timothy's name.

The "style-argument," that the language of Hebrews is different because Paul wrote in Hebrew, Calvin refutes with two interesting points, interesting because I have not seen them made earlier. The first, at the start reminiscent of Erasmus and Cajetan, is that if the epistle were written initially in Hebrew, the word testament (διαθήκη) would not have been used and so extensively, because ברית *(berith)* means only covenant. Calvin then makes the interesting point that (διαθήκη) has

---

omnes, qui patrum fidem non sequuntur. Hoc ad Evangelii commendationem non parum valet, quod nobis in eo cum universa, quae ab initio mundi fuit, Ecclesia consensus est ac societas. Duo, quae supersunt, capita varias formandae vitae praeceptiones continet, de spe, de tolerantia crucis, de perseverantia, de gratitudine erga Deum, de obedientia, de misericordia et charitatis officiis, de castitate, et similibus. Demum Epistolam precatione claudit: nisi quod spem illis facit adventus sui. *Commentarii in epistolam ad Hebraeos* (1549), pp. 1–4.

two meanings (testament and covenant). His second, also interesting point, is that few Jews knew Hebrew anyway and that Greek was more widely known.

Also the teaching and Heb. 2.3 "sufficiently show that Paul was not the author." In his commentary on Heb. 2.3, Calvin repeats his introductory assertion that the text militates against Pauline authorship.[123] In his comments on 6.6, Calvin says that, while the Novatians might have found support in this text, "once the mind of the apostle is laid bare," it will be clear that "there is nothing here to support such a stupid mistake." Calvin opposes the "majority" medieval view that 6.4–6 denies second baptism, and the view (held by Lyra) that "impossible" means "hard." Calvin's explanation follows the line of Bugenhagen, that 6.4–6 refers to the sin against the Holy Spirit.[124] Consistent with his view that the authority of Hebrews is apostolic though the author is not Paul, Calvin throughout his commentary refers to the author as "the apostle."

"We shall proceed now to the *Argumentum.*" Calvin's main point is that the apostle in Hebrews was not out to prove something about the person of Jesus Christ; Jesus as the Christ is taken for granted. The object of Hebrews was to prove somethings about the "office of Christ," the "what" of his work. The work, "the end, the effect, and the advantages of His coming," is described in terms of the end of ceremonies and rituals.

The other 16th century exegetes we have studied described the work of Christ in different terms. Luther and Bugenhagen do so in contrary terms. Luther and, in more intensified terms, Bugenhagen discusses Christ as the end of the (whole) law. Calvin and others do not see such a dichotomy between law and gospel. Erasmus talked in terms of the end of shadows and observances, and Titelmans in terms of the end of figures and carnal observances of the law. Bullinger and Zwingli said that old shadows, priesthood and sacrifices were antiquated by Christ, and that Christ is the fulfillment and perfection of the law. Dietrich also used "fulfillment" language. Contarini said that Christ is the end of the shadow of the old law, and Gagny, that Christ is the end of the priesthood of the old law. Except for Luther and Bugenhagen, what seems common among these exegetes, including Calvin, is a view that Christ marked the end to certain aspects of the old Jewish order, but

---

[123] *Ibid.*, p. 20.

[124] *Ibid.*, pp. 72–73.

not, as Luther and Bugenhagen would see it, the end to the law itself. For Calvin there is "agreement between the law and the gospel."[125] In fact for Calvin, Hebrews was directed against a false view of the law (held by Jews and contemporary papists).

For Calvin there was continuity between the old and the new. The priesthood of Christ "was more excellent *(praestantius)*." The new covenant "was simply an improvement *(correctio)* on the old." There was "likeness and similitude *(similitudine congruentiaque)* between the shadows and the reality exhibited in Christ." The comparison between Christ's dignity and the angels and Moses shows that Christ is "far superior to all others." The foundation for the continuity and comparison between the old and the new is God.[126]

In his discussion of Christ's dignity, Calvin has a turn of phrase that is striking, in terms of the humanity of Christ. Most exegetes of Hebrews, and Calvin as well, dwell on the divine origins of Christ's dignity. For Calvin, in the early chapters of Hebrews, the apostle sets Christ "in the supreme step *(gradu)* of power," and "at the same time he sets Him forth . . . as our Brother in our flesh."

---

[125] *Ibid.*, p. 5.

[126] *Ibid.*, pp. 5–6.

Part Two

Politus to Bèze 1551–1598

Ambrosius Catharinus Politus (1483–1553)[1]

Preface to the Epistle of blessed Paul the Apostle to the Hebrews

Formerly certain heretics, as Jerome testifies in his argument to the epistle to Titus, attempted to argue that this epistle to the Hebrews did not belong to blessed Paul the Apostle, and some of our own people follow them in this unhappy time. They allege two points in particular which seem to convince them. First, there is no name of the author prefixed to this epistle. Second, the style of this epistle is not in accord with the style of the other epistles. The first is elegantly blunted by the response of blessed Jerome. If this epistle is not Paul's because his name is not given, it is equally no one else's, because no name is prefixed. Rather, it is to be ascribed to blessed Paul and he did this, because, since he was offensive to the Hebrews, he was unwilling to prevent their profitable reading of it by prefixing his name which was odious to them. They add that this epistle in eloquence and style is not in accord with the others, and is by far superior to them, for the reason that blessed Paul wrote only this one in the Hebrew tongue, without doubt his own, and the others in Greek. Whence it is not surprising if this one stands out in eloquence. However, if we consider the style, whose is it like? They say, Clement's. God have mercy on them, since neither the style nor anything else accords with him. For even the author of this epistle most clearly showed that he is Hebrew in origin (as we will note in the proper places). There are so many and so important authorities, both Pontiffs and weighty authors asserting such strong arguments that this epistle is Paul's, that I marvel vehemently with what boldness anyone (who wished to appear Christian) is able to dare to contrive anything against such great judgments. I have written copiously about this both against Cajetan and in another special book, where I have brought forth many councils and decrees of Pontiffs and testimonies of so many fathers and saints, besides the long standing usage of all

---

[1] *Commentaria . . . in omnes divi Pauli, et alias septem canonicas epistolas* (Venice: Vincenzo Valgrisi, 1551). "Commentaria in eandem epistolam beati Pauli ad Hebraeos," *In omnes divi Pauli apostoli, et alias septem canonicas epistolas R. P. Fratris Ambrosii Catharini Politi Senensis, Episcopi Minoriensis, commentaria* (Paris: Bernardus Turrisanus, 1566), pp. 453–521, which I have used.

the churches, so that he who wishes to contend against such a cloud of witnesses shall have clearly shown himself without doubt to be of an impudent, obstinate and heretical spirit, and so unworthy of debate.

It may however be asked with greater reason, why this epistle, filled with weighty judgments and so much doctrine, nevertheless acquired the last place in order. We have already responded to this in our treatment of Romans. The Hebrews rejected apostolic, and especially Paul's, preaching. Therefore, as though despised by God so that they would for a time give way to the Gentiles, it was fair and just that they receive last place, just as finally they will come at the last time when the fullness of the Gentiles will have entered. Thus the Apostle preferred Philemon, a private man, to them, just as they deserved. Therefore because they are converted last, it is fitting that they here hold the last place. And then they will acknowledge that blessed Paul was truthful and that he had fulfilled his office and function diligently for the last, which they will then turn out to be.[2]

---

[2] Praefatio in epistolam B. Pauli Apostoli ad Hebraeos:

Quidam haereticorum olim, quemadmodum B. Hieronymus in argumento epistolae ad Titum testatur, suadere conati sunt hanc ad Hebraeos epistolam non esse B. Pauli Apostoli. Quos et quidam ex nostris hac infoelici tempestate sectati sunt. Duo autem praecipue afferebant, quae facere suasionem videbantur. Primum, quod huic epistolae non est nomen authoris praescriptum. Alterum, quoniam stylus huius non convenit cum caeterarum epistolarum stylo. Sed primum eleganter B. Hieronymi responso retunditur. Nam si ob hoc non est B. Pauli, quia eius nomine non inscribitur, nec ullius pariter erit: quia nullius habet nomen praescriptum. Quod vero sit potius credenda B. Pauli, vel hoc ipsum facit, quod cum esset Hebraeis infensus, noluit praefixione odiosi sui apud eos nominis utilitatem excludere lectionis. Quod vero addebant, non convenire hanc epistolam eloquio et stylo cum caeteris, et esse longe illis superiorem, ob id esse, quia hanc solam B. Paulus lingua hebraica scripsit, nimirum propria: caeteras vero Graeca. Unde non mirum si haec eloquio praestat: quanquam si stylum expendimus, cuius erit stylo similis? Aiunt, Clementis. Parcat illis Deus, cum nec stylus, nec reliquorum quicquam illi conveniat. Nam et huius epistolae author se genere Hebraeum esse (ut suis locis annotabimus) quam manifestissime insinuavit. Sunt vero tot, tantaeque authoritates et Pontificum, et gravissimorum authorum, taliaque argumenta, eam B. Pauli esse asserverantia, ut vehementissime sim miratus, quanam fronte quisquam audere potuerit (qui Christianus videri volebat) adversus tanta praeiudicia quicquam comminisci. De qua re et in Caietanum, et alio proprio libello copiose scripsi, ubi multa concilia, et decreta Pontificum, et tot patrum, et Sanctorum testimonia produxi, praeter diuturnum omnium ecclesiarum usum, ut qui contra tantam nubem testium velit contendere, haud dubium protervi, et contumacis, atque haeretici animi seipsum perspicue prodiderit, et sic indignum cum quo disputetur.

Quaeri autem maiori cum ratione posset, cur haec epistola gravitate sententiarum et tanta doctrina referta, postremum tamen nacta sit in ordine locum. Huic quaestioni iam respondimus in ea quae ad Romanos. Spreverunt enim Hebraei apostolicam, et praesertim B. Pauli, praedicationem. Et ideo tanquam spreti a Deo ut interim cedant Gentibus, aequum fuit et iustum eos postremum obtinere locum, sicut et postremo tandem tempore venient, quum intraverit plenitudo Gentium: ita ut Apostolus Philemonem privatum hominem ipsis praetulerit, quemadmodum fuerunt digni. Quia ergo in novissimis convertuntur, novissimum hic eos locum tenere oportuit. Et tunc agnoscent B. Paulum veracem, et diligenter suo officio ac munere pro novissimis, qui tunc invenientur, fuisse functum.

The two points that Politus raised regarding the question of authorship were often discussed by the medievals: *modus scribendi* – no name, and *stilus* – more eloquent. His answers, which he generally acknowledges, are also medieval. Politus' brief *"Argumentum"* represents the consensus of medieval emphases: the *"eminentia Christi"* over Angels and Moses, of gospel over law, New Testament over Old Testament and priesthood of Christ over Levitical priesthood, and exhortation to faith as *"fundamentum."* The reference to his writing against Cajetan would be Politus' *Annotationes* (1535), to which, it has been noted, Gagny made reference. In the body of his commentary Politus makes several critical comments about Cajetan's interpretation, and not only Cajetan's views of authorship.[3]

The one point in Politus' preface that stands out is his question and answer about why the weighty epistle to the Hebrews is fourteenth. This question has "greater reason" to it than all the questions about authorship. The answer, with reference to Rom. 9–11, is that Hebrews is last because the Jews as a people will be last (in the eschatological timetable, as it is said today). Even the epistle to a converted private citizen precedes.

Andreas Gerhard Hyperius (1511–64)[4]

The sections in the *"Prolegomena"* of Hyperius are as follows: "Hebrews," occasion, parts, genus, status, *"Loci* of Christian doctrine" and authorship.

EPISTOLAE ARGUMENTUM:

Congruentissime haec epistola, et opportunissime ostendit Apostolus Hebraeis eminentiam Christi prae Angelis et Mose: ac propterea eminentiam Evangelicae gratiae prae lege, sive testamenti novi prae vetere: et eminentiam sacerdotii Christi, prae sacerdotio Levitico, quod mandatur in lege. Et hinc docet supervenientem legis inutilitatem, et sacerdotii antiqui, et idcirco eius cessationem, utpote quae legitime functa erat suo officio, adveniente utilitate ac sempiternitate novi testamenti, et evangelii aeterni. Et iis patefactis hortatur eos ad fidem, ut fundamentum totius aedificii, et ad opera charitatis cum tolerantia passionum in spe mercedis magnae, et immortalis. "Commentaria in eandem epistolam beati Pauli ad Hebraeos," (1566), p. 453.

[3] E.g., Politus, pp. 457, 459, 463, 465, 496.

[4] *Commentarii D. Andreae Hyperii, doctissimi . . . Theologi, in epistolam D. Pauli Apostoli ad Hebraeos, nunc primum opera Ioannis Mylii in lucem editi* (Zürich: Christoph Froschouer, 1584). In his Preface (f. 5r), Mylius comments that some will not be grateful for the posthumous work, both because the author could not revise the work (composed between 1544 and 1548), and because he could not elaborate on the 617 pages *(4°)*, as he intended to

One type of introduction, very explicit in Calvin, has been the *Argumentum,* where author and theme(s) are discussed. The type of introduction that is developing at this time is an expanded type of introduction, where other questions are asked as well. Politus thought that the question with "greater reason" was why Hebrews is the 14th epistle.

The first question in Hyperius' ten page introduction is, "Who were the Hebrews?" His argument is that the word does not come from Heber but from Abraham, for four reasons. 1) Since it is not Hebrer or Hebre but Heber, it is more difficult to derive Hebraei from Heber. 2) In Scripture, we do not find descendents from Heber called Hebraei, but first they are called sons of Abraham (Abrahae). 3) The Jews pride themselves in being descendents from Abraham. 4) From etymology, the Hebrew word עברים (Ibraim) means those who go over *("transeuntes")* or the foreigners *("peregrinos"),* which agrees with the word Abram, who went from Mesopotamia over to Canaan and lived there as a foreigner. Why is the epistle not addressed "to the Jews"? The name Hebrew is more honorific (2 Cor. 2; Phil. 3); besides, it comes from the first and most honorific patriarch, Abraham, and not from his much inferior descendant, Judah.[5]

"Why was it written, or what was the occasion?": to confirm pious Hebrews, lest they defect from Christ and the gospel, and to preach the preeminence of Christ, the gospel and faith.[6] The "Genus" is didactic (Bullinger said that part of it was). The "Status" or "general proposition of the whole epistle" is threefold: Christ by nature is God, his priesthood true and perfect, righteousness through faith.[7] The section on "whether Paul wrote this epistle" gives most of the arguments which have already been given for Pauline authorship.[8]

The section that stands out in Hyperius' introduction is the one entitled, "How great its utility, or how many various *loci* of Christian doctrine are there in it?" There are twenty-nine – in part one. In a previous section on, "What it contains, or how many are its parts?" Hyperius discusses in the usual manner, the contents of the epistle by theme and chapter. There are in Hebrews two principal parts, according

---

do, but his death in 1564 "interrupted" the work. For a chronological list of his works, cf. Gerhard Krause, *Andreas Gerhard Hyperius* ("Beiträge zur historischen Theologie," Vol. 56; Tübingen: Mohr, 1977), pp. 130–58.

[5] Hyperius, p. 1.

[6] *Ibid.,* p. 2.

[7] *Ibid.,* p. 5.

[8] *Ibid.,* pp. 6–10.

to him. The first (to the middle of chapter 12) is about the divinity of Christ, abrogation of the law, preeminence of the gospel, and justification by faith. The second (to the end) is about the doctrine of charity. At the end of his list of *loci,* he chooses not to enumerate the *loci* contained in the second principal part.

Most of the *loci* touch upon law and gospel: the gospel was revealed through the son of God himself; law and gospel come from one and the same God; the difference between law and gospel is excellence; a "prominent locus" concerns the abrogation of the legal priesthood and simultaneously the abrogation of the whole law [redolent of Luther's reading of chapter 7]; the law was incapable of leading to perfection and only capable of leading to Christ or the gospel; the gospel remains forever; the law was a shadow of the gospel. There are four *loci* concerning the rejection of the gospel.[9]

---

[9] *Ibid.*, pp. 5–6:

1. Evangelium esse revelatum per ipsum filium Dei. Unde dignitas eius elucescit ad confirmandas conscientias.
2. Unum eundemque esse Deum, a quo Lex, et a quo evangelium.
3. Christum esse filium Dei et verum Deum: contra Iudaeos et omnes negantes divinitatem Christi.
4. Quam periculosum sit, contemnere verbum, seu oblatum evangelium: ad terrendos hostes evangelii.
5. Evangelicam veritatem certissimis et plurimis testimoniis comprobatam: ad confirmandas conscientias credentium.
6. Christum esse verum hominem, et quare hominem fieri decuerit: cui loco non pauca ad dignitatem Christi, et consolationem nostram pertinentia sunt inserta: ut quod Christus diaboli, peccati et mortis aboleverit imperium: quod frater noster sit: quod factus miseriarum nostrarum conscius et participes: quodque propositus misericors pontifex et intercessor.
7. Discrimen inter legem et evangelium huiusque praestantia.
8. Occasionem amplectendi evangelium, et sanam doctrinam, non sinendam avolare.
9. Per incredulitatem excludi homines a participatione Evangelii et regni Dei.
10. E diverso suscipientes sermonem cum fide, ingredi in requiem, seu accipere promissiones evangelicas.
11. Verbi Dei efficacia ac dignitas.
12. Per solum Christum verum pontificem obtingere misericordiam et gratiam: ubi mox capite quinto multa de dignitate Christi sequuntur, in quibus illud amplissimum et mire consolatorium, quod fuerit caussa salutis aeternae.
13. Omnibus semper ad pleniorem cognitionem et profectum in fide enitendum.
14. Lapsos difficulter quidem resurgere, non tamen de eis desperandum.
15. Deum respicere opera ex charitate prodeuntia, praemiisque afficere.
16. Plena et certa spe perstandum in fide.
17. Confirmandam spem certitudine divinarum promissionum, et ex iisdem consolationem omni tempore accipiendam.
18. Insignis locus de abrogatione legalis sacerdotii, simulque totius legis.

The *Loci* section would be of interest to those who seek to locate Hyperius between Luther and Zwingli. Of interest for this study is both the form and content of an introduction which identifies the utility of Hebrews with *Loci* of Christian doctrine.

Sébastien Châteillon (1515–63)[10]

Basilius Zanchius (d. 1560)[11]

Prior to selected notes, Zanchius makes the different and unusual comment that Paul did not preface himself as the Apostle Paul because of what he would say about Christ in 3.1: "Having therefore the first priest and Apostle of our confession, Jesus"; it would be incongruent for Paul to be called Apostle where Christ was to be called Apostle.[12]

---

19. Legem per se fuisse imbecillem, inutilem, nihil ad ducentem ad perfectionem, et tantum introducentem ad Christum seu evangelium.

20. Christi sacerdotium simulque evangelium manere aeternum, neque aliam legem praestantiorem expectandam.

21. Legem tantum fuisse exemplar et umbras evangelii, seu novi testamenti, et istud in lege ac prophetis fuisse promissum.

22. Promissiones evangelicas de remissione peccatorum esse, et universales.

23. Sacrificia veteris legis nihil potuisse efficere ad purgationem conscientiarum, seu iustitiam coram Deo, sed id vere effecisse unicum sacrificium sanguinis Christi, propter cuius efficaciam omnia alia sacrificia cessare debent.

24. Credentes et purgatos sanguine Christi, debere proferre etiam fidei suae fructus.

25. Contemptores evangelii graviter a Deo puniri.

26. Consolationis locus de non abiienda spe in afflictionibus.

27. Homines fide iustificari, deque eius effectibus ac dignitate.

28. Quis usus exemplorum veteris testamenti, et quomodo ea ad evangelicam doctrinam confirmandam accommodari debeant.

29. Pios, permittente Deo, utiliter et salutariter affligi.

[10] "Ad Hebraeos," *Biblia . . . una cum eiusdem annotationibus* (Basel: Oporin, 1551), col. 267–78; also Basel, 1556, 1573; also in *Critici Sacri*. The notes are few and short.

[11] "*Basilii Zanchii in omnes divinos libros notationes* (Rome, 1553; also Spire, 1558). I have used, "In epistolam ad Hebraeos," *B Z, Bergomatis, canonici ordinis lateranensis, in omnes s. scripturae libros Notationes* (Cologne: Mylius, 1602), cols. 216–20.

[12] Et in Epistola ad Hebraeos intelligere possumus propterea Paulum solita consuetudine nomen suum, nec Apostoli vocabulum praeposuisse, quia de Christo erat dicturus: Habentes ergo principem sacerdotum, et Apostolum confessionis nostrae Iesum; nec fuisse congruum, ut ubi Christus, Apostolus dicendus erat, ibi etiam Paulus Apostolus poneretur. "In epistolam ad Hebraeos," col. 216.

Jean Arboreus (d. c. 1569)[13]

Preface

In this epistle, which is quite learned, weighty, distinguished, full of meaning, and truly difficult to understand, Paul teaches that God, always mindful of the human race, expressed formerly in many ways his mind, his design, his will through prophets and angels. Finally in these last days, in order to declare his love towards us and to make for us faith in the most holy trinity fuller and more certain, he deemed it worthy to speak through his only son Jesus Christ, having with him dominion over the whole world, to whom all angels are subjected as to the only author of eternal salvation and the supreme leader of heaven and earth. They will not escape the avenging wrath of God who neglect to accept and revere this Savior and redeemer with blameless holiness of life and worship him with the highest cultivation of religion. For this High Priest voluntarily offered a sacrifice for us, by his victorious death overthrew, destroyed and dissipated the furious ruler of death, namely the devil, and liberated us, subject to the dominion of satan, from the law of sin and death. Although Moses was the most learned legislator of the Judaic nation, and quite loved and intimate with God, nevertheless he was unworthy to be compared with this sacrificial Christ, lest the Jews, roused to such pride, indeed fallen into the pit of blindness, exalt their Moses and worship him in place of the Messiah. On account of them, the Lord, vehemently offended and angered, vowed that he would reject them on account of their persistent ingratitude and obstinate incredulity, although promises of eternal inheritance were first made to them. On the other hand, the Gentiles (whom they detested as profane and impious) who, believing with sincere faith in Christ and obeying the divine commands from the heart, will enter into eternal rest and enjoy the comradeship of celestial citizens and all the saints. It is fitting that we designate in this most blameless Pontiff the anchor of our hope and salvation, for he made propitiation for our trespasses by his blood, and is always prepared to have compassion on our infirmities and to help those who are afflicted with many calamities and various temptations. Let the Jews cease to praise so much their great pontiff namely Aaron, because he offered to God victims and sacrifices for the people, and ministered perpetually to God with sacred duties, and no other high priest is to be compared with him. Christ by a long distance and by the magnitude of powers and prophetic signs surpasses that ancient Pontiff. For the former offered sacrifices to God both for his own sin and the transgressions of the whole people. But this later holy Pontiff, innocent and unstained, and instituted the greatest and most illustrious priest according to the order of Melchisedec, offered himself in sacrifice not for

---

[13] b. Laon, *doctor surbonicus* (1536). *Theosophiae complectens sanam et luculentam difficillimorum locorum cum Veteris tum Novi Testamenti expositionem,* tomes I and II (Paris: Simon Colinaeus, 1540); *Tertius tomus Theosophiae . . . complecitur sanam et luculentam in omnes divi Pauli Epistolas explanationem* (Paris, 1553). "In Pauli ad Hebraeos Epistolam," *Doctissimi et lepidissimi Commentarii Ioannis Arborei Laudonensis . . . in omnes divi Pauli epistolas* (Paris: Jean Roigny, 1553), ff. 245^{v}–87^{v}, which I have used.

his own sin (because he did no sin) but for the crimes of his people. That the promise of heavenly reward might be more certain (which we are to acquire by faith and endurance of all evils) he pledged an oath so that through two unalterable things we have firm consolation amid the perils of this world. Let us understand that Christ did not take his priesthood from the Levitical tribe, from which Aaron was, for that tribe finally perished on account of its weakness; but from heaven he was made high priest according to the order of Melchisedec forever; on this account his priesthood will be forever. Since this mediator of the new testament illumined the world, he thus engraved and inscribed his law in our hearts, so that no one will greatly need to be instructed by his neighbor. Moreover this most select Pontiff did not enter only once every year into the holy of holies to offer the blood of cattle for his and the people's transgressions, but he offered his own blood to God in order to liberate the whole of the human race from all sins and to purify our conscience from dead works. Let us convince ourselves that the shadows of the Mosaic law ceased when the gospel of Christ shone forth, and that salvation is to be hoped for not from the observance of imperfect law but from sincere and evangelical faith, through which the saints of old, greatly distinguished by a most blameless life and duties of piety, pleased God, to whom also Christian soldiers were wonderfully pleasing, who, by the example of Christ, suffered calamities and afflictions of this world with an unconquerable greatness of spirit. Moreover let us know from the doctrine of Paul that no one will reach that heavenly Jerusalem nor the church of the first members unless he cast off his burden of faults and serve God with fear and reverence, and value his neighbor with sincere disposition of charity. Paul writes this letter to faithful Jews who were of Palestine and Jerusalem, and exhorts them not to lose heart because of innumerable calamities inflicted by their fellow kinsmen, nor to be destroyed by grief; but they should endure everything with a steadfast heart for the glory of Christ.

And not to be turned into doubt and controversy is whether this epistle written to the Hebrews is Paul's. For in the holy, Nicene Synod, the universal church received it as written by the Apostle Paul, and decreed that it ought to be held as such. Then also divine Dionysius, instituted in the divine mysteries of the sacred faith by Paul, in his works cites testimony from this epistle as written by his teacher. Also blessed Chrysostom in his Homilies published on this epistle affirms it was written at Rome by blessed Paul. Besides this, Damascene, *On the Orthodox Faith,* book 4, chapter 18, asserts that there are fourteen epistles of the Apostle Paul, which would not be true if that one which is to the Hebrews were not Paul's. Moreover, Jerome in his epistle to Dardanus says . . . Although this epistle does not have an opening salutation, nevertheless it does have a closing one, inasmuch as Paul says in the last chapter: "And I beseech you, brethren, that you suffer the word of consolation. For I have written to you in a few words. Know that our brother Timothy is set at liberty, with whom (if he comes shortly) I will see you. Salute all your prelates, and all the saints. The brethren from Italy salute you." Jacques Lefèvre was moved by these words to receive this epistle as written by Paul. ["] The reason why we do not have the first salutation, is thought to be that neither the Greeks nor the Latins, have the original, for the Apostle wrote it in his paternal, Hebrew tongue. ["] Therefore Cajetan appears to me to be raving and to think contrary to the ancient writers, in affirming that this epistle was not written in the Hebrew language. And a quite frivolous conjecture leads to his conclusion: "Paul says Melchisedec is interpreted to mean King of justice. If the epistle were written in Hebrew, in what language, I ask, is Melchisedec interpreted as King of justice? For Melchisedec in Hebrew is a compound word from king and justice. Thus in Hebrew he would have had to say, Melchisedec means Melchisedec." But this reason is groundless. For, although Melchisedec among the Hebrews says King of justice, nevertheless the translator expressed for us in Latin words what Melchisedec signifies. And Melchisedec among the Hebrews is not composed of king and justice, for a Hebrew compound word is not composed from Latin words but from their own native words. For who among the Greeks would say that *morosophos* is composed of *stulto* and *sapiente*? It is composed of *moros* and *sophos*. In such a manner Melchisedec among the Hebrews is composed of *melchi* or *malci* which means my King and *Zedec* which means justice. And that doctor hesitates about the author of this epistle after the definition by the church . . .[14]

[14] Praefatio:

Docet Paulus in hac epistola admodum docta, gravi, luculenta, sententiosa, verum intellectu difficili, Deum nunquam non humano generi consulentem, olim multis modis suam mentem, suum consilium suam voluntatem per Prophetas et Angelos expressisse: tandem hisce temporibus extremis ut declararet suam erga nos charitatem, nobisque pleniorem et certiorem sanctissimae Trinitatis fidem faceret, loqui dignatus est per unicum filium suum Iesum Christum, habentem secum totius orbis dominium, cui ut aeternae salutis autori unico, coelique et terrae dominatori maximo, Angeli omnes subiiciuntur: et propterea iram Dei etiam ultricem non effugient, qui neglexerint hunc Salvatorem et redemptorem inculpatissima vitae sanctimonia, summoque religionis cultu colere, suspicere et revereri. Hic enim Pontifex summus ultro in sacrificium pro nobis oblatus, sua victrici morte furiosum necis Imperatorem, diabolum scilicet, profligavit, dissipavit et abolevit, nosque servituti satanae obnoxios, a lege peccati et mortis liberavit. Et licet Moses fuerit Iudaicae nationis legislator peritissimus, Deoque admodum dilectus et familiaris, indignus tamen erat qui cum hoc sacrifico Christo conferretur, ne Iudaei in superbiam tantopere elati, imo in caecutientiae foveam collapsi, suum Mosem iactarent et loco Messiae colerent: a quibus Dominus vehementer offensus et exacerbatus, deiuravit se reiecturum illos ob suam pertinacem ingratitudinem et obstinatam incredulitatem, licet illis aeternae haereditatis pollicitationes primo factae fuerint. Ex adverso Gentiles (quos illi ut prophanos et impios abominabantur) syncera fide credentes in Christum, divinisque iussis ex animo obsequentes, in requiem aeternam ingredientur, civiumque caelestium et sanctorum omnium contubernio fruentur. Designamus igitur oportet nostrae spei et salutis anchoram in hoc inculpatissimo Pontifice, nam delicta nostra suo sanguine repropiciavit, et semper paratus est compati nostris infirmitatibus, et opitulari illis, qui multis calamitatibus et variis tentationibus affiictantur. Desinant Iudaei suum magnum Pontificem, Aaron scilicet, tantopere extollere, quod offerret Deo victimas et sacrificia pro populo, sacrisque officiis Deo iugiter ministraret, nec ullum antistitem cum eo conferendum esse. Nam Christus longo intervallo, et virtutum ac prodigiorum magnitudine illum veterem Pontificem praecellit. Siquidem ille et pro suo peccato, et totius populi delictis, Deo sacrificia offerebat. Hic vero Pontifex sanctus, innocens et impollutus, et secundum ordinem Melchisedech institutus sacerdos maximus et illustrissimus, non pro suo peccato (quia peccatum non fecit) sed pro flagitiis sui populi seipsum obtulit in sacrificium. Verum

In the light of earlier descriptions of the content of this "weighty epistle," the parallels between Erasmus and Arboreus are extensive.

ut praemii coelestis promissio (quam sumus fide et malorum omnium tolerantia assequuturi) certior fieret, interposuit iusiurandum, ut per duas res immobiles firmam haberemus consolationem in huius mundi procellis. Intelligamus Christum non desumpsisse suum sacerdotium a tribu Leviticae, de qua erat Aaron: nam illud aliquando ob suam infirmitatem periit, sed divinitus secundum ordinem Melchisedech in aeternum, creatum fuisse summum sacerdotem, hinc eius sacerdotium futurum est sempiternum. Et cum hic novi testamenti mediator illuxit mundo, suam legem nostris cordibus ita insculpsit et inscripsit, ut non magnopere quis indigeat ut a suo proximo erudiatur. Adhaec, hic selectissimus Pontifex non ingrediebatur semel duntaxat singulis annis in sancta sanctorum, ut sanguinem pecudum pro suis et populi delictis offerret, sed proprium suum sanguinem obtulit Deo, ut universum hominum genus ab omnibus peccatis liberaret, nostramque conscientiam ob operibus mortuis purificaret. Persuadeamus et nobis umbras Mosaycae legis cessasse cum Evangelium Christi effulsit, nec ab observatione legis imperfectae sperandam esse salutem, sed a syncera et evangelica fide, per quam veteres sancti ab inculpatissima vita et pietatis officiis magnopere commendati, Deo placuerunt. cui etiam mirum in modum placebunt Christiani milites, qui exemplo Christi calamitates et afflictiones huius seculi invicta animi magnitudine sufferent. Insuper sciamus ex Pauli doctrina neminem ad coelestem illam Hierusalem, et ecclesiam primitivorum accessurum nisi posita vitiorum sarcina Deo cum metu et reverentia inserviat, suumque proximum syncero charitatis affectu complectatur. Scribit autem Paulus hanc epistolam ad Iudaeos fideles, qui Palestinae et Hierosolymis erant, eosque adhortatur ne ob innumera mala sibi a contribulibus suis ingesta, concidant animo, aut maerore conficiantur, sed constanti animo pro gloria Christi adversa quaeque sufferant. Nec in dubium et controversiam vertendum est, sinam haec epistola ad Hebraeos scripta, sit Pauli. Nam in sacrosancta Synodo Nicaena, Ecclesia universalis eam recepit tanquam ab Apostolo Paulo scriptam, ipsamque talem haberi debere sanxit. Tum quoque divus Dionysius a Paulo divinis mysteriis sacrae fidei institutus, in operibus suis citat testimonium ex illa epistola tanquam a suo praeceptore composita. Beatus etiam Chrysostomus in suis Homeliis in hanc epistolam editis, affirmat eandem esse Romae a beato Paulo scriptam. Adhaec, Damascenus libro. 4. orthodoxae fidei. cap. 18. asserit Pauli Apostoli epistolas esse quatuordecim, quod verum non esset si illa quae est ad Hebraeos, non esset Pauli. Insuper Hieronymus in epistola ad Dardanum dicit, "Illud nostris dicendum est hanc epistolam quae inscribitur ad Hebraeos, non solum ab ecclesiis Orientis, sed ab omnibus retro ecclesiis Graeci sermonis scriptoribus, quasi Pauli Apostoli suscipi. Licet plerique eam vel Barnabae vel Clementis arbitrentur, et nihil interesse, cuius sit, cum ecclesiastici viri sit, et quotidie ecclesiarum lectione celebretur. Quos si eam Latinorum consuetudo non recipit inter scripturas canonicas, nec Graecorum quidem ecclesiae Apocalypsim Ioannis eadem libertate suscipiunt, et tamen nos utraque suscipimus, nequaquam huius temporis consuetudinem, sed veterum scriptorum authoritatem sequentes." [*PL* 22.1103] Haec ille. Et licet haec epistola praeviam salutationem non habeat, finalem tamen habet: Siquidem in ultimo capite dicit Paulus, "Rogo autem vos fratres, ut sufferatis verbum solatii: etenim perpaucis scripsi vobis, Cognoscite fratrem nostrum Timotheum dimissum, cum quo (si celerius venerit) videbo vos. Salutate omnes praepositos vestros, et omnes sanctos. Salutant vos de Italia fratres." His verbis movetur Iacobus Faber ad recipiendum hanc epistolam ut a Paulo scriptam. Quod autem primam salutationem non habeamus, arbitratur factum, quod archetypum neque Graeci neque Latini habeant: nam patrio Hebraeoque sermone, eam conscripsit Apostolus. [Faber, f. 230^{v}.] Quare mihi videtur Caietanus delirare, et contra veteres scriptores sentire, affirmando hanc epistolam non esse Hebraico sermone scriptam.

Proceeding in Erasmus' order, the Jews are "obstinate;" for Erasmus, no people have "more obstinate souls"; for Arboreus, they are rejected because of "obstinate incredulity." The Jews were "hostile" towards Paul, for Erasmus; they "hated" him, for Arboreus.[15] The law is "antiquated," for Erasmus; it is "imperfect" for Arboreus. Paul wrote to believing Jews in Jerusalem who were suffering calamities, for both Erasmus and Arboreus. The saints of old are examples of the virtuous life, for both, along with the example of Christ, for Erasmus; the example of Christ for Arboreus motivated Christian soldiers who suffered calamities. The hope of eternal reward is there for both. The gospel of Christ comes as "light, and the shadows of the Mosaic law cease," is stated by both commentators, as is the fact that "one cannot be saved by an imperfect law but by faith, through which the saints of old pleased God."

In Arboreus there are several strong words and phrases that describe the person and work of him for whom the believing Jews should endure everything with a steadfast soul. Christ has dominion over the whole world; angels are subject to him; he is the greatest leader of heaven and earth. He is the "highest priest," the "sacrificial Christ," the "most blameless Pontiff," "the anchor of our hope and salvation," "compassionate," "innocent and unstained," "the greatest and most illustrious

---

Et frivola admodum coniectura ducitur ad id suadendum, "Dicit Paulus Melchisedech, interpretatur Rex iustitiae. Si hebraice, inquit, scripta est epistola, in quo quaeso idiomate interpretatur Melchisedech, Rex iustitiae? Melchisedech enim apud Hebraeos dictio composita est ex rex et iustitiae: Unde in Hebraeo debuisset dicere Melchisedech, interpretatur Melchisedech." [Cajetan, p. 329.] Sed inanis est haec ratio: licet enim Melchisedech apud Hebraeos sonet Regem iustitiae: tamen interpres nobis verbis latinis expressit quid Melchisedech significaret. Nec Melchisedech apud Hebraeos componitur ex Rex et iustitiae: non enim dictio Hebraea composita, ex latinis dictionibus componitur, sed suis nativis et germanis. Quis enim diceret morosophos apud Graecos componi ex stulto et sapiente? sed ex moros et sophos: Ita Melchisedech apud Hebraeos componitur ex melchi, sive malci, quod Rex meus dicitur, et zedec iustitia. haesitavit et ille doctor etiam post definitionem ecclesiae de autore huiusce epistolae. Nec ex eo dicendum est hanc epistolam non esse Pauli, quia non meminit sui nominis suique apostolatus. Nam suppressit suum nomen Iudaeis invisum et odiosum. Siquidem quamprimum fuit conversus, acerrime tutatus est partes Christi, quem prius persequebatur. Et ob id non meminit sui apostolatus, quia non erat Apostolus Iudaeorum, sed Gentium. Scripsit et elegantius in hac epistola, et cum diligentiori et accuratiori verborum et rerum serie, quod sua lingua nativa scripserit: magis enim, et multo uberius callebat linguam Hebraeam, quam Graecam. "In Pauli ad Hebraeos Epistolam," (1553), ff. 245^{v}–246^{v}.

[15] Stated at the end of the Preface, not translated, because of its general and traditional nature.

priest," "the most select Pontiff." No other priest is to be compared with this truly holy Pontiff.

In his discussion of authorship Arboreus refers to several authorities: Nicaea, Dionysius, Chrysostom, John of Damascus and Jerome. The reference to Damascene (title, book and chapter) has not appeared in other commentaries, nor has the citation of Jacques Lefèvre (Faber). And all of these are cited without "doubt and controversy," about Pauline authorship. Furthermore, Arboreus' argument against Cajetan's argument about Melchisedec and the language of the epistle is different. It is different and difficult. Cajetan's point was that the epistle could not have been written in Hebrew, because it would then have to read, king of justice means king of justice (in Hebrew). Cajetan's reasoning was that the explanation of Melchisedec was due to the fact that the epistle was written in Greek. Nobody has suggested that the epistle was written in Latin or that a translator would add anything.

The real issue seems to be as follows, and it demonstrates the effectiveness of Cajetan's point: the authority of this "distinguished" epistle rests upon Pauline authorship, and Pauline authorship raises the *stylus*-question, and the proponents of Paul's authorship traditionally answer the *stylus*-question by arguing for a Hebrew original.

Nicolas-Tacite Zegers (d. 1559)[16]

Adam Sasbout (1516–53)[17]

Sasbout's "*Argumentum*" admittedly follows Chrysostom. Paul wrote to weak Jews about the priesthood of Christ and the new law, and to afflicted Jews that they should persevere in faith.[18]

---

[16] Seghers was initiated into biblical studies at Louvain by Titelmans, whom he replaced (up to 1548) in Scripture; after moving around, he returned to Louvain in 1558. *Scholion in omnes Novi Testamenti Libros* (Cologne: Birckman, 1553); also in *Critici Sacri*.

[17] After Zegers; Sasbout occupied Titelmans' chair of Scripture until his death (1553). *In omnes fere Pauli, et quorumdam aliorum Apostolorum, epistolas explicatio*, ed. C. Verburch (Louvain: Bergagne, 1556; Antwerp, 1561). In *Opera Omnia* (Cologne: Birckman, 1568, 1575), ad Hebraeos, pp. 553–80. I have used, "Epistola D. Pauli ad Hebraeos expositio Fratris Adami Sasbout," *Biblicus Apparatus*, ed. R. Walton (Zürich: Bodmer, 1673), pp. 531–56, which ends in c. 7.

[18] "Epistola D. Pauli ad Hebraeos," (1673), p. 531.

Joachim Camerarius (1500–74)[19]

At the beginning of his comments, Kammermeister notes that some ancient doctors of the church questioned the authorship, that many Greeks received it as Pauline while many call this into doubt, and that Chrysostom argued that Paul wished to write to the Hebrews. "But we will not examine our judgment on this at the moment," nor does he in the body of his observations. He does observe that διαθήκη means both *testamentum* and *pactum*.[20]

Genevan Version (1560)[21]

The Argument

Forasmuche as diuers, bothe of the Greke writers and Latines witnesse, that the writer of this Epistle for iuste causes wolde not haue his name knowen, it were curiositie of our parte to labour muche therein. For seing the Spirit of God is the autor thereof, it diminisheth nothing the authoritie althogh we knowe not with what penne he wrote it. Whether it were Paul (as it is not like) or Luke, or Barnabas, or Clement, or some other, his chief purpose is to persuade vnto the Ebrewes (whereby he principally meaneth them that abode at Ierusalem, and vnder them all the rest of the Iewes) that Christ Iesus was not onely the redemer, but also that at his comming all ceremonies must haue an end: forasmuche as his doctrine was the conclusion of all the prophecies, and therefore not onely Moses

---

[19] "De epistola scripta ad Hebraeos," *Notatio figurarum orationis et mutatae simplicis elocutionis in apostolicis scriptis* (Leipzig: Papa, 1556) [16 fols.], which I have used. Also, Leipzig, 1572.

[20] [f. 10] on 7.22.

[21] "The Epistle to the Ebrewes," *The Bible and Holy Scriptures Conteyned in the Olde and Newe Testament. . . With Moste Profitable Annotations upon all the hard places. . .* (Geneva: Rowland Hall, 1560), ff. 102^r–106^v. Translators were Whittingham, who was probably general editor of the New Testament, Gilby, Sampson and others. By 1575, it was so popular that "from 1575 until 1618 at least one new edition of the Geneva Bible appeared each year." From 1560–1611 (King James version) there were over 120 editions (Lloyd Berry, "Introduction," *The Geneva Bible. A facsimile of the 1560 edition* [Madison: University of Wisconsin Press, 1969], p. 14).

The New Testament of the "Genevan version" was a revision of William Whittingham's New Testament (Geneva: Conrad Badius, 1557), "due to a further comparison with Beza's Latin translation" (A. S. Herbert, *Historical Catalogue of Printed Editions of the English Bible 1525–1961* [London: The British and Foreign Bible Society, 1968]. #106, 107).

In 1556 Théodore de Bèze published his annotated Latin translation of the Greek New Testament; the colophon is dated 1557: "Epistola Pauli ad Hebraeos," *Novum D. N. Jesu Christi testamentum. Latine iam olim a Veteri interprete, nunc denuo a Theodoro Beza versum: cum eiusdem annotationibus, in quibus ratio interpretationis redditur* (Geneva: R. Estienne, 1556/7), ff. 284^r–299^v. The other editions of Beza will be discussed below.

was inferior to him, but also the Angels: for they all were seruants, and he the Lord, but so Lord, that he hathe also taken our flesh, and is made our brother to assure vs of our saluation through him self: for he is that eternal Priest, whereof all the Leuitical Priests were but shadowes, and therefore at his comming they oght to cease, and all sacrifices for sinne to be abolished, as he proueth from the seuenth chap. verse 11. vnto the 12. chap. verse 18. Also he was that Prophet of whome all the Prophetes in time past witnessed, as is declared from the 12. chapter, verse 18. to the twentie and fiue verse of the same chapter: yea, and is the King to whome all things are subiect, as appeareth from that verse 25. to the beginning of the last chapter. Wherefore according to the examples of the olde fathers we must constantly beleue in him, that being sanctified by his iustice, taught by his wisdome, and gouerned by his power, we may stedfastly, and courageously perseuere euen to the end in hope of that ioye that is set before our eyes, occupying our selues in Christian exercises that we may bothe be thankeful to God, and duetiful to our neighbour.[22]

The Geneva Bible dismisses the authorship question along the lines taken by Bèze (1556). Bèze had written that there never was universal agreement about authorship; while the Greeks accepted it, the style and "other probable conjectures" make it appear that it was neither Paul's nor written in Hebrew; but "what is to be gained by arguing about the name of the writer when the writer himself chose to be hidden"; finally, Bèze held, "let it suffice to know this, that it was truly dictated by the Holy Spirit."[23]

"The Argument" of the Bible makes similar points. One, the author chose – for good reasons – to conceal his name. Two, "to labour muche" about the question reflects undue inquisitiveness ("curiositie"; "conjecture" for Bèze). Three, the important point is that the Holy Spirit is the author and nothing is to be gained by trifling about "with what penne he wrote it."

The points "The Argument" makes about the content and "chief

---

[22] "The Epistle to the Ebrews," f. 102ʳ.

[23] Epistola Pauli, ἐπιστολη Παύλου

Ita scriptum invenimus in omnibus nostris codicibus, uno tantum excepto, in quo duntaxat scriptum erat, πρὸς Ἑβραίους ad Hebraeos. Hoc quidem constat nunquam satis convenisse a quo scripta esset: quanvis Graeci theologi certatim Paulo vendicent a quo scilicet scripta quidem fuerit, sed Hebraice, id est lingua tum in Iudaea familiari: quam deinde Lucas in Graecum sermonem converterit. Certe mira est styli dissimilitudo, et aliae probabiles coniecturae non desunt ex quibus nec Pauli esse, nec Hebraice unquam fuisse scriptam appareat: quas suo loco attingemus. Verum quid attinet de scriptoris nomine contendere quod scriptor ipse celatus voluit? Sufficiat hoc nosse, vere esse dictatam a Spiritu sancto, quae luculentissimam ac plane Apostolicam Veteris foederis cum Novo collationem atque adeo Novi foederis veluti singularem quandam promulgationem ac sanctionem complectatur. "Epistola Pauli ad Hebraeos," (1556/7), f. 284ʳ.

purpose" of the epistle are similar to Calvin's "Argument," and in Calvin's order. For both, the chief point is that Christ is the end of ceremonies. He is the "conclusion" of prophecy. "Conclusion" is a better rendering of *"clausula"* (Calvin) than the modern translation ("fulfilment"). The points about Moses, Angels and Levitical priests are also in Calvin, as well as the description of the Lord, who was such a Lord ("so Lord"), that he became our brother in our flesh.

The Bible also agrees with Calvin: "No" on Paul, "Yes" on authority.

Niels Hemmingsen (1513–1600)[24]

The Argument of the Epistle to the Hebrews

Many Greeks affirm that the epistle to the Hebrews is the Apostle Paul's, which some of the Latins call into doubt. Thus, Eusebius witnesses to this with these words (*EH*, bk. 3): "There are clearly fourteen epistles of Paul, which are held to be authentic, although I know that the Latins have doubt about the epistle written to the Hebrews."

Although there can be some doubt about the instrument through which the Holy Spirit gave this epistle to the church of God, nevertheless, having rejected useless disputations about the human author, let us venerate its maker, the Spirit of Christ, and be thankful to God for this enormous treasure which he gave to his church, since the church, especially the Greek church, holds it as catholic and the Spirit of God clearly puts himself forth as its author.

Moreover, it is disputed whether it was written in Hebrew or Greek. While opinions differ, certain arguments drawn from the force of Greek words are convincing that it was written in Greek without any doubt.

But omitting these let us talk about the things which the argument of this epistle opens up to us: let us see what the occasion was for writing, what the principal point or question was, and what was the order of proceeding or method. For knowing these things well, we will have the way prepared for understanding this epistle more clearly.[25]

---

[24] *Commentarius in epistolam apostolicam ad Hebraeos* (Wittenberg, 1568). The preface is dated 1567. "Ad Hebraeos," *Commentaria in omnes epistolas Apostolorum, Pauli, Petri, Iudae, Iohannis, Iacobi, et in eam quae ad Hebraeos* (Leipzig: Andreas Schneider, typis Voegelianis, 1572; Frankfurt a. M.: Georg Corvinus, 1579; Strasbourg: Theodosius Rihelius, 1586), pp. 830–915. I have used the 1579 printing. For a chronological list of works, see Kjell Barnekow, *Niels Hemmingsens teologiska åskådning* (diss. Lund, 1940), VIII–XII.

[25] Argumentum in Epistolam ad Hebraeos.

Graecorum plerique epistolam ad Hebraeos scriptam Pauli Apostoli esse affirmant, id quod Latinorum nonnulli in dubium revocarunt. Quemadmodum Eusebius libro tertio Ecclesiasticae historiae, his verbis testatur: Pauli quoque manifeste quatuordecim sunt Epistolae, quae in autoritate habentur, licet sciam apud Latinos de Epistola, quae ad Hebraeos scribitur, haberi dubitationem. Haec Eusebius.

So, for Hemmingsen, as for Bèze (1556) and the Genevan version, it is useless to argue about the human author of the epistle. The real matters about what an *"Argumentum"* should concern itself are not authorship and language, but the occasion, point and method of this treasure authored by the Holy Spirit. After all, the purpose of an *"Argumentum"* is to prepare the way for understanding, and understanding the epistle is not helped by knowing that Paul did or did not write the thing.

The "Occasion" of Hebrews was those converted Jews who wanted to join the gospel of Christ with the ceremonies of Moses. "They were addicted to too many Mosaic rites." The occasion, then, on the part of a man of God, full of the Spirit, was the concern to root out this "crass error."[26]

The "Principal Point or *Quaestio*" is that the "one and only" sacrifice of Christ is the propitiation for the sins of the world, which means the end of Levitical sacrifices. The genre of the epistle is principally didactic, mixed with the genre of persuasion, in order to apply the doctrine. This mixture exists throughout Scripture in order to bond a covenant between the doctrine and the hearer.[27]

The Order or Method of Proceeding

The order of proceeding is based most wisely and clearly on the rule of rhetoricians. For he puts in first place the narrative or exposition concerning the person and office of the son of God. This exposition is the material from which the remaining structure of this whole epistle is built. Then he unravels the exposition by analysis, and discourses *(disputat)* about each of its parts copiously and most learnedly. Because he has mentioned the son of God, he first discourses on his twofold nature and office. Then he builds the exhortation so that the Hebrews will hear him. Afterwards, because it said in the narration that the purgation of sins was made through Christ, he begins a discourse *(disputatio)*

Etsi autem de organo, per quod Spiritus sanctus hanc Epistolam Ecclesiae Dei dedit, ista dubitatio esse potest tamen cum Ecclesia, praesertim Graeca, eam pro Catholica habuerit, et ipse spiritus Dei se eius autorem manifeste prodat, reiectis inutilibus de autore homine disputationibus, eius artificem spiritum Christi, veneremur, ac Deo grati simus pro hoc ingenti thesauro, quo suam Ecclesiam donavit.

Praeterea disputatur, Hebraice ne an Graece scripta sit. Alii enim aliter sentiunt, sed argumenta nonnulla, ex virtute Graecarum vocum petita, convincunt eam procul omni dubio Graece scriptam esse.

Sed his disputationibus omissis dicamus de rebus, quae nobis huius Epistolae argumentum aperiant: atque videamus quae fuerit scribendi occasio, quis status seu quaestio principalis, et quis tractationis ordo seu Methodus, his enim probe cognitis, viam paratam habebimus, ad hanc Epistolam planius intelligendam. "Ad Hebraeos," (1579), p. 830.

[26] *Ibid.*

[27] *Ibid.*

most copiously on the priesthood of Christ, and teaches that by the sacrifice of Christ alone the saints are consummated forever, showing that it is the end of Levitical sacrifices. Hence, because the application of the sacrifice of Christ is made through faith, he exhorts to faith, with many examples of the saints. Finally, by adding common precepts of life, he ends the epistle.[28]

Hemmingsen's discussion of the occasion and principal point of the epistle is familiar. What stands out in Hemmingsen's "*Argumentum*" is the explicit statement that its purpose is to prepare the way for understanding, and this is done by a systematic structuring of the epistle with the "order or method" of rhetoric and "*disputatio.*" The epistle begins with the principal doctrine of the person and office of Christ. Emphasized is the sacrifice of Christ. The covenant between the doctrine of Christ's sacrifice as once and for all and the hearer "is made through faith." The epistle is didactic, the method of applying the doctrine for the hearer is persuasion.

The last time we, in this study, have seen Hebrews handled in Wittenberg as a commentary was Luther's lectures in 1517/18. There is considerable difference in these two interpretations. The book by the Professor at Copenhagen holds that the main point of the epistle is that Christ's unique sacrifice marks the end of Levitical sacrifices. In his disputation on Hebrews 7.12 ("Once there is a change in the priesthood there is a change in the law as well") Hemmingsen says, "Priesthood and law (this is the covenant of priesthood) are joined in nature so that they either remain or perish simultaneously [*simul*]. If therefore the priesthood is changed, it is necessary that the covenant be changed also; but the Levitical priesthood is already changed, and the priesthood of Christ succeeded it. Therefore, the covenant of Christ's priesthood succeeds the law or covenant of the Levitical priesthood. Then, we also conclude here that the ceremonial Mosaic law, which was the covenant

---

[28] Ordo, seu Tractationis Methodus.

Ordo tractationis sapientissime et plane ex Rhetorum praescripto institutus est. Primo enim loco Narrationem seu expositionem de persona et officio filii Dei collocat. Quae expositio est tanquam materia, ex qua reliquum corpus totius huius Epistolae extruitur. Deinde expositionem Analysi retexit, ac de singulis eius membris fuse et doctissime disputat: ac primum quidem, quia filii Dei mentionem fecit, de eius duplici natura et officio disputat. Unde et exhortationem extruit, ut ipsum audiant Hebraei. Postea, quia in Narratione dixerat, per Christum fieri purgationem peccatorum, de Sacerdotio Christi instituit disputationem copiosissime, ac docet solius Christi sacrificio consummari sanctos in perpetuum, ostendens iam finem esse Leviticorum sacrificiorum. Hinc, quia applicatio sacrificii Christi fit per fidem, hortatur ad fidem, idque pluribus Sanctorum exemplis. Tandem additis communibus vitae praeceptis finit Epistolam. *Ibid.*, p. 831.

of the Levitical priesthood, ought to have an end with the coming of Christ's new priesthood."[29] In his lectures on 7.12, Luther said that "law" can be understood in two different ways. The "inferior understanding" reads "law" as ceremonial law only. The "superior understanding" reads "law" in Hebrews the way Paul uses it elsewhere as "everything that is prescribed by God and man, be it ceremonial, judicial or moral."[30] For Luther the gospel completely replaces the law in all its aspects. Thus, the testament of Christ alone, for Luther, is the main point of Hebrews. Luther's opening statement about Hebrews summarized its contents. Hemmingsen's introduction is concerned with the prolegomena (historical, literary, methodological) for understanding the contents.

Matthias Flacius Illyricus (1520–75)[31]

The "Preface" by Flacius begins with a long discussion of authorship and is among the most extensive to date. The importance of the question for Flacius rests on the importance of the "doctrines" treated in Hebrews. These doctrines are "necessary," and the full revelation of Scripture would be considerably lessened *(mutila)* without the authority (Pauline authorship) of this epistle.[32]

The format of the discussion is a list of four reasons given against Pauline authorship, Flacius' response to each of these, followed by a development of fifteen reasons for Pauline authorship.

The four reasons against Pauline authorship are the traditional ones: 1) no name, 2) 2.3, 3) style, 4) cc. 6 & 10. In Flacius' order, his response to # 4 is that penance for the lapsed is not denied because Christ has compassion on infirmities. His response to # 1 is the very customary "odious – argument." The responses to # 2 and # 3 are nuanced and not customary.

Flacius' argument regarding 2.3 *("in nos confirmata")* is that it was typical for Paul (and Peter) to identify himself with his hearers. The

[29] *Ibid.*, p. 867.

[30] Luther, *WA* 57.III. 192.16–25.

[31] "In epistolam Pauli apostoli ad Hebraeos," ΤΗΣ ΤΟΥ ΥΙΟΥ ΘΕΟΥ ΚΑΙΝΗΣ ΔΙΑΘΗΚΗΣ ΑΠΑΝΤΑ. *Novum Testamentum Iesu Christi Filii Dei, ex versione Erasmi, innumeris in locis ad Graecam veritatem, genuinumque sensum emendata. Glossa compendiaria M. M. Fl. Ill. Albonensis in novum Testamentum* (Basel: Perna and Dietrich, 1570), pp. 1101–1196. For chronological list of printed works cf. Wilhelm Preger, *M. F. Ill. und seine Zeit* (Erlangen: Bläsing, 1859), II, 539–72.

[32] Flacius Illyricus, p. 1103.

reasons why Paul excludes himself from those who heard the word from the Lord are that he was not one of the twelve, nor was he an early convert, and he thought himself unworthy of the name apostle because he persecuted the church. Furthermore, "in" signifies time (in our time), not the hearers.

The response to the style-argument is that an author's style often changes (e.g. Cicero and Aristotle; Corinthians differs from Ephesians). The reason the language is clearer and more splendid is that Paul is not writing to one church or person, but to the whole Hebrew nation. He thus packed more power into it. Is not the Holy Spirit able to vary the style out of "the necessity of things, times and hearers"?[33]

The Holy Spirit definitely altered Paul's style in Hebrews. There are fifteen reasons why it had to be written by Paul. Outside of appeals to ancient authorities (arguments one and nine) and language (five and fifteen), there are basically two points why it had to be Paul's: the importance of the teaching (3, 4, 6, 8, 12) and certain circumstantial evidence present and lacking (2, 7, 10, 11, 13, 14).

In order: 1) Eusebius' reference to Clement. 2) Any disciple of the apostles would have had to cite a New Testament writing or his apostolic teacher in this case of such sublime mysteries, and this is not the case. 3) Everyone agrees that the epistle contains outstanding explication, thus the highest of Apostles is the author. 4) Without this epistle the full revelation of Scripture would be nearly mutilated, especially regarding the eternal priesthood of Christ, the expiation of sins and the relationship between the two Testaments. 5) It was not written in Hebrew, cf. 7.1 [on 7.1, Flacius appeals to Cajetan's argument about the definition of Melchisedek]. 6) It contains extremely necessary doctrine; if it is not apostolic or its authorship is in doubt, the merits of the epistle, namely its teaching about faith, are in doubt. 7) Given the authority of the Hebrew churches, only an apostle of Christ would have been received by the churches. 8) The most serious questions and dogmas are treated in this epistle with dignity and authority, and without citing more recent testimony; no pious disciple of the Apostles would have dared do this. 9) The ancient Greeks did not doubt the author (Paul) of the epistle (Origen, Irenaeus). 10) Only Paul was captive so long in Italy, and wrote from there. 11) No ignoble man is the author of the epistle, since he told the Hebrews of his captivity,

[33] *Ibid.*, pp. 1101–1103.

urged them to pray for him and promised them a visit soon, just as Paul and Philemon did in other epistles. 12) This epistle has *"multa Paulina"*: "the just shall live by his faith." 13) The author lived during the time of the Apostles and was one of them, because he says that God spoke first through the prophets, then through the Son, not adding through the Apostles, which a disciple of the Apostles would have done. The epistle speaks of sacrifices and rites of Moses; if it had been written after the fall of the temple and Jerusalem, some mention would have been made regarding such a great change. 14) At the end he shows that he had a most well-known ministry; no one had a more famous ministry than Paul. 15) It was written in Greek – by Paul.[34]

There are twists to each point, and only the main theses of each point have been summarized here, yet Flacius' overriding concern (and argument) is that Paul being Paul, the theology of Paul being what it was, the theology of Hebrews being what it was, the Hebrew situation being what it was, and the importance, authority and necessity of all this, means that it all comes together with Paul authoring Hebrews.

The next section concerns the "occasion," "scope" and "order" of this epistle. These all overlap. The emphasis in all three is on the one true priesthood and one true sacrifice of Christ. The occasion was those Jewish converts who wanted to mix Moses and Christ. The scope was to explain the person of Christ, two natures in one person, his office of priesthood and his benefits.[35]

In treating the "order of the material," Flacius distinguishes between "four primary or major parts" and "in last place, as it were, an appendix." The four major sections are chapters on 1) the divinity and humility of Christ, 2) the exhortation to hear and embrace this Messiah, 3 "and primary") the priesthood, sacrifice and benefits of Christ, and 4) faith, or the one instrument by which we receive this priest with all his works and benefits. "In last place," and necessarily so, as Flacius goes on to explain, there is a chapter (13) on virtue, obedience and piety. The doctrine of the pious and holy life is treated by Christ and the Apostles in "the last parts," to show that it is the fruit and effect of the prior, and not in any way as noble and excellent as the prior. What is at stake here is that the doctrine of the holy life "must not be dangerously mixed in with the article of justification."[36]

[34] *Ibid.*, pp. 1103–1105.

[35] *Ibid.*, p. 1105.

[36] *Ibid.*, pp. 1105–1107.

It is striking in the light of previous interpretation that the necessary, Pauline doctrine of faith relates to the doctrine of the new obedience as chapters 11 and 12 relate to chapter 13, as "primary and major" to "appendix."

Georg Major (1502–74)[37]

Major starts out by claiming that "I will say nothing about the author of this epistle, since there are such various judgments by many people." He does manage to say a few things, however, the conclusion of which is that he is uncertain and noncommittal. He mentions the argument about 2.3. "Whoever, however, was the author, it appears to have been a great and eloquent man, and powerful in writing, assisted by the Spirit; of such it was written about Apollos (Acts 18), to whom they assign this epistle." The "they" sounds like Luther and Bugenhagen. What is important is not the author but "the doctrine which is handed down."[38]

The *"loci"* of doctrines that Major discusses as *"utiles," "insignis"* and *"praecipuus,"* are similar to the ones previously emphasized by Hyperius, Hemmingsen and Flacius: the two natures of Christ, the priesthood of Christ, and faith (the doctrine of application). The "efficacy" of faith is given more prominence by Major, of course, than was the case with Flacius. Discussing the last chapters Major writes, "where also he shows and commemorates the definition of faith (in chapter 11) and its efficacy with extensive and historical narration of the examples of those who were saved from the beginning of the church up to his own time." Also in the *"status"* survey, Major emphasizes the "hard struggle and dangerous wars" Christians must "fight not only against blood and flesh, but also against principalities, powers, lords of the world . . . just as it says in chapter 12, in the conclusion of this epistle, 'let us run with patience the race that is set before us. . .' "[39]

Johann Brenz (Son, 1539–96)[40]

---

[37] *Enarratio epistolae ad Hebraeos, praelecta a D. Georgio Maiore Wittenbergae* (Wittenberg: Joannes Lufft, 1571).

[38] Major, f. 1^r.

[39] *Ibid.*, ff. 1^r–2^r.

[40] *In epistolam, quam Paulus Apostolus ad Hebraeos scripsit de persona et officio Domini nostri Iesu Christi Commentarius. Authore Ioanne Brentio F. Theologiae Doctore et Professore publico in*

Edward Dering (1540?–76)[41]

The Praelections of Edward Deering vpon certaine of the first chapters of the Epistle to the Hebrues.

The first Lecture vpon the first verse of the first Chapter.

'At sundrise times and in diuers manners, God spoke in the olde time to our fathers by the prophets: in these last daies, he hath spoken vnto vs by his sonne.'

'At sundrie times and in diuers manners,' & c. Before we begin the exposition of this Epistle, I will brieflie speake somewhat of these three points: Why this Epistle was written, by whome, and at what time. And first touching the cause of the writing, though we knowe assuredlie, it was cause sufficient to leaue so excellent doctrine vnto the Church of God: yet a speciall occasion then giuen, was vndoubtedly this; The Iewes were stubbernlie set to the maintenance and defence of the lawe of Moses, holding fast all the ceremonies of it, as things necessarie. neuer to bee abrogate, but perpetuallie to be vsed in the worship of God. Among the residue, they did especiallie striue for Circumcision; next vnto it, for the obseruation of meates, and drinkes, and times, and feastes, and sundrie purifyings, as these things are namelie mentioded in the Scripture: besides these, other ceremonies, which they imbraced, and loued. And though manie thousands (as it is in the xxj. of the Actes) did beleeue: yet were they still zealous for the Lawe, nor would possibly heare of the abrogation of it. Insomuch, that they and their forefathers had made this an article of their faith, and it is the ninth article of their Creede, and they holde it to this daie: GOD gaue his LAWE to his faithful seruant Moses, and hee will neuer alter it, nor change it for anie other. And this their opinion, as it was rooted in them, so they had verie manie, and plausible perswasions for it: they stroue not for the inuentions of man, but for the Lawe of God; not holden by traditions, but written by Moses; not in doubtfull testimonie, but in manifest shewe of the glorie of God. And this their opinion, they did not thinke was anie coniecturall exposition, but the manifest word, as it was often repeated, that this should be an ordinance to them for euer. For this cause, the Apostle hauing compassion vpon his weake brethren, who beleeued in Christ (but were also thus addicted to the Lawe,) hee writeth vnto them this Epistle, by all meanes perswading them,

---

Schola Tubingensi. (Tübingen, 1571). The argument on authorship concludes, from very general points, that the Holy Spirit is the internal author and Paul the external.

[41] *A Lecture or Exposition upon a part of the V.* [5.7–9] *chapter of the Epistle to the Hebrues. As it was read in Paules the 6. day of December. 1572. By Edward Derying* (London: John Awdeley, 1573). *XXVII. Lectures, or readings, upon part of the Epistle written to the Hebrues. Made by Maister Edward Deering, Bachelour of Divinitie* (London, 1576, 1577, 1578, 1583, 1590); the 1590 edition used here, is, in *M. Derings workes. More at large then ever hath heere-to-fore been printed in any one Volume* (London: Linly & Flasket, 1597; "The English Experience," Vol. 448, Amsterdam and New York, 1972).

neuer to ioyne together our Sauiour Christ with the Ceremonies of the Law, whose glorie is perfect in himselfe alone, and all height must be abased before him. . .

Now touching the Author of this Epistle, who it was, it skilleth not. For if the name had been heere, what had it shewed, but that GOD vsed the ministerie of such a man? and now the name is not knowen, it teacheth expresly, the doctrine is of God. And for this cause, to the bookes of holie Scripture, names are sometimes added, sometime not; that the doctrine of the Lord might bee vnto vs, without respect of person. And for my part, who wrote this Epistle, I cannot tell, nor I see no cause, why I should seeke it. For when the Spirite of God hath left it out, can I thinke it the better, if I should adde it? I remember 'Athanasius' saith; that since the Gospell was first preached, this Epistle was euer thought to bee 'Paules.' But 'Eusebius,' as boldlie on the other side, saith; that he dareth constantly affirme, as the sense is the Apostles, so the phrase and penning is some other mans, but whose God knoweth. And thus much of the Author, whom we will leaue as wee finde him, a faithful witness of Iesus Christ, euen to the endes of the world, but whose name we knowe not.

Now for the time in which it was written. It is certeine it was in the Apostles dayes: For if it had been after the destruction of 'Ierusalem,' threatning so oft the anger of God to those who would despise his Sonne, no doubt he would haue mentioned so singular an example. Besides this, he maketh mention of 'Timothie' as his companion and fellowe, who was famous among the Apostles. And it is like that this Epistle was written about the latter ende of the Apostles age, because hee saith; that this doctrine first preached by the Lord, hath now been confirmed vnto vs by them that heard it. And noting the time how long the Gospell had been preached afore, he saith; that time required that nowe they should bee able to bee teachers of it. Againe, in the x. Chapter he putteth them in remembrance, that in times past they had suffered great and manifold afflictions for the Gospels sake. So that wee easely see this Epistle, as it is holie and apostolicall in the truth of doctrine, so it hath also the honor of their time. And thus farre of the occasion, Author, and time of this Epistle.[42]

In response to the question "why" Hebrews, Dering repeats the standard, what might be called, "mix-theory": converted Jews wanted to mix Moses and Christ. What is not standard is Dering's explanation of that type of Jewish-Christian thinking, based on "the ninth article of their Creede," that God will never change his law, given to Moses. The eighth article of the well known "creed" of Maimonides is that God gave his Law to Moses and the ninth is that he will never alter it.

On authorship, Dering takes a position, seen previously in this study in Bèze (1556) and the Genevan version. In Dering's words, "it matters [skilleth] not"; or, "it is of no help" to know the author's name, seeing that the Holy Spirit did not supply it. The Holy Spirit wrote it; "the

[42] *XXVII. Lectures,* A 1–A 3.

doctrine is of God." There is "no cause" to seek any further. "for when the Spirite of God hath left it out, can I thinke it the better, if I should adde it?"

Dering's questions go beyond occasion and authorship to include the more historical question, "at what time was it written?"

Franciscus Lucas Brugensis (1549–1619)[43]

Benedictus Aretius (ca. 1522–1574)[44]

Rhemes NT, 1582[45]

Let the Christian Reader note the corruption and impudent boldnes of our Adversaries, that upon a false private persuasion of their owne, that S. Paul was not the author of this Epistle, leave out his name in the title of the same, contrarie to the authentical copies both Greeke and Latin. In old time there was some doubt who should be the writer of it. but then, when it was no lesse doubted whether it were Canonical Scripture at al. Afterward the whole Church (by which onely we know the true Scriptures from other writings) held it and delivered it, as now she doth, to the faithful, for Canonical, and for S. Paules Epistle. Notwithstanding the Adversaries would have refused the Epistle, as wel as they do the Author, but that they falsely imagine certaine places thereof to make against the Sacrifice of the Masse.[46]

Lucas Osiander I. (1534–1604)[47]

The opening discussion about authorship is identical to Luther's (1522, 1537); it will not be reported here. The description of content

[43] *Notationes in sacra Biblia* (Antwerp: in-fol., 1580, 1583²; in 4°, 1581); also in *Critici Sacri*.

[44] *Commentarii in epistolam ad Hebraeos* (Bern: Joannes le Preux, 1581, 1583 [with *Isagoge in ipsam epistolam*]). *Commentarii in omnes epistolas D. Pauli, et canonicas, itemque in Apocalypsin D. Ioannis* (Bern: Preux, 1583, 1589, 1596). In his *"Dispositio"* to the epistle, Benedikt Mart covers several items; authorship, "Hebrews," occasion, argument, *"propositio*, genus and parts. The discussion is a report of the positions of others. On authorship, Aretius begins, "The judgement of learned men concerning Hebrews is. . ." On "Who the Hebrews were," he "finds three opinions" ("In epistolam ad Hebraeos" [1589], pp. 587–89). Because the material has been given previously, it will not be repeated here.

[45] "The Epistle of Paul the Apostle to the Hebrewes," *The New Testament of Iesus Christ, Translated Faithfully into English, out of the authentical Latin. . . With Arguments. . . Annotations, and other necessarie helpes, for the better understanding of the text, and specially for the discoverie of the Corruptions of divers late translations, and for cleering the Controversies in religion, of these daies: In the English College of Rhemes* (Rheims: J. Fogny, 1582), pp. 603–39.

[46] *Ibid.*, p. 603.

[47] *Epistola ad Hebraeos, Iacobi . . . et Apocalypsis Ioannis,* Vol. 8 (Tübingen: Georg

echoes previous material. Between 1582 and 1588, our *terminus ad quem* (Bèze), there is little to report, except the existence of four more commentaries. As in Osiander, the arguments are repetitious of previous work.

Giles Hunn(ius) (1550–1603)[48]

Benito Arias Montano (1527–98)[49]

Johann Jakob Grynäus (1540–1617)[50]

Giovanni Antonio Delfino (1504–60)[51]

Théodore de Bèze (1519–1605)[52]

In 1556 and continuing in 1565 (second edition) and 1582 (third edition) Bèze prefaced his Annotations with a brief introduction on

---

Gruppenbach, 1585), *ad Heb.*, pp. 4–106, in: *Quinque libris Moysis* [and the other books of the Bible] *iuxta veterem seu vulgatam translationem, ad Hebraeam veritatem (ad Graecum textum) emendati, et breve . . . explicatione illustrati, insertis etiam praecipuis locis communibus in lectione sacra observandis,* 9 Vols. (Tübingen: Gruppenbach, 1573–86).

[48] *Exegesis epistolae ad Hebraeos* (Frankfurt a. M.: Johann Spies, 1586).

[49] "In epistolam D. Pauli ad Hebraeos elucidationes," *Benedicti Ariae Montani Elucidationes in omnia sanctorum Apostolorum scripta* (Antwerp: Christopher Plantin, 1588), pp. 299–351 (dated 1586).

[50] *Explanatio epistolae S. Apostoli Pauli, ad Hebraeos* (Basel: Sebastian Henricpetri, 1587).

[51] *Commentarii in Evang. Ioannis, et in epistolam Pauli ad Hebraeos,* ed. Cardinal Constantius Torri Sarnanus (Buccafuoco, d. 1595) (Rome, 1587).

[52] In 1556/7, as was noted (under the Genevan Version), Bèze published the first of five editions of the New Testament, his annotated Latin translation of the Greek New Testament: "Epistola Pauli ad Hebraeos," *Novum D. N. Jesu Christi testamentum. Latine iam olim a Veteri interprete, nunc denuo a Theodoro Beza versum: cum eiusdem annotationisbus, in quibus ratio interpretationis redditur* (Geneva: R. Estienne, 1556/7), ff. 284^r–299^v. The second edition of Bèze's New Testament had three columns of text, Greek (using Codex Bezae and Claromontanus), "new translation" (Bèze's), "old" (Vulgate), along with the Annotations: *Iesu Christi D. N. Novum testamentum, sive Novum foedus. Cuius Graeco textui respondent interpretationes duae: una, vetus: altera, nova, Theodori Bezae, diligenter ab eo recognita. Eiusdem Th. Bezae Annotationes, quas itidem hac secunda editione.* (Geneva: H. Estienne, 1565^2, 1582^3, H. Estienne II, 1588^4; E. Vignon, 1598^5). In 1594 the "Greater Annotations" (cf. 1588 fourth edition) were published separately: "Epistola Pauli Apostoli ad Hebraeos. Annotationes, in quibus ratio interpretationis redditur," *Theodori Bezae Annotationes maiores in Novum D. N. Iesu Christi Testamentum* ([Geneva: E. Vignon], 1594), II, pp. 483–546. Bèze also published Greek and Latin New Testaments with very brief notes.

authorship, content and "Hebrews." In 1588 (4th), and continuing in 1594 *("Maiores")* and 1598 (5th), Bèze changes his treatment of authorship.

The first set (with variants of 1565² and 1582³ noted in brackets) is as follows:

The Epistle of Paul to the Hebrews

"The Epistle of Paul." Ἐπιστολὴ Παύλου. In all our codices we find it so written, with the one exception in which it was simply written, Πρὸς Ἑβραίους "to the Hebrews." It is indeed well known that it has never been sufficiently agreed upon by whom it was written [this epistle: 1565², 1582³]. However, the Greek theologians claim vigorously that Paul wrote it, but in Hebrew, that is, in the language then common in Judea, which then Luke [or a certain Clement: 1582³], translated into Greek. The difference of style is certainly remarkable, and other probable conjectures are not lacking from which it appears that neither was it Paul's nor was it ever written in Hebrew, which [conjectures] we will touch upon in the proper place. Indeed, what is to be gained by arguing the name of the writer when the writer himself chose to be hidden?

Let it suffice to know this, that it was truly dictated by the Holy Spirit; it embraces the most brilliant and clearly apostolic joining of the Old covenant with the New and, what is more, the giving and sanctioning of the New as unique.

"To the Hebrews," Πρὸς Ἑβραίους, that is, to the churches of Judaea and especially the one at Jerusalem. For the name Jews then designated everyone generally of that people. Thus with a particular name, the provincials, that is those who were dispersed throughout the world, especially in the West and the regions of Asia Minor, were distinguished from those who maintained some [the ancient: 1582³] dwelling places. The former were called ἑλληνισταί [Hellenists], the latter were called by the ancient name of the people, Hebrews, as appears in Acts 6.1, from which text it is clear that the churches of Palestine had been gathered from these two types of Jews. And it is not surprising that those from the region as well as those from the greater multitude are both designated by the common name of Hebrews.

[The summary of this epistle is this, that Christ is that true, eternal and unique Prophet, King and Priest, unto whom all the fathers looked through faith and by whom it is fitting that the whole church be taught, ruled and sanctified: 1565², 1582³].[53]

[53] Epistola Pauli, Ἐπιστολὴ Παύλου. Ita scriptum invenimus in omnibus nostris codicibus, uno tantum excepto, in quo duntaxat scriptum eratΠρὸς Ἑβραίους ad Hebraeos. Hoc quidem constat nunquam satis convenisse a quo scripta esset [sit haec epistola]: quanvis Graeci theologi certatim Paulo vendicent a quo scilicet scripta quidem fuerit, sed Hebraice, id est lingua tum in Iudaea familiari: quam deinde Lucas [vel Clemens nescio quis], in Graecum sermonem converterit. Certe mira est styli dissimilitudo, et aliae probabiles coniecturae non desunt ex quibus nec Pauli esse, nec Hebraice unquam fuisse

The point on content is that Hebrews contains apostolic teaching. The point on the word, "Hebrews," is that they were the Jews, especially at Jerusalem, who were from both the region and the provinces (Hellenists; Acts 6.1).

The main point on authorship is that there is no point in arguing about it, since the Holy Spirit dictated the epistle. He admits, however, to "probable conjectures" that it was not Paul's nor written in Hebrew. On 9.16, (*re* διαθήκη) he maintains that it appears to have been written in Greek, which is not surprising because Greek was known throughout the orient.[54] The conjecture on "not Paul's," he briefly attacks in his comments on 2.3.[55] The usual problem of 6.4–6 is not discussed. The main sentiment is "what is to be gained by arguing about the name of the writer when the writer himself chose to be hidden?"

But argue he does in the fourth and fifth editions (1588[4], 1594, 1598[5]):

The Epistle of Paul to the Hebrews

'The Epistle of Paul,' Ἐπιστολη Παύλου. In all our codices we find it so written, with the one exception in which it was simply written, Πρὸς Ἑβραίους, "to the Hebrews." It is indeed well known that it has never been sufficiently agreed upon by all who wrote this epistle. However the Greeks claim vigorously that Paul wrote it, but in Hebrew, that is in the language then common in Judea, which then Luke or a certain Clement translated into Greek. The following [arguments], moreover, tend to be proposed by those who deny it is Paul's. First, that Paul was accustomed in all his epistles to prefix his name. Next, that the author of this epistle in 2.3 enumerates himself with the hearers of the Apostles. The third argument proposed is taken from the word διαθήκη

---

scriptam appareat: quas suo loco attingemus. Verum quid attinet de scriptoris nomine contendere quod scriptor ipse celatus voluit? Sufficiat hoc nosse, vere esse dictatam a Spiritu sancto, quae luculentissimam ac plane Apostolicam Veteris foederis cum Novo collationem atque adeo Novi foederis veluti singularem quandam promulgationem ac sanctionem complectatur.

Ad Hebraeos Πρὸς Ἑβραίους Id est ad Ecclesias Iudaeae, ac praesertim ad Hierosolymitanam. Nam Iudaeorum nomen omnes eius gentis homines in genere tum designabat. Itaque speciali appellatione provinciales, id est qui per orbem terrarum, ac praesertim in Occidente et Asiae minoris regionibus erant dispersi, ab iis distinguebantur qui aliquas [antiquas] sedes obtinebant. Illi ἑλληνισταὶ isti antiqua gentis appellatione Hebraei dicebantur, ut apparet ex Act. 6.a.1. ex quo tamen loco satis liquet Palaestinae Ecclesias ex duobus istis Iudaeorum generibus fuisse coactas. neque tamen mirum est tum a situ, tum a maiore multitudine, utrosque communi Hebraeorum nomine significari. [Summa autem huius epistolae haec est, Christum esse verum illum aeternum et unicum Prophetam, Regem ac Pontificem, in quem omnes Patres per fidem respexerunt, et a quo doceri, regi ac sanctificari totam Ecclesiam oportet.] "Epistola Pauli ad Hebraeos" (1556), f. 284[r].

[54] *Ibid.*, f. 293[v]. Cf. Luther (on 2.7), *WA* 57.III. 118.6–8.

[55] *Ibid.*, f. 285[r].

(9.16) which is not Hebrew. Fourth, that from the appendix (13.23), it seems possible to infer that the writer of this epistle was not a prisoner when he wrote it. These [arguments] are opposed, however, by all the things written in II Peter 3.15, which certainly seems to point to this epistle with an extended finger. I respond as follows. If it is not to be considered Paul's because the name of Paul is not manifest, then let it be no one's, because the name of no one is manifest. I, on the contrary, on the basis of this itself, would contend that it is rather Paul's than anyone else's. For why would someone else keep his name silent? With Paul there was just cause why he would send an [anonymous] epistle to Jerusalem; that was surely not, I think, because he was the special Apostle of the Gentiles, as Peter was of the circumcision, but because he knew that his name was highly hated at Jerusalem among the enemies of the Christian name. Therefore he was unwilling to inflame their anger against the church, by affixing his name, their anger already aroused and perhaps exasperated on the occasion of the captivity of Paul himself, as can be gathered from 10.33, 34. This is also the reason, I think, why in 2.3, as if avoiding jealousy of his apostolate, he enumerates himself among those hearers who heard Christ himself speaking, with that figure which orators call ἀνακοίνωσιν, of which we also have an example in I Peter 4.3. As far as the word διαθήκη is concerned, it was already used by the Chaldaeans and Syrians, and on the testimony of the Hebrew grammarians, was used before in the ancient Jerusalem paraphrase: Gen. 24.10. For with Daniel himself there are also found many Greek words so inflected, undoubtedly taken from Ionic Greeks interested in music; just as in these writings we count many words taken from Latin – Matt. 5.26, Mk. 14.3, and II Tim. 4.13, and also the name περιοχῆς (Acts 8.32) from Hebrew; thus already at that time these languages were mixed together. We will speak about the appendix of this epistle in its own place. In several places we have noted that there are not a few words in this epistle which are written in Paul's writings almost word for word. Well, let there be free judgments of men here, but let us all agree on this, that this epistle was truly dictated by the Holy Spirit and that it has been for a long time preserved in the church as a most valuable treasure; no other epistle shows more divinely and skilfully that the old rite was an analogy to spiritual truth, nor more openly and copiously describes the office of our illustrius mediator, written with as much excellence as with exact method. Thus (unless perhaps Apollos can be considered to have written it, whose erudition and eloquence joined with the highest piety is praised so much, Acts 18.24, 28, and who in particular is said to have refuted the Jews), scarcely anyone other than Paul could have been the writer of this epistle.

Let it suffice to know this, that it was truly dictated by the Holy Spirit; it embraces the most brilliant and clearly apostolic joining of the Old covenant with the New and, what is more, the giving and sanctioning of the New as unique.[56]

---

[56] Epistola Pauli, Ἐπιστολὴ Παύλου. Ita scriptum invenimus in omnibus nostris codicibus, uno tantum excepto, in quo duntaxat scriptum erat [inter omnes], ad Hebraeos. Hoc quidem constat nunquam satis convenisse a quo scripta esset [sit haec epistola]: quanvis Graeci theologi [Graeci] certatim Paulo vendicent a quo scilicet scripta quidem

The section " 'To the Hebrews' " also appears in these last editions and is identical to the first edition and the following. The section, "The summary of this epistle," is also in these editions and is identical to the second edition and the following.

A change has taken place in Bèze's 1588 introduction concerning authorship. The first hint is the addition of "by all," "it has never been sufficiently agreed upon by all who wrote the epistle." The next change is that the sentence, "The difference of style . . . other probable

---

fuerit, sed Hebraice, id est lingua tum in Iudaea familiari: quam deinde Lucas [vel Clemens quidam] in Graecum sermonem converterit. Haec autem afferri solent ab iis qui Pauli esse negant. Primum quod Paulus nomen suum praescribere epistolis suis omnibus consuevit. Deinde quod auctor huius epistolae cap. 2.3. sese auditoribus Apostolorum annumeret. Tertio affertur argumentum sumptum a nomine διαθήκη quod Hebraeum non est. 9.16. Quarto quod ex appendice 13.23. videatur colligi posse scriptorem huius epistolae non fuisse captivum quum illam scriberet. Opponuntur autem his omnibus quae scribuntur 2 Petri 3.15. quae certe videntur hanc epistolam velut intento digito monstrare. Ad illa vero obiecta sigillatim sic respondeo. Si Pauli non esse existimanda est quoniam Pauli nomen non praefert, Ergo nullius esto, quum nullius nomen praeferat. Ego vero contra ex hoc ipso contenderim Pauli potius esse quam alterius cuiusquam. Cur enim quispiam alius suum nomen reticuisset? At Paulo iusta causa fuit cur ἀνώνυμον epistolam Hierosolymam mitteret: non illa certe, opinor, quod Gentium esset peculiaris Apostolus, ut Petrus circumcisionis: sed quod summe exosum sciret esse suum nomen Hierosolymitanis, Christiani nominis hostibus, ac proinde illorum rabiem iam grassantem, et occasione fortasse captivitatis ipsius Pauli exacerbatam, ut coniicere licet ex cap. 10.33 et 34. nollet apposito suo nomine adversus Ecclesiam inflammare. Et hanc etiam causam esse arbitror cur cap. 2.3. quasi sui Apostolatus invidiam evitans, sese accenseat eorum auditoribus qui Christum ipsum loquentem audierant, ea figura quam Oratores ἀνακλοίνωσιν appellant: cuius etiam durioris exemplum habemus 1. Petri 4.3. Quod autem attinet ad vocem διαθήκης fuit illa iam pridem Chaldaeis et Syris usitata, testantibus Hebraeis Grammaticis iam olim in paraphrasi Hierosolymitana antiquissima usurpatam: Gen. 24.10. Nam apud Danielem ipsum plures quoque voces Graecae sic inflexae reperiuntur, a Graecis Ionibus musices studiosis proculdubio desumptae: sicut in his scriptis plurimas voces a Latinis desumptas recensuimus Matth. 5.26. Mar. 14.3. et 2. Timoth. 4.13. et ex Hebraeo quoque nomen περιοχῆς Act. 8.32. ut iam tum hae linguae permiscebantur. De appendice autem huius epistolae dicemus suo loco. Certe non pauca sunt in hac epistola quae alibi apud Paulum totidem pene verbis scribi aliquot locis notavimus. Sed age libera hic sunto hominum iudicia, modo in eo consentiamus omnes, vere dictatam hanc epistolam fuisse a Spiritu Sancto, et ut longe pretiosissimum thesaurum in Ecclesia conservatam, qua certe nulla divinius et artificiosius ostendit veterum rituum cum spirituali veritate analogiam, nec apertius, vel copiosius describit Mediatoris illius nostri officium: tam excellente denique et tam exacta methodo scriptam, ut (nisi fortassis Apollos illam scripsisse existimari possit, cuius et eruditio et eloquentia cum maxima pietate coniuncta tantopere commendatur Act. 18.24 et 28. et qui speciatim Iudaeos dicitur coarguissse) vix alius quam Paulus huius epistolae scriptor esse potuerit. Sufficiat hoc nosse, vere esse dictatam a Spiritu sancto, quae luculentissimam ac plane Apostolicam Veteris foederis cum Novo collationem atque adeo Novi foederis veluti singularem quandam promulgationem ac sanctionem complectatur. "Epistola Pauli Apostoli ad Hebraeos," (1588), p. 359.

conjectures . . . it was not Paul's . . .," is lacking. Also lacking is the sentence that nothing is to be gained "by arguing." And finally, there is the addition of a considerable discussion of four points "alleged by those who deny it is Paul's": first the four points are given, then Bèze reponds to these "accusations."

The first three points against Paul have been seen throughout this study: 1) no name, 2) 2.3, 3) διαθήκη. The fourth "alleged" point is curious, because it has usually been used the other way around. The argument from the appendix has been used to argue for Pauline authorship, since the author seems to be in prison. He chooses not to respond in the introduction to the fourth point and dismisses it at the end of his Annotations.

Bèze's response to the first accusation (from no name to no Paul) takes the position of Erasmus (1535) and Politus, both of whom cited Jerome (no name: no Paul:: no name: no one). Then Bèze follows with the "odious-argument" for "no Paul."

The "odious-argument" leads him to conclude, vis-à-vis the second point (2.3), that 2.3 was intended to avoid "jealousy of his apostolate" on the part of his readers.

His response to the third point (διαθήκη is not Hebrew) takes a new twist: the ancient languages "were mixed together."

Bèze prefaced his response to all four accusations by saying that II Peter 3.15 ("Paul wrote to you") points to the Hebrews "with an extended finger." He concludes his response with the emphasis that, while "there are the free judgments of men," it was certainly dictated by the Holy Spirit, the theology of Hebrews regarding the old and new is unsurpassed, "thus . . . scarcely anyone other than Paul could have written it."

For Bèze and others after Calvin some points of general interest can be briefly summarized:

1) They increasingly emphasize that the Holy Spirit is the author of Hebrews. The identity of the human person, of such concern earlier, is unimportant. For some the authorship question is too speculative and conjectural. Yet for others extensive arguments *for* Paul are given. In case it has not been noticed: no one argued against Paul.

2) Introductions expand to include more items than the traditional authorship and theme. Such items are more historical (e.g. *occasio*) literary (e.g. *genus*) methodological (e.g. *loci*) and linguistic (e.g. *Hebraeos*).

3) Given the doctrinal/theological weight of the epistle it must be canonical *(apostolic)*.

4) Many medieval concerns continue: name and style, relationship of Old and New.

5) Erasmus (especially διαθήκη) and Cajetan (Melchisedek) are of concern.

Conclusion

A fair number of obscure texts have been brought to light. This study would support the claim that among the epistles, the one to the Hebrews was most controversial. The authorship question alone, after Erasmus (1516), lifted the discussion to a more textual and historical *(humanistica)* level, and posed severe theological problems. Without the authority of this epistle, central doctrines are without foundation. And Hebrews also raises questions about Old Testament interpretation, law, gospel, Christ, priesthood, sacrifice, faith, works.

A fair cross section of confessional view points have been seen at work on Hebrews. One advantage of working on *exegetica* is that the text under analysis provides two controls: one, the control that the Bible itself provides; two, the control a common section *(pericope)* provides. In other words, this study has provided a fairly constant and focused view of a near century of work on sacred matters.

Having worked on the medieval period previously and now on the 16th century, there have been several surprises during this study – surprises in the sense of interesting finds for one interested in Hebrews:

1) Luther, except for Bugenhagen, was not followed on the basic understanding of the relationship between Old and New Testament. Of course, his lectures on Hebrews were not printed in that century, but his thoughts on the subject were not limited to these lectures.

2) Cajetan's handling of authorship was very critical and devastating, and, one is tempted to add, modern. Cajetan shook one of the two medieval pillars for upholding Pauline authorship: the style-argument, based on a Hebrew original. Paul would not have been so stupid as to tell Jews that Melchisedek means Melchisedek, "I will be to him a father and he shall be to me a son" refers to Christ and not Solomon, or that covenant means testament.

3) The exegete who emphasized faith so much was a Roman Catholic (Contarini).

4) The customary praise for Calvin as exegete is justified. The basis for this, perhaps subjective, comment is the experience of struggling

from one obscure and technical commentary to another, and then with Calvin to see real balance, depth, and reasoned judgment.

5) Denominational lines of interpretation are virtually non-existent. One cannot isolate or predict a Lutheran or Reformed or Roman Catholic interpretation of Hebrews. Yet theological differences did influence (e.g. Flacius and Major on faith-good works).

6) Differences between testament and covenant continue to be noted.

7) Arguments on authorship are endlessly nuanced: what is to be gained by arguing about which pen the Holy Spirit used? (Genevan Version); since the Holy Spirit left the name off, is it better that I should add it? (Dering); the author is whoever he is (Luther). Also amusing was Politus' point that Hebrews is the last epistle because the Jews will be the last to enter.

Bibliography

Primary. Sources

Aquinas, Thomas, "Super epistolam ad Hebraeos lectura." *Super epistolas sancti Pauli lectura.* Ed. P. Raphaelis Cai, O. P. Vol. 2, 8th ed. Rome, 1953, pp. 335–506.

Arboreus, Jean, *Theosophiae complectens sanam et luculentam difficulliorum locorum cum Veteris tum Novi Testamenti expositionem.* Paris: Simon Colinaeus, 1540.

–, "In Pauli ad Hebraeos Epistolam." *Doctissimi et lepidissimi commentarii Joannis Arborei Laudonensis . . . in omnes divi Pauli epistolas.* Paris: Jean Roigny, 1553, ff. 245–287.

–, *Tertius tomus Theosophiae . . . complicitur sanam et luculentam in omnes divi Pauli Epistolas explanationem.* Paris, 1553.

Aretius, Benedictus, *Isagoge ad lectionem Epistolarum Divi Pauli Apostoli.* Lausanne: Franciscus le Preux, 1574.

–, "In Epistolam ad Hebraeos Commentarii." *Commentarii in omnes epistolas Divi Pauli, et Canonicas, itemque in Apocalypsin Divi Ioannis: A. D. Benedicto Aretio.* Bern: Io. le Preux, 1583, 1589, 1596, pp. 590–684.

–, *Commentarii in domini nostri Jesu Christi Novum Testamentum.* Bern: le Preux, 1607.

Arias Montanus, Benito, ed., *Biblia Sacra. Hebraice, Chaldaice, Graece, et Latine,* 8 vols. Antwerp: Christopher Plantin, 1569–72.

–, *Novum Testamentum graecum, cum vulgata interpretatione latina graeci contextus lineis inserta.* Antwerp: Christopher Plantin, 1584.

–, "In epistolam Divi Pauli ad Hebraeos elucidationes." *Elucidationes in omnia sanctorum Apostolorum scripta.* Antwerp: Christopher Plantin, 1588, pp. 299–351.

Balduin, Friedrich, *Analysis epistolae ad Hebraeos.* Wittenberg, 1608.

–, *Commentarius in omnes epistolas Pauli ad Rom . . . nec non XI ad Hebraeos.* Frankfurt: Mevius, 1654–55. Frankfurt: Wustius, 1691.

Bence, Jean, *Manuale in omnes Divi Pauli Epistolas et in septem Canonicas.* Paris, 1638.

Benoît, Jean, *Novum testamentum, haud poenitendis sacrorum Doctorum scholiis, . . . illustratum.* Paris, 1543, 1551, 1554, 1564.

Bèze, Theodore, "Epistola Pauli ad Hebraeos." *Novum Domini Nostri Jesu Christi Testamentum. Latine iam olim a Veteri interprete, nunc denuo a Theodoro Beza versum: cum eiusdem annotationibus, in quibus ratio interpretationis redditur.* Geneva: R. Estienne, 1556, ff. 284^{r}–299^{v}.

–, Της καινης διαθηκης ἅπαντα. . *Novum Iesu Christi . . . Testamentum . . . cum eiusdem annotationibus.* Zürich, 1559; Basel: Barbirii and Courteau, 1559.

–, *Jesu Christi Domini Nostri Novum Testamentum sive Novum foedus. Cuius graeco textui respondent interpretationes duae: una vetus: altera nova, Theodori Bezae, diligenter ab eo recognita.* Geneva: H. Estienne, 1565[2].

–, *Jesu Christi Domini Nostri Novum Testamentum, Graece et Latine, Theodoro Beza interprete. Additae sunt eodem authore, summae breves doctrinae uno quoque Evang. et Acta Apost . . . Item, Methodi Apostolicarum Epistolarum brevis explicatio.* Geneva: H. Estienne, 1565.

–, *The Newe Testament of our Lord Iesus Christ, translated out of Greek by Theodore Beza. Whereunto are adjoined brief summaries of doctrine upon the Evangelistes and Actes of the Apostles, together with the methode of the Epistles of the Apostles, by the said Theodore Beza . . . Englished by L. Thomson.* London: Christopher Barker, 1579.

–, *Jesu Christi Domini Nostri Novum Testamentum sive Novum Foedus.* Geneva: H. Estienne, 1582[3]; H. Estienne II, 1588[4].

–, *Test. Veteris Biblia sacra . . . brevibusque scholiis illustrati ab Immanuele Tremellio et Francisco Junio . . . quibus etiam adjunximus Novi Testamenti libros ex sermone syro ab eodem Tremellio, et ex graeco a Theodoro Beza . . . notisque itidem illustratus. Secunda cura Francisci Junii.* Geneva, 1590.

–, "Epistola Pauli Apostoli ad Hebraeos. Annotationes, in quibus ratio interpretationis redditur." *Theodori Bezae Annotationes maiores in Novum Domini nostri Jesu Christi Testamentum. In duas distinctae partes . . . posterior vero in Epistolas et Apoc. continet . . . Nova autem haec editio multo correctior et emendatior priore . . .* Geneva: E. Vignon, 1594, Vol. II, pp. 483–546.

–, *Jesu Christi Domini Nostri Novum Testamentum sive Novum foedus. Cuius Graeco contextui respondent . . . Bezae. Eiusdem Th. Bezae Annotationes in quibus ratione Interpretationis vocum reddita, additur synopsis doctrinae.* Geneva: E. Vignon, 1598[5].

Biblia cum Glossa ordinaria, Walafrida Strasbonis aliorumque et interlineari Anselmi Laudurensis. 4 vols. Strasbourg: Rusch for Koberger, n. d.

Biblia cum Glossa ordinaria, Nicolai de Lyra postilla, moralitatibus eiusdem, Pauli Burgensis additionibus, Matthiae Thoring replicis. 6 vols. Basel: Johan Froben, 1506–1508.

Biblia . . . cum concordantiis . . . summariis omnium capitum, divisionibus, quattuor repertoriis propositis . . . una cum vera nominum Hebraicorum interpretatione. Basel: Johan Froben, 1509.

Biblia cum concordantiis veteris et novi testamenti necnon et iuris canonici, ac diversitatibus textuum, canonibusque evangeliorum ac quibusdam temporum incidentibus in margine positis et accentu singularum dictionum. Venice, 1511.

BIRD, SAMUEL, *The Lectures of Samuel Bird . . . upon the 11. chapter of the Epistle to the Hebrewes, and upon the 38. Psalme.* Cambridge: John Legate, 1598.

BONADE, FRANCOIS, *Divi Pauli Apostoli gentium, ac Christi Jesu ecclesiae doctoris evangelici, epistolae divinae ad Orphicam lyram traductae Francisco Bonado Anderiae Presbytero paraphraste.* Basel: Bartholomaeus Westhemer, 1537; Paris: Simon du Bois, 1537.

BRENZ, JOHANN, *In epistolam, quam Paulus Apostolus ad Hebraeos scripsit de persona et officio Domini nostri Iesu Christi Commentarius. Authore Ioanne Brentio. F. Theologiae Doctore et Professore publico in Schola Tubingensi.* Tübingen, 1571.

BUGENHAGEN, JOHN, *Annotationes in Deuteronomium, in duos libros Regum.* Basel: Adamus Petri, 1524.

–, *Annotationes Ioan. Bugenhagii Pomerani in decem Epistolas Pauli, sc. ad Eph., Philipp., Col., Thess. primam et secun., Tim. primam et secun., Tit., Philem., Hebraeos.* Nuremberg: Joannes Petrejus, 1524.

–, *Ioannis Pomerani Bugenhagii in librum Psalmorum interpretatio, Wittembergae publica lecta.* Basel: Adamus Petri, 1524.

–, *Von der Evangelischen Messz was die Messz sey . . .* Wittenberg, 1524.

–, "In epistolam ad Hebraeos Ioannis Pomerani Annotationes." *Annotationes . . . in* [XI] *epistolas Pauli.* Strasbourg: Johann Knoblouch, 1525, ff. 138^{r}–159^{v}.

–, *In Epistolam Pauli ad Romanos interpretatio, ipso in schola interpretante, a Doctore Ambrosio Maiobano, ut licuit, excepta.* Hagenau: Iohann Secer, 1527.

BULLINGER, HEINRICH, *In piam et eruditam Pauli ad Hebraeos epistolam, Heinrychi Bullingeri commentarius.* Zürich: Christoph Froschouer, 1532.

–, *De testamento seu foedere dei unico et aeterno.* Zürich: Christoph Froschouer, 1534.

–, *Commentarii in omnes Pauli Apostoli epistolas.* Zürich: Christoph Froschouer, 1535.

–, *In Acta apostolorum H. B. commentariorum libri VI.* Zürich: Christoph Froschouer, 1535.

–, *In omnes Apostolicas epistolas . . . commentarii.* Zürich: Christoph Froschouer, 1537, 1539, 1544, 1549, 1558.

–, *De Scripturae sanctae authoritate, certitudine, et firmitate absoluta.* Zürich: Christoph Froschouer, 1538.

–, *Novi Testamenti Historia Evangelica . . . omnibusque Apostolicis Epistolis, nempe S. Pauli XIII . . .* Zürich: Christoph Froschouer, 1554.

–, *Compendium Christianae religionis.* Zürich: Christoph Froschouer, 1556.

–, *Summa christlicher Religion.* Zürich: Christoph Froschouer, 1556.

–, *Catechesis pro adultioribus scripta . . . De Foedere dei et vero dei cultu. . .* Zürich: Christoph Froschouer, 1559.

–, "In piam et eruditam Pauli ad Hebraeos epistolam Heinrychi Bullingeri." *Commentarii in omnes Pauli apostoli epistolas, atque etiam in epistolam ad Hebraeos.* Zürich: Christoph Froschouer, 1582.

CAJETAN, THOMAS, *Epistolae Pauli, et aliorum apostolorum ad Graecam veritatem castigatae, et per . . . Thomam de Vio . . . juxta sensum literalem enarratae.* Paris, 1532, 1537, 1540, 1542.

–, "In epistolam ad Hebraeos commentarii." *Opera Omnia,* V. Lyons: Prost, 1639.

CALVIN, JOHN, *Commentarii in Epistolam ad Hebraeos.* Geneva: Joannes Girardus, 1549.

–, *Ioannis Calvini in omnes Divi Pauli epistolas, atque etiam in epistolam ad Hebraeos commentaria luculentissima. Ex postrema authoris recognitione.* Geneva: Joannes Girardus, 1551.

–, "In epistolam ad Hebraeos." *In omnes Pauli Apostoli Epistolas atque etiam in*

Epistolam ad Hebraeos, item in canonicas . . . Ioh. Calvini Commentarii. Hanc commentariorum postremam esse recognitionem. Geneva: Estienne, 1556, pp. 675–775.

–, *Commentarius in epistolam ad Hebraeos. Opera Omnia,* edited by Baum, Cunitz and Reuss. Vol. 55, Brunswick, 1896, Cols. 1–198. CR, Vol. 83.

–, "The Epistle of Paul the Apostle to the Hebrews." *Calvin's Commentaries,* tr. by William B. Johnston. London: Oliver and Boyd, 1963.

CAMERARIUS, JOACHIM, "De epistola scripta ad Hebraeos." *Notatio figurarum orationis et mutatae simplicis elocutionis in apostolicis scriptis.* Leipzig: Papa, 1556, [16 fols.].

–, *Commentarius in Novum Foedus: in quo et figurae sermonis et verborum significatio, et orationis sententia, ad illius foedus intelligentiam certiorem, tractantur. Elaboratus studio et diligentia Joachim Camerarii Pabepergensis.* Cambridge: Roger Daniel, 1642.

CAMERON, JOHN, "Ad quaestiones in epistolam ad Hebraeos." *Praelectiones in selectaria quaedam Novi Testamenti loca Salmurii habitarum.* 3 vols. Salmurum: Girard and Lerpiner, 1626–28; III, pp. 129–267.

–, "Ad Hebraeos." *Myrothecium Evangelicum.* Geneva: Peter Aubert, 1632, pp. 286–337.

CAPPEL, JACQUES, *Observationes in epistolam ad Hebraeos.* Amsterdam: Elzivirius, 1657.

CASAUBON, ISAAC, *In Novi Testamenti Libros Notae.* Geneva, 1587.

–, ΤΗΣ ΚΑΙΝΗΣ ΔΙΑΘΗΚΣ ΑΠΑΝΤΑ *Novi Testamenti libri omnes.* Lugduni Batavorum: ex officiana Elseviriana, 1641.

CHATEILLON, SEBASTIAN, "Ad Hebraeos." *Biblia . . . una cum eiusdem annotationibus.* Basel: Oporin, 1551, Cols. 267–278.

–, *Biblia Sacra . . . cum annotationibus eiusdem.* Basel: Petrus Perna, 1573.

–, *Novum Jesu Christi Testamentum a Sebastiano Castalione Latine redditum, in usum scholarum.* London, 1696.

CHRYSOSTOM, ST. JOHN, *Homilae XXXIV in epistolam ad Hebaeos.* PG 63, Paris, 1862, pp. 237–456.

CLARIUS, ISIDORUS, "Epistola Beati Pauli Apostoli ad Hebraeos." *Novi Testamenti Vulgata quidem aeditio, sed quae ad vetustissimorum utriusque linguae exemplarium fidem, nunc demum emendata est diligentissime, ut nova non desideretur, adiectis scholiis, et doctis et piis . . .* 2 vols. Venice: Petrus Schaeffer, 1541, II, pp. 327–380.

–, *Vulgata aeditio Veteris ac Novi Testamenti, quorum alterum ad Hebraicam, alterum ad Graecam veritatem emendata est diligentissime . . . adiectis ex eruditis scriptoribus scholiis.* 3 vols. Venice: Petrus Schaeffer, 1542.

–, *Vulgata,* Antwerp, 1544.

–, *Biblia sacrosancta Veteris ac Novi Testamenti . . . ex secunda eius recognitione.* Venice: Iunta, 1557.

–, *Biblia sacrosancta Veteris ac Novi Testamenti.* Venice: Iunta, 1564.

CONTARINI, GASPARO, "Epistola ad Hebraeos." *Scholia in epistolas divi Pauli, Opera.* Paris: Sebastian Nivelle, 1571, pp. 515–529. Venice, 1578, 1589.

DELFINO, GIOVANNI ANTONIO, *Commentarii in Evang. Ioannis, et in Epistolam Pauli ad Hebraeos, Magistri Antonii Delphini e Casali Maiore, Convent. Francis-*

cani: a. F. Constantio eiusdem Ord. Card. Samano summa industria expoliti, notatisque marginibus illustrati. Rome, 1587.

DERING, EDWARD, *A Lecture or Exposition upon a part of the V. chapter of the Epistle to the Hebrues. As it was read in Paules the 6. day of December, 1572. By Edward Deryng.* London: John Awdeley, 1573, 1574, 1583.

–, *XXVI Lectures, or readings, upon part of the Epistle to the Hebrues.* London, 1576, 1577, 1578, 1583, 1590.

–, *Lectures, or readings, upon part of the Epistle written to the Hebrues. Made by Maister Edward Deering, Bachelour of Divinitie.* London: Woodcocke, 1590. *M. Dering's workes. More at large then ever hath here-to-fore been printed in any one volume.* London: Lineley and Flasket, 1597.

DES GALLARS, NICOLAS, *La Bible . . . on a adiousté des Annotations.* Geneva: François Iaguy, 1562.

–, *Le Nouveau Testament . . .* Lyon, 1563.

DICKSON, DAVID, *A Short Explanation of the Epistle of Paul to the Hebrews.* Aberdene: Raban, 1635; Dublin: Society of Stationers, 1637; Cambridge: Daniel, 1649.

–, *Expositio analytica omnium Apostolicarum Epistolarum: seu brevis introductio ad pleniores commentarios in usum studiosorum theologiae: Opera Davidis Dicsoni.* Glasguae: Andersonus, 1645.

–, *An exposition of all St. Paul's epistles, together with an Explanation of those other Epistles . . . Wherein the sense of every Chapter and Verse is Analytically unfolded,* [translated from Latin by Wm. Retchford]. London: Eglesfield, 1659.

–, *Method of healing diseases of the conscience concerning Regeneration.* Edinburgh, 1695.

DIETRICH, VEIT, "Summaria in epistolam sancti Pauli ad Hebraeos." *Annotationes compendiariae in novum testamentum. Quibus summatim in singula capita praecipui loci et selectiones sententiae explicantur, annotanturque . . . Per M. Vitum Theodorum.* Frankfurt: Christian Egenolph, 1545, ff. 249r–259v.

–, *Summaria uber die gantze Bibel, das Alte und Neue Testament . . .* Nuremberg, 1553. [German translation of Latin *Annotationes*]

DIONYSIUS THE CARTHUSIAN, "Enarratio in epistolam beati Pauli ad Hebraeos." *Enarrationes piae ac eruditae in beati Pauli epistolas. Omnia Opera,* XIII. Monstrolius, 1901, pp. 469–531.

DOWNHAM, JOHN, *Annotations upon all the Books of the Old and New Testament.* London, 1645. 2nd. ed., London: John Legatt, 1651. 3rd ed., London: Tyler, 1657.

DRUSIUS, JOANNES, *Iohannis Drusi ad voces hebraicas Novi Testamenti commentarius.* Antwerp: Christopher Plantin, 1582.

–, *Annotationum in totum Jesu Christi Testamentum sive Praeteritorum Libri decem.* Franeker: Aegidius Radaeus, 1612.

DU PREAU, GABRIEL, *Omnes divi Pauli atque canonicae epistolae quatuor libris digestae par G. P.* Louvain, 1568.

ERASMUS, DESIDERIUS, *Novum instrumentum cum annotationibus.* Basel: Johan Froben, 1516.

–, *Apologia ad Jacobum Fabrum Stapulensem.* 1517. LB IX, 17–50, Lugduni Batavorum, 1706.

–, *Novum Testamentum omne, multo quam antehac diligentius ab Erasmo Roterodamo recognitum.* Basel: Johan Froben, 1519.

–, *In epistolam Pauli ad Hebraeos paraphrasis per Erasmum Roterodamum extrema.* Basel: Johan Froben, 1521.

–, *Paraphrases Erasmi Roterodami in omnes Epistolas Pauli germanas et in omnes canonicas.* Basel: Johan Froben, 1521.

–, "In epistolam Pauli ad Hebraeos Annotationes Des. Eras. Rot." *Des. Erasmi Roterodami in Novum Testamentum ab eodem tertio recognitum.* Basel: Johan Froben, 1522; pp. 561–589. 4th ed., Basel: Froben, 1527. 5th ed., Basel: Froben, 1535.

–, "Enchiridion militis christiani (1501/1503)." *Des Eras. Roter., Ausgewählte Werke.* Edited by Hajo Holborn. Munich, 1933, pp. 22–136.

–, "Annotationes in epistolam Pauli ad Hebraeos," *Paraphrases in Novum Testamentum.* Vol VII of *Opera Omnia.* Paris, 1631.

–, *Opus Epistolarum Des. Erasmi Roterodami.* 11 vols. Edited by Percy S. and H. M. Allen. Oxford: Oxford University Press, 1906–1947.

Estienne, Robert, *Biblia.* Paris, 1527–1528.

–, *Biblia.* Paris, 1532, 1540.

–, *Index rerum et sententiarum quae in Veteri et Novi Testamenti libris continentur.* Paris, 1532. Antwerp, 1534.

–, *Ed. et Annot. Evangelium Secundum Matt . . . Marci . . . Luc . . . Johan. . . . Pauli apostoli epistolae . . . Breves variarum tralationum annotationes.* Paris, 1541, 1543, 1545.

–, "Epistola Pauli Apostoli ad Hebraeos." *Pauli Apostoli Epistolae ad Rom . . . ad Heb . . . Breves variarum tralationum annotationes.* Paris, 1541; ff. 97^v–111^r.

Estius, Gulielmus, "In epistolam Beati Pauli apostoli ad Hebraeos commentarius." *In Omnes Pauli Epistolas item in Catholicas Commentarii.* Edited by Sausen. Moguntiae, 1841–45, VI, 1–498.

Flacius Illiricus, Matthias, *Clavis scripturae sacrae.* Basel: Paul Quecus, 1567.

–, "In Epistolam Pauli Apostoli ad Hebraeos." Τῆς τοῦ υἱοῦ θεοῦ καὶνης διαθήκης ἁπάντα *Novum Testamentum Jesu Christi Filii Dei ex versione Erasmi, innumeris in locis ad Graecam veritatem, genuinumque sensum emendata. Glossa compendiaria M. M. Fl. Ill. Albonensis in Novum Testamentum.* Basel: Perna and Dietrich, 1570, pp. 1101–1196.

–, *De ratione cognoscendi sacras literas.* Edited by Lutz Geldsetzer. Düsseldorf, 1968.

Froidmont, Libert, *Commentaria in omnes Beati Pauli Apostoli et septem canonicas aliorum Apostolorum epistolas.* Louvain, 1663, 1679.

–, *Commentaria in Sanctam Scripturam.* 2 vols. Paris, 1670, 1671, 1673, 1674.

Gagny, Jean de, *Divi Pauli Apostoli epistolae brevissimis . . . scholiis . . . illustratae.* Paris: Simon Colinaeus, 1539.

–, *Brevissima et facillima in omnes Pauli epistolas scholia.* Paris: Simon Colinaeus, 1543. Paris: Vivant Gaultherot, 1547, 1550.

–, "Epistola divi Pauli ad Hebraeos." *Brevissima et facillima in omnes Divi Pauli epistolas scholia, ultra priores editiones ex antiquissimis Graecorum authoribus, abunde locupletata. Itidem in septem canonicas epistolas et Divi Ioannis Apocalypsim, brevissima scholia recens edita*. Paris: Sebastian Nivelle, 1563, ff. 149r–188v.

GARNIER, JEAN, *De epistola Sancti Pauli ad Hebraeos declamatio*. Marburg, 1559.

The Geneva Bible: "The Epistle to the Ebrewes." *The Bible and Holy Scriptures conteyned in the Olde and Newe Testament. Translated according to the Ebrue and Greke . . . with moste profitable annotations upon all the hard places. . . .* Geneva: Rowland Hall, 1560, ff. 102r–106v.

The Geneva Bible. A facsimile of the 1560 edition. Madison: The University of Wisconsin Press, 1969.

GERHARD, JOHN, *Commentarius super epistolam ad Hebraeos*. Iena: Reiffenbergeri, 1641.

GIUSTINIANI, LE P. BENEDETTO, *In omnes Beati Pauli Apostoli epistolas explanationum* tom. I, II. Lyon: H. Cardon, 1612, 1613.

GODEAU, ANTOINE, *Paraphrase sur l'Epistre de sainct Paul aux Hébreux, par Ant. Godeau*. Paris: J. Camusat, 1637, 1641, 1651. Rouen, 1653, 1667. Lyon: L. Plaignard, 1685.

–, *Elevations to Jesus Christ: being Christian Meditations on St. Paul's Epistle to the Hebrews*. Translated by Joshua Smith. London: Sare, 1715.

GOMARUS, FRANCISCUS BRUGENSIS, *Oratio de foedere dei*. Leiden, 1594.

–, "Analysis Epistolae Pauli Apostoli ad Hebraeos." *Opera Theologica Omnia*. 2 vols. Amsterdam, 1644, II, pp. 285–369.

GORDON, JAMES, *Biblia sacra cum commentariis ad sensum literae, et explicationem temporum, locorum, rerumque. . . .* 3 vols. Paris, 1632.

GOUGE, WILLIAM, *A learned and very useful commentary on the whole Epistle to the Hebrews. Being the substance of Thirty Years' Wednesday's lectures at Blackfriars, London*. London: A. M., T. W., and S. G., for Joshua Kirton, 1655.

–, *Annotations upon all the books of the Old and Newe Testament: this third . . . edition*. 2 vols. London: Evan Tyler, 1657.

GROTIUS, HUGO, "Ad Hebraeos." *Annotationes in Acta Apostolorum et in epistolas catholicas*. Paris, 1646, pp. 787–896.

GRYNÄUS, JOHANN JAKOB, *Epitomes Sacrorum Biblion, pars prima, complectens Veteris Testamenti. . .* Basel: Henricpetri, 1577.

–, *Explanatio epistolae S. Apostoli Pauli, ad Hebraeos*. Basel: Sebastiani Henricpetri, 1587.

GUALTHER, RUDOLF, *Argumentorum in sacra Biblia*. 2 vols. Frankfurt: Weygandt Han, 1556.

–, "In epistolam Divi Pauli Apostoli ad Hebraeos D. Rodolphi Gualtheri Pastoris Ecclesiae Tigurinae Homiliarum archetypi." *In Divi Pauli Apostoli Epistolas omnes . . . Homiliarum archetypi*. Edited by H. Vuolphius. Zürich: Christoph Froschouer, 1589, ff. 318–352.

GUILLEBERT, NICOLAS, *L'Épistre de saint Pol aux Hébreux, avec toutes les Épistres canoniques*. Paris: Vue de N. Buon, 1638.

GUILLIAUD, CLAUDE, "Epistola beati Pauli ad Hebraeos." *Collatio in omnes divi Pauli apostoli epistolas*. Lyon: Sebastian Gryphius, 1543, pp. 441–527. Paris, 1548, 1550, 1552.

GUISARDIUS, HENRICUS, *Vindiciae testamentariae . . . in IX . . . ad Hebraeos*. Geneva: Chouët, 1656.

HEINSIUS, DANIEL, *Exercitationes sacrae ad Novum Testamentum*. Lugdunum Batavorum, 1639. 2nd ed., Cambridge: Roger Daniel, 1640.

HEMMINGSEN, NIELS, *Commentarius in epistolam apostolicam ad Hebraeos*. Wittenberg, 1568.

–, "Ad Hebraeos." *Commentaria in omnes epistolas Apostolorum, Pauli, Petri, Iudae, Iohannis, Iacobi et in eam quae ad Hebraeos inscribitur*. Leipzig: Andreas Schneider, typis Voegelianis, 1572, pp. 830–915.

–, *Commentaria in omnes Epistolas Apostolorum, Pauli, Petri, Iudae, Ioannis, Iacobi, et in eam quae ad Hebraeos inscribitur*. Frankfurt: Georg Corvinus, 1579.

–, *Commentaria in omnes epistolas apostolorum et in eam quae ad Hebraeos inscribitur*. Strasbourg: Theodosius Rihelius, 1586.

–, *Opuscula theologica*. Geneva, 1586.

HORNEIUS, CONRAD, *In epistolam sancti Apostoli Pauli ad Hebraeos expositio litteralis*. Brunswick: Dunckeri, 1655.

HUNNIUS, GILES, *Exegesis epistolae ad Hebraeos*. Frankfurt am Main: Johann Spies, 1586.

HYPERIUS, ANDREAS GERHARD, *De formandis concionibus sacris, seu de interpretatione scriptuarum populari libri II*. Marburg: Andreas Colibius, 1553.

–, *De theologo, seu de ratione studii theologici libri IIII*. Basel: Johannes Oporinus, 1559.

–, *De sacrae Scripturae lectione ac meditatione quotidiana*. 2 vols. Basel: Johannes Oporinus, 1561.

–, *Methodi theologiae sive praecipuorum Christinae religionis locorum communium libri III*. Basel: Johannes Oporinus, 1567.

–, *Commentarii . . . in omnes Divi Pauli Apostoli Epistolas, atque etiam in Epistolam Divi Judae, nunc primum opera Ioannis Mylii in lucem editi*. 5 vols. in 2. Zürich: Christoph Froschouer, 1582–1584.

–, *Commentarii D. Andreae Hyperii, doctissimi . . . Theologi, ad Hebraeos, nunc primum opera Ioannis Mylii in lucem editi*. Zürich: Christoph Froschouer, 1584.

JONES, WILLIAM, *A Commentary upon the Epistles of St. Paul to Philemon, and to the Hebrewes, together with a compendious explication of the second and third epistles of St. John*. London, 1636.

JUNIUS, FRANCISCUS, *Sacrorum Parallelorum libri tres: . . . tertio, Epistolae ad Hebraeos . . . commentarius*. Heidelberg, 1588. London: Bishop, 1588^{2}, 1591.

LAPIDE, CORNELIUS A, "Ad Hebraeos." *Commentaria in omnes Divi Pauli epistolas*. Antwerp, 1614, Paris, 1868, XIX, 347–524. Paris, 1631 (*ad Heb.*, 879–1036). Antwerp, 1635 (831–976).

LAWSON, GEORGE, *An exposition of the Epistle to the Hebrews*. London, 1662.

LEFEVRE D'ÉTAPLES, JAQUES, "Commentariorum in epistolas beati Pauli apostoli liber quartusdecimus qui est in epistolam ad Hebraeos." *Epistolae Pauli Apostoli*. Paris: Henri Estienne, 1512, 1515, 1531. Basel, 1527. Cologne, 1515, 1531. Antwerp, 1540.

–, *The Prefatory Epistles*. Edited by Eugene F. Rice, Jr. New York: Columbia University Press, 1972.

LE GRAND, NICOLAS, *In divi Pauli Epistolam ad Hebraeos enarratio a fratre Nicolao Grandis*. Paris: Ponset le Preux, 1537, 1552.

–, *In epistolas ad Romanos et Hebraeos*. Paris: le Preux, 1546.

LIGHTFOOT, JOHN, *The Harmony, Chronicle and Order of the New Testament*, London, 1655.

LINCK, WENZESLAUS, *Das zwölfft Capitel der Epistel an die Ebreer mit kurtzer einfältiger Auslegung*. 1544.

LUCAS BRUGENSIS, FRANCISCUS, *Notationes in Sacra Biblia*. Antwerp, 1580, 1581, 1583².

LUSHINGTON, THOMAS, TR. *The Expiation of A Sinner*. London: Thomas Harper, 1646.

LUTHER, MARTIN, "Die Epistell der hohen messen am Christag auss Heb. primo." *Kirchenpostille 1522*. WA 10, 1,1, Weimar: Hermann Böhlau, 1910, pp. 142–180.

–, "Vorrhede auff die Epistel zu den Ebreern." *Das Newe Testament Deutzsch* (1522). WA, DB 7. Weimar: Hermann Böhlau, 1931, p. 344.

–, "Alius Sermo. I Corinth: 3. 'Ego Sum Cephae' Vyl fast nuezlicher punet." *Aussgezogen auss etzlichen Predigen dess Gottes gelahrtn Doctoris Martini Lutheri* (1537). WA 45. Weimar: Hermann Böhlau, 1911, pp. 389–392.

–, *Divi Pauli apostoli ad Hebreos epistola*. WA 57. III. Weimar: Hermann Böhlau, 1929, pp. 1–238.

LYSERIUS, POLYCARP (filius), *Commentarius in epistolam ad Ebraeos*. Wittenberg, 1616.

MAJOR, GEORG, *De origine et autoritate verbi Dei*. Wittenberg: Joannes Lufft, 1550.

–, *Testamentum Doctoris Georgii Maioris*. Wittenberg: Joannes Lufft, 1570.

–, *Enarratio epistolae ad Hebraeos, praelecta a D. Georgio Maiore Wittenbergae*. Wittenberg: Joannes Lufft, 1571.

MARIANA, LE P. JUAN DE, *Scholia in Vetus et Novum Testamentum*. Paris, 1620.

MENOCHIO, LE P. GIOVANI STEPHANO, *Brevis explicatio sensus literalis Sacrae Scripturae*. Cologne, 1630. Lyon, 1631, 1697.

MESTREZAT, JEAN, *Sermons Sur Les Deux Premiers Chapitres De L'Epistre aux Hebreux*. Paris, 1639.

–, *En Sermon Exposition de l'Epistre aux Hebreux*. Geneva, 1639–55.

–, *Sermons Sur Les Chapitres Troisiéme Quartiéme, Cinquiéme et Sixiéme de L'Epistre Aux Hebreux*. Geneva: Samuel Chouët, 1653.

MORE, ALEXANDER, "Ad Hebraeos." *Ad quaedam loca Novi Foederis Notae*. London, 1661, pp. 162–176. Cf. Tena.

NAHUM, IODOCI, *Commentarius in epistolam ad Ebraeos*. Hannover, 1602.

NOVARINI, LUIGI, "Ad Hebraeos." *Paulus expensus notis, monitisque sacris, qua ex linguarum fontibus, qua ex variarum versionum collatione, qua ex sanctorum Patrum aliorumque probae notae auctorum observationibus, quae ad mores informandos praecipue spectant, illustratus*. Verona: F. de Rubeis, 1644, pp. 370–400. Lyon: haered. G. Boissat et L. Anisson.

OECOLAMPADIUS, JOHANNES, *Die verdeutscht Antwort die der doctor Eck in seynem Sendbrieff an dem Bischoff tzu Meyssen hat die ungelärten Lutherischen Thumherrn genandt*. Wittenberg: Johann Rhau-Grunenberg, 1520.

–, *De Gaudio resurrectionis sermone, in quo de mysterio tridui contra sophistas*. Augsburg: Sigismund Grim und Marcus Wirsung, 1521.

–, *Ein sonderliche lehre und bewerung . . . durch Jo. Haussschein sunst genant Oeco-*

lampadius sant Birgiten ordens. Augsburg: Sigismund Grim und Marcus Wirsung, 1521.

–, *In Epistolam Ioannis Apostoli Catholicam primam, Ioannis Oecolampadii Demegoriae, hoc est, Homiliae una et viginti*. Nuremberg: Johann Petreius, 1524.

–, *In Epistolam ad Hebraeos, Ioannis Oecolampadii, explanationes, ut ex ore praelegentis exceptae, per quosdam ex auditoribus digestae sunt*. Strasbourg: Matthias Apiarius, 1534.

OSIANDER, LUCAS, "Epistola ad Hebraeos; Iacobi; prima et secunda Petri; prima, secunda, et tertia Ioannis; Iudae; et Apocalypsis Ioannis." *Quinque libri Moysis . . . iuxta veterem seu vulgatam translationem, ad Hebraeam veritatem (ad Graecum textum) emendati, et breve . . . explicatione illustrati, insertis etiam praecipuis locis communibus in lectione sacra observandis. Lucas Osiander*. Vol. 9. Tübingen: Georg Gruppenbach, 1573–1586.

OWEN, JOHN, *Exercitations on the epistle to the Hebrews. Also concerning the Messiah*, 4 vols. London, Robert White, for Nathaniel Ponder, 1668–1684.

–, "An exposition of the Epistle to the Hebrews with Preliminary Exercitations." *The Works of John Owen, D. D.* Edited by William H. Goold, vols. 18 and 19. Edinburgh: Johnstone and Hunter, 1854.

PALACIOS, MIGUEL DE, *Enarrationes in epistolam Beati Pauli Apostoli ad Hebraeos*. Salamanca: Ferdinand, 1590.

PAREUS, DAVID, *In divinam ad Hebraeos Sancti Pauli Apostoli epistolam commentarius*. Geneva: Aubertum, 1614.

–, *Operum Theologicorum Exegeticorum* tom. I. pars prima . . . Frankfurt, 1647.

PAYNELL, THOMAS, *A frutefull booke of the comon places of all St. Pauls Epistles . . . especially for those of the ministerye dyligentslye sette foorthe by Thomas Paniell*. London: John Tisdale, 1562.

PEARSON, JOHN, *Critici Sacri: sive doctissimorum virorum in SS. Biblia annotationes et tractatus*. 9 vols. London, 1660. Frankfurt, 1695–1696 (9 vols. in 7). Amsterdam, 1698 (8 vols. in 9). Amsterdam, 1698–1732 (13 vols.).

–, "Annotata in epistolam ad Hebraeos." *Critici Sacri: sive annotata doctissimorum virorum in Vetus ac Novum Testamentum. Quibus accedunt tractatus varii theologico-philologici*. Amsterdam: Boom, 1698, VII, cols. 883–1190.
Includes the following exegetes of Hebrews: Laurentius Valla, Erasmus, Franciscus Vatablus, Sebastianus Castalio, Isidorus Clarius, Nicolaus Zegerus, Lucas Brugensis, Henricus Stephanus, Johannes Drusius, Josephus Scaliger, Isaacus Casaubonus, Joannes Camero, Jacobus Cappelus, Ludovicus Cappelus and Hugo Grotius.

–, *Minor theological works*. 2 vols. Oxford: Oxford University Press, 1844.

PELLIKAN, KONRAD, "Commentarium in epistolam D. Pauli apostoli ad Hebraeos." *Commentaria Bibliorum*. Preface by Heinrich Bullinger. Zürich: Christoph Froschouer, 1539 VII, pp. 608–680.

–, *In omnes apostolicas epistolas commentaria*. Zürich, 1582.

PERKINS, WILLIAM, *A Cloud of Faithful Witnesses . . . or a Commentary upon the eleventh Chapter to the Hebrewes*. London: H. Fetherstone, 1622.

–, "A Cloud of Faithful Witnesses: Leading to the Heavenly Canaan, or, A Commentarie upon the Eleventh Chapter to the Hebrews, preached in Cambridge by that godly and judicious Divine, Mr. William Perkins."

Recorded "from his mouth" by Crashaw and Pierson. *The Works of that Famous and Worthy Minister of Christ.* London: Haviland, 1631, III, pp. 1–199.

–, "A Commentarie upon Part of the Twelfth Chapter to the Hebrews." *The Works of the Famous and Worthy Minister of Christ.* London: Haviland, 1631, III, pp. 199–206.

–, *The Works of William Perkins.* Edited by Ian Breward. Abingdon: Sutton Courtenay Press, 1970.

PISCATOR, JOHANNES, *Analysis lofica [sic] quinque . . . epistolarum Pauli.* Herborn: Christoph Corvinus, 1590.

–, *Commentarii in omnes libros Novi Testamenti.* 3rd. ed., Herborn, 1638.

POLITUS, AMBROSIUS CATHARINUS, *Annotationes . . . in Excerpta quaedam de Commentariis . . . Cardinalis Caietani Sancti Christi Dogmata.* Paris: Simon Colinaeus, 1535.

–, *Annotationes in Commentaria Caietani, denuo multo locupletiores et castigatiores redditae.* Lyon: Joannes Bonhomme, 1542.

–, *Commentaria . . . in omnes divi Pauli, et alias septem canonicas epistolas.* Venice: Vincenzo Valgris, 1551.

–, "Commentaria in eandem epistolam beati Pauli ad Hebraeos." *In omnes divi Pauli apostoli, et alias septem canonicas epistolas R. P. Fratris Ambrosii Catharini Politi Senensis, Episcopi Minoriensis, commentaria.* Paris: Bernardus Turrisanus, 1566, pp. 453–521.

PS.-HUGH of ST. VICTOR, "In epistolam ad Hebraeos." *Quaestiones et decisiones in epistolas divi Pauli.* PL 175. Paris, 1879, pp. 607–634.

QUISTORP, JOHANN, *In divinam ad Hebraeos epistolam commentarius analyticus.* Rostock: J. Reusneri, 1638.

–, *Annotationes in omnes libros biblicos.* 2 vols. in 1. Frankfurt et Rostock: Wildium, 1648.

RAPINE, CHARLES, *Exposition paraphrastique de l'Épistre de l'apostre S. Paul aux Hébreux.* Paris: C. Sonnius, 1636.

The Rheims New Testament: "The Epistle of Paul the Apostle to the Hebrewes." *The New Testament of Iesus Christ, Translated Faithfully into English, out of the authentical Latin . . . With Arguments . . . Annotations, and other necessarie helpes, for the better understanding of the text, and specially for the discoverie of the Corruptions of divers late translations, and for cleering the Controversies in religion, of these daies: In the English College of Rhemes.* Rheims: J. Fogny, 1582, pp. 603–639.

RIBERIA, FRANCISCO, *Commentarius in epistolam Beati Pauli ad Hebraeos.* Salamanca: Petrus Lassus, 1598.

–, *In epistolam b. Pauli apostoli ad Hebraeos commentarii.* Turoni: C. Michaelem, 1601.

ROLLOCK, ROBERT, *Analysis logica in epistolam ad Hebraeos. Authore D. Roberto Rolloco Scoto . . . Accessit . . . tractatus de Justificatione eodem Authore.* Edinburgh, 1605; Geneva, 1610.

RUNGIUS, DAVID, *Analysis et disputationes in epistolam ad Ebraeos.* Wittenberg, 1600.

SA, EMMANUEL, *Notationes in totam Scripturam sacram.* Antwerp: Joannes Moretus, 1598.

SAINT-MARTIAL, JEAN DE, *Explication familière de l'épistre de S. Paul aux Hébreux.* Paris: Josse, 1644.

SALMERON, ALFONSE, *Disputationum in Epistolas divi Pauli tomus tertius. In quo alii duo libri continetur. Septimus . . . Octavus in Epistolam ad Hebraeos.* Madrid: Sanchez, 1602.

SASBOUT, ADAM, *In omnes fere Pauli, et quorumdam aliorum Apostolorum, epistolas explicatio.* Edited by C. Verburch. Louvain: Bergagne, 1556. Antwerp, 1561.

–, *In omnes divi Pauli et quorumdam aliorum Apostolorum epistolas. Opera Omnia.* Cologne: Pirchman, 1568, 1575.

–, "Epistola divi Pauli ad Hebraeos expositio Fratris Adami Sasbout." *Biblicus Apparatus.* Edited by R. Walton. Zürich: Bodmer, 1673.

SCAINO, ANTONIO, *Paraphrasis in omnes Sancti Pauli Epistolas, cum adnotationibus . . . Auctore Antonio Scayno Salodiensi.* Venice: Nicolinus, 1589.

SCALIGER, JOSEPH, Της Καινης Διαθηκης ἁπαντα. *Novum Iesu Christi D. N. Testamentum cum notis Iosephi Scaligeri.* Geneva, 1620. London, 1622, 1633, 1641.

SCHLICHTING, JONASZ, *Commentaria in epistolam ad Hebraeos.* Rakau: P. Sternacius, 1634.

–, *Jonae Slichtingii de Bukowiec Commentaria posthuma in plerosque Novi Testamenti libros.* Irenopoli, post a. 1656.

SELNECKER, NIKOLAUS, *Nicolai Selnecceri D. In omnes epistolas Divi Pauli apostoli, commentarius plenissimus, continens . . .* Leipzig: Apelii. 1595.

SERARIUS, NICOLAS, *Prolegomena Bibliaca, et Commentaria in omnes epistolas canonicas.* Moguntiaci: Lippius, 1612.

SISTO DA SIENA, *Bibliotheca sancta.* 8 vols. Lyon: Presnot, 1575.

SPANHEIM, FRIEDRICH, cf. Tena.

STEVARTIUS, PIERRE, *Epistolae divi Pauli ad Hebraeos, septem priorum capitum brevis explicatio, publice ad disputandum in Catholica Ingolstadiensium academia proposita, Praeside Petro Stevartio Leodio . . .* Ingolstadt: David Sartorius, 1588.

STRESO, CASPAR, *Commentarius analytico – practicus in epistolam ad Hebraeos.* Hegae-Comitum: C. Doll et M. Van Heyningen, 1661.

STRIGEL, VICTOR, ed. ΥΠΟΜΝΗΜΑΤΑ – *in omnes libros Novi Testamenti.* 2 vols. in 1. Leipzig: Ernesti Voegelini Constantiensis, 1565.

TARANTASIA, PETRUS, DE, "In epistolam beati Pauli ad Hebraeos." *In omnes divi Pauli epistolas ennarratio.* Edited by Nicolas de Gorran. Lyon, 1692, II, pp. 160–282.

TENA, LUIS DE, *Commentaria et disputationes in Epistolam D. Pauli ad Hebraeos, auctore D. Ludovico Tena . . . Quibus adduntur ob argumenti similitudinem hi tractatus: Fr. Spanhemii Exercitationes de autore et epistola ad Hebraeos; Ambr. Catharini. Dissertatio de epistola ad Hebraeos; Christoph Schlegelii Quaestiones de persona Melchisedeci; Henrico Guisardi Vindiciae testamentariae in IX. ad Hebraeos; Joh. Hopkinsoni Descriptio paradisi; Christophoro Helvici de Libris adversus Judaeos; Alex Mori Ad quaedam loca Novi Foederis notae nunc primum editae.* London: R. Scott, 1661.

TIRINIUS, JACOBUS, *Commentarius in Sacram Scripturam,* 2 parts. Antwerp, 1632. Venice: Nicolaum Pezzane, 1724.

TITELMANS, FRANCISCUS, "Elucidatio in epistolam ad Hebraeos, beati Pauli.

apostoli." *In omnes epistolas apostolicas . . . elucidatio*. Paris, 1543, ff. 184^{v}–215^{v}. Antwerp, 1528, 1529, 1532, 1540. Paris, 1532, 1543, 1551, 1553. Lyon, 1553.

TYNDALE, WILLIAM *The newe Testament yet once agayne corrected by Wilyam Tindale. . .* Antwerp: De Keyser, 1535.

–, *The First New Testament Printed in the English Language (1525 or 1526), . . . reproduced in facsimile*. Edited by Francis Fry, Bristol, 1862.

–, *The New Testament Translated by William Tyndale, 1534. A reprint of the edition of 1534 with the translator's preface and notes and variants of the edition of 1535*. Edited by N. H. Wallis. Cambridge: The Cambridge University Press, 1938.

URSINS, CHARLOTTE DES, *Homilies sur l'Épistre de Saint Paul aux Hébreux*. Paris: C. Rouillard, 1634.

VALLA, LORENZO, *Adnotationes in latinam Novi Testamenti interpretationem*. Edited by Desiderius Erasmus. Paris, 1505.

VAN DER HAER, FRANCISCUS, *Expositio ss. patrum in epistolas Pauli*. Antwerp, 1615.

VATABLE, FRANCOIS, *Biblia sacra, cum . . . annotationibus*. Paris: Estienne, 1545. Geneva, 1557. Basel, 1564. Salamanca, 1584. Leiden, 1599.

WALTER, MICHAEL, *Der güldene schlüssel des Alten und der süsse kern des Newen Testaments: das ist Gründliche, ordentliche und aussführliche erläuterung der über alle massen tiefsinngen Epistel S. Pauli an die Ebraeer, in hundert sermonen angestellet durch Michaelem Waltherum . . .* Nuremberg, 1646.

WHITTINGHAM, WILLIAM, *The Newe Testament of our Lord Jesus Christ*. Geneva: Conrad Badius, 1557.

ZANCHIUS, BASILIUS, *Basilii Zanchii in omnes divinos libros notationes*. Rome, 1553. Spire, 1558.

–, "In epistolam ad Hebraeos." *B. Z. Bergomatis, canonici ordinis lateranensis, in omnes s. scripturae libros Notationes*. Cologne: Arnold Mylius, 1602. Cols. 216–220.

ZEGERS, NICOLAS-TACITE, *Scholion in omnes Novi Testamenti Libros*. Cologne: Birckman, 1553.

ZWINGLI, HULDRYCH, *In evangelicam historicam de domino nostro Iesu Christo, per Matthaeum, Marcum, Lucam, et Joannem conscriptam, epistolasque aliquot Pauli, annotationes D. Huldrychi Zwinglii per Leonem Iudae exceptae et aeditae. Adjecta est epistola Pauli ad Hebraeos, et Joannis Apostoli epistola per Gasparem Megandrum*. Zürich: Christoph Froschouer, 1539.

–, *Opera, Zwingli*. Zürich: Christoph Froschouer, 1545, 1581.

–, "In epistolam beati Pauli ad Hebraeos expositio brevis." *Zwingli Opera*. Edited by Schuler and Schulthess. Zürich: Schulthess, 1838, VI, 2, pp. 291–319,

–, *The Latin Works and Correspondence of Huldreich Zwingli*. Edited by Samuel Macauley Jackson and others. 3 vols. New York: G. P. Putnam's Sons, 1912–1929.

Bibliographic Aids

BELLARMINE, ROBERT, "Index explanatorum sacrae scripturae." *De scriptoribus ecclesiasticis*. Opera Omnia, VI. Naples: J. Giuliano, 1862, pp. 111–116.

BESTERMAN, THEODORE, *Early Printed Books to the End of the Sixteenth Century. A Bibliography of Bibliographies*. 2nd ed., Geneva: Societas Bibliographica, 1961.

Bibliographie de la littérature francaise du seizième siècle. Edited by Alexander Cioranescu, Paris: C. Klencksieck, 1959.

BRANDES, WALTHER, *Bibliotheca bibliographica Aureliana*. Bibliographie der niedersächsischen Frühdrucke bis zum Jahre 1600. Baden-Baden, 1960.

CROWE, WILLIAM, *The Catalogue of our English writers on the Old and Newe Testament, either in whole, or in part: whether commentators. . .* London: Williams, 1668.

DAGENS, JEAN, *Bibliographie chronologique de la littérature de spiritualité et de ses sources, 1501–1610*. Paris: Desclée de Brouwer, 1952.

Dictionnaire des lettres française. Vol I: Le Seizième Siècle. 5 Volumes. Paris: A. Fayard, 1951–1971.

EYS, W. J. VAN, *Bibliographie des Bibles et des Nouveaux Testaments en langue française des XVme* et XVIme siècles. 2 vols. Geneva, 1900–1902; reprint ed., Nieuwkoop: Graaf, 1963.

FINSLER, GEORG, *Zwingli Bibliographie. Verzeichnis der gedruckten Schriften von und über Ulrich Zwingli*. Zürich, 1897; reprint ed., Nieuwkoop: Graaf. 1962.

GÄBLER, ULRICH, *Huldrych Zwingli im 20. Jahrhundert. Forschungsbericht und annotierte Bibliographie, 1897–1972*. Zürich: Theologischer Verlag, 1975.

GARDY, FRÉDÉRIC, *Bibliographie des oeuvres, théologiques, littéraires, historiques et juridiques, de Théodore de Bèze*. Geneva: Librairie E. Droz, 1960.

GEISENHOF, GEORG, *Bibliotheca Bugenhagiana*. Quellen und Darstellungen aus der Geschichte des Reformationsjahrhunderts, no. 6. Leipzig, 1908; reprint ed., Nieuwkoop: Graaf, 1963.

HAEGHEN, FERDINAND VAN DER, *Bibliotheca Erasmiana. Répertoire des Oeuvres D'Érasme*. Nieuwkoop: Graaf, 1961.

HERBERT, A. S., (Doulow, T. H. and Moule, H. F.). *Historical Catalogue of the Printed Editions of Holy Scripture in the Library of the British and Foreign Bible Society*. Vol. 1 (English Versions), 1903. Revised and expanded by A. S. Herbert. London: The British and Foreign Bible Society, 1968.

HURTER, HUGO, *Nomenclator literarius theologiae catholicae*. Innsbruck: Libraria academica Wagnerana, 1933 f.

Index Aureliensii: Catalogus librorum sedecimo saeculo impressorum. Baden-Baden, 1962.

KRISTELLER, P. O., *Latin Manuscript Books before 1600*. New York: Fordham, 1960.

–, and Cranz, eds. *Catalogus, translationum et commentariorum: Medieval and Renaissance Latin translations and commentaries*. Washington, D. C.: Catholic University of America Press, 1960–1976.

KRÜGER, W., *Die ältesten Altenburger Linck- und Luther- drucke der Thüring*. Landesbibliothek zu Altenburg. Altenburg: Bonde, 1932.

MALCLÈS, L.-N., *Les sources du travail bibliographique*. 3 vols. in 4. Geneva, 1950–1958.

MALCOLM, HOWARD, *References to the Principal Works in Every Department of Religious Literature*. Boston: Gould and Lincoln, 1868.

MARGOLIN, JEAN CLAUDE, *Douze années de bibliographie Érasmienne (1950–1961)*. Paris: J. Vrin, 1963.

PELLECHET, M., *Catalogue des livres de la bibliothèque d'un chanoine d'autun Claude Guilliaud, 1493–1551*. Paris: Picard, 1890.

PIPKIN, H. WAYNE, *A Zwingli Bibliography*. Pittsburgh: Clifford E. Barhour Library, Pittsburgh Theological Seminary, 1972.

RIGAUX, B., *Saint Paul. Les Épitres aux Thessaloniciens*. Paris: Lecoffre, 1956.

RITTER, FRANCOIS, *Catalogue des incunables et livres du XVI*[e] siècle de la Bibliothèque Municipale de Strasbourg. Strasbourg: P. H. Heitz, 1948.

RODRÍGUEZ MOÑINO, ANTONIO R. *La Bibliotheca de Benito Arias Montano*. Badajoz: Institucíon de Servicios Culturales, 1929.

SCHETELIG, CHRISTOPH H. *Bibliotheca disputationum theologico – philologico – exegeticarum in Vetus et Novum Testamentum*. 3 vols. Hamburg: Literis Saalicothianu, 1736–1737.

SHAABER, MATTHIAS A., *Sixteenth Century Imprints in the Libraries of the University of Pennsylvania*. Philadelphia: The University of Pennsylvania Press, 1976.

SIMON, RICHARD, *Histoire critique des principaux commentateurs de Nouveau Testament, depuis le commencement du christianisme jusques à nôtre tems*. Rotterdam, 1693; reprint ed., Frankfurt: Minerva, 1969.

SOMMERVOGEL, CARLOS, ed. *Bibliothèque de la Compagnie de Jésus*. Toulouse: L'auteur, 1911.

STAEDTKE, JOACHIM, *Beschreibendes Verzeichnis der gedruckten Werke von Heinrich Bullinger*. Vol. I. of *Heinrich Bullinger Bibliographie*. Zürich: Theologischer Verlag, 1972.

STAEHELIN, ERNST, *Oekolampad-Bibliographie*. Basler Zeitschrift für Geschichte und Altertumskunde, no. 17 and 27; 2nd ed. Nieuwkoop: Graaf, 1963.

STEGMÜLLER, FRIDERICUS, *Repertorium Biblicum Medii Aevi*. 7 vols. Madrid, 1950–1961.

Troisième centenaire de la mort de Th. de Bèze. Compte rendu publié par la Geneva: Société du musée historique de la reformation, 1906.

VIGOUROUX, FULERAN G., *Dictionnaire de la Bible*. 5 vols. Paris: Letouzey et Ané, 1907–1912.

WALCH, JOHANN G. *Bibliotheca theologica selecta*. 4 vols. Iena: Johann Rudolph Crökers, 1757–1765.

Secondary Sources

ALDRIDGE, JOHN W., *The Hermeneutic of Erasmus*. Richmond: John Knox Press, 1966.

ARMSTRONG, ELISABETH, *Robert Estienne, Royal Printer*. Cambridge: Harvard University Press, 1954.

BAINTON, ROLAND H., *Erasmus of Christendom*. New York: Charles Scribner's Sons, 1969.

BAKER, WAYNE, "Covenant and Society: The *Respublica Christiana* in the Thought of Heinrich Bullinger." Ph. D. dissertation, University of Iowa, 1970.

BARNEKOW, KJELL, "Niels Hemmingsens Teologiska Åskådning: En Dogmhistorisk Studie." Theological Dissertation, University of Lund, 1940.

BENTLEY, JERRY, "Erasmus' *Annotationes in Novum Testamentum.*" ARG 67 (1976): 33–53.

BLANKE, FRITZ, "Zu Zwinglis Vorrede an Luther in der Schrift 'Amica Exegesis' 1527." *Zwingliana* 5 (1930): 185–192.

BOENDERMAKER, J. P., *Luthers Commentaar op de Brief aan de Hebreën*. Assen: Van Gorcum and Co., 1965.

BOUT, H., "Calvijn en het Oude Testament." *Theologia Reformata* 3 (1960): 6–31.

BRAY, JOHN S., *Theodore Beza's Doctrine of Predestination*. Nieuwkoop: Graaf, 1975.

CASTREN, OLAVI, *Die Bibeldeutung Calvins*. Annales Academiae Scientiarum Fennicae, B LVI, 3. Helsinki, 1946.

CUNO, FR. W. *Franciscus Junius der Aeltere Professor der Theologie und Pastor (1545–1602)*. Amsterdam: Schaffer and Co., 1891.

DEMAREST, BRUCE, *A History of Interpretation of Hebrews 7, 1–10 from the Reformation to the Present*. Beiträge zur Geschichte der biblischen Exegese, no. 19. Tübingen: J. C. B. Mohr, 1976.

DITTRICH, FRANZ, *Gasparo Contarini 1483–1542. Eine Monographie*. Braunsberg: J. A. Wichert, 1885.

EMERSON, EVERETT H., "Calvin and Covenant Theology." CH 25 (1956): 136–144.

FARNER, OSKAR, *Huldrych Zwingli*, 4 vols. Zürich: Zwingli-Verlag, 1943–1960.

FAST, HEINOLD, *Heinrich Bullinger und die Täufer. Ein Beitrag zur Historiographie und Theologie im 16. Jahrhundert*. Schriftenreihe des Mennonitischen Geschichtsverein, no. 7. Weierhof: Pfalz, 1959.

FELD, HELMUT, *Martin Luthers und Wendelin Steinbachs Vorlesungen über den Hebräerbrief. Eine Studie zur Geschichte der neutestamentlichen Exegese und Theologie*. Veröffentlichungen des Institutes für europäische Geschichte Mainz, no. 62. Wiesbaden: F. Steiner, 1971.

FÉRET, PIERRE, *La Faculté de Théologie de Paris et ses docteurs les plus célèbres: Epoque moderne*, 7 vols. in 4. Paris: Alph. Picard et Fils, 1900–1910.

FRIELINGHAUS, DIETER, *Ecclesia und vita. Eine Untersuchung zur Ekklesiologie des Andreas Hyperius*. Neukirchen-Vluyn: 1966.

GEISENDORF, PAUL F., *Théodore de Bèze*. Geneva: Labor et fides, 1949.

GREENSLADE, STANLEY LAWRENCE, ed., *The Cambridge History of the Bible*, 3 vols. Cambridge: Cambridge University Press, 1963–70.

GRIN, E., "L'unité des deux Testaments selon Calvin." TZ 17 (1961): 175–186.

HAAG, ÉMILE, *La France Protestant*, 10 vols. 2nd ed., Paris, 1877–1888.

HAGEN, KENNETH G., "Luther's Lectures on Hebrews in the Light of Medieval

Commentaries on Hebrews." Th. D. dissertation, Harvard University, 1966.

–, "From Testament to Covenant in the Early Sixteenth Century." SCJ 3 (April, 1972): 1–24.

–, *A Theology of Testament in the Young Luther: The Lectures on Hebrews.* Studies in Medieval and Reformation Thought, no. 12. Leiden: E. J. Brill, 1974.

HAGENBACH, KARL R., *Johann Oekolampad und Oswald Myconius die Reformatoren Basels.* Leben und Ausgewählte Schriften reformierten. . ., no. 2. Elberfeld: R. L. Friderichs, 1859.

HERZOG, J. J. Das Leben Johannes Oekolampads und die Reformation der Kirche zu Basel, 2 vols. in 1. Basel: Schweighauser, 1843.

HOEKEMA, ANTHONY, "The Covenant of Grace in Calvin's Teaching." *Calvin Theological Journal* 2 (1967): 133–161.

HOLLWEG, WALTER, *Heinrich Bullingers Hausbuch. Eine Untersuchung über die Anfänge der reformierten Predigtliteratur.* Beiträge zur Geschichte und Lehre der reformierten Kirche, no. 8. Neukirchen Kreis Moers: Verlag der Buchhandlung des Erziehungsvereins, 1956.

HOOFT, ANTONIUS JOHANNES VAN T', *De Theologie van Heinrich Bullinger in betrekking tot de Nederlandsche Reformatié.* Amsterdam: I. de Hoogh, 1888.

HORST, ULRICH, "Der Streit um die hl. Scrift zwischen Kardinal Cajetan und Ambrosius Catharinus." In *Wahrheit und Verkündigung,* Vol I., pp. 551–77. Edited by Leo Scheffczyk. Munich: Schöningh, 1967.

JACKSON, SAMUEL M., *Huldreich Zwingli: The Reformer of German Switzerland, 1484–1531.* New York: G. P. Putnam's Sons, 1901; reprint ed., New York: AMS, 1972.

KIRCH, GUIDO, "Humanistic Jurisprudence." *Studies in the Renaissance* 8 (1961): 71–87.

KÖHLER, WALTER, *Huldrych Zwingli.* Leipzig: Kochler and Amelang, 1943/54.

KOHLS, ERNST-WILHELM, *Die Theologie des Erasmus.* Basel: Friedrich Reinhardt Verlag, 1966.

KRAUSE, GERHARD, *Andreas Gerhard Hyperius.* Beiträge zur historischen Theologie, no. 56. Tübingen: J. C. B. Mohr, 1977.

KÜNZLI, EDWIN, "Zwinglis theologische Wertung des Alten Testaments." *Der Kirchenfreund* 83 (1949): 244–248, 276–284.

–, "Quellenproblem und mystischer Schriftsinn in Zwinglis Genesis- und Exoduskommentar." *Zwingliana* 5 (1950–51): 185 ff., 253 ff.

–, "Zwingli als Ausleger des Alten Testamentes." CR 101 (14), Zürich: Berichthaus, 1959, pp. 869–899.

LAUCHERT, FRIEDRICH, *Die italienischen literarischen Gegner Luthers,* Erläuterungen und Ergänzungen zu Janssens Geschichte des deutschen Volkes, no. 8. Freiburg i. B.: Herder, 1912.

–, *Der italienische Benediktiner Isidorus Clarius und seine Schrift für den religiösen Frieden.* Studien und Mitteilungen zur Geschichte des Benediktiner Ordens, no. 29. 1908.

LAURENT, M.-H., "Quelques documents des Archives Vaticanes (1517–1534)." *Revue Thomiste* 17 (1934): 126–129.

LIEBING, H., "Die Schriftauslegung Sebastian Castellio." Dissertation, University of Tübingen, 1953.

LOCHER, GOTTFRIED, *Die Theologie Huldrych Zwinglis im Lichte seiner Christologie*. Zürich: Zwingli-Verlag, 1952.

–, "Das Geschichtsbild Huldrych Zwinglis." *Theologische Zeitschrift* 9 (1953): 275–302.

MACGREGOR, MALCOLM, *The Sources and Literature of Scottish Church History*. Glasgow: John McCallum and Co., 1934.

Nordisk Teologisk Uppslagsbok. Lund, 1952.

OORTHUYS, G. ANASTASIUS, *"Wechuyser," Bullingers "Huysboeck" en Calvyns "Institutie" vergeleken in hun leer van God en Mensch*. Leiden: E. J. Brill, 1919.

OTTO, J. K. T. *De Victorino Strigelio liberioris mentis in ecclesia Lutheria vindice*. Iena: Friderici Mauke, 1843.

PARKER, T. H. L., *Calvin's New Testament Commentaries*. Grand Rapids: Eerdmans, 1971.

–, *John Calvin: A Biography*. Philadelphia: The Westminster Press, 1975.

POPE, HUGH, *English Versions of the Bible,* revised by Sebastian Bullough. London: Herder, 1952.

PREGER, WILHELM, *Matthias Flacius Illyricus und seine Zeit,* 2 vols. in 1. Erlangen: T. Blösing, 1859–1861; new edition, Hildesheim: G. Olms, 1964.

RABIL, ALBERT, Jr., *Erasmus and the New Testament. The Mind of a Christian Humanist*. San Antonio: Trinity University Press, 1972.

RAITT, JILL, *The Eucharistic Theology of Theodore Beza: Development of the Reformed Doctrine*. American Academy of Religion Studies in Religion, no. 4. Missoula: Scholars Press, 1972.

RAUTENBERG, WERNER, *Johann Bugenhagen. Beiträge zu seinem 400. Todestag*. Berlin: Evangelische Verlagsanstalt, 1958.

REID, HENRY, *The Divinity Professors in the University of Glasgow, 1640–1903*. Glasgow: Maclehose, Jackson and Co., 1923.

REKERS, BERNARD, *Benito Arias Montano (1527–98)*. Studies of the Warburg Institute, no. 33. London: The Warburg Institute, 1972.

RENAUDET, AUGUSTIN, *Études érasmiennes, 1521–29*. Paris, 1939.

REUSS, RUDOLPHE, *Notes pour servir a l'histoire de l'eglise française de Strasbourg, 1538–1794*. Strasbourg: Treuttel et Würtz, 1880.

RICH, ARTHUR, *Die Anfänge der Theologie Huldrych Zwinglis*. Zürich: Zwingli-Verlag, 1949.

RIGGENBACH, EDUARD, *Historische Studien zum Hebräerbrief*. Part I: *Die ältesten lateinischen Kommentare zum Hebräerbrief*. Forschungen zur Geschichte des neutestamentlichen Kanons und der altkirchlichen Literatur. Leipzig: A. Deichert, 1907.

RILLIET, JEAN, *Zwingli, Third Man of the Reformation,* translated by Harold Knight. Philadelphia: The Westminster Press, 1964.

RUPP, E. G., *Patterns of the Reformation*. Philadelphia: Fortress Press, 1969.

SCHILD, MAURICE, *Abendländische Bibelvorreden bis zur Lutherbibel*. Quellen und Forschungen zur Reformationsgeschichte, no. 39. Gütersloh: G. Mohn, 1970.

SCHLINGENSIEPEN, HERMANN, "Erasmus als Exeget." ZKG 48 (1929): 16–57.

SCHWARZ, WERNER, *Principles and Problems of Biblical Translation. Some Reformation Controversies and their Background.* Cambridge: Cambridge University Press, 1955.

SIMON, M., "Die Beziehung zwischen Altem und Neuem Testament in der Schriftauslegung Calvins." *Reformierte Kirchenzeitung* 82 (1932): 17–21, 25–28, 33–35.

SMEND, JULIUS, "Das Testament Jesu Christi." *Die evangelische deutsche Messe bis zu Luthers Deutscher Messe.* Göttingen: Vandenhoeck and Ruprecht, 1896; reprint ed., Nieuwkoop: Graaf, 1967.

STAEDTKE, JOACHIM, *Die Theologie des jungen Bullinger.* Studien zur Dogmengeschichte und systematischen Theologie, no. 16. Zürich: Theologischer Verlag, 1962.

STAEHELIN, ERNST, ed., *Brief und Akten zum Leben Oekolampads.* Quellen und Forschungen zur Reformationsgeschichte, nos. 10 and 19. Leipzig: M. Heinsius, 1927 and 1934.

–, *Das theologische Lebenswerk Johannes Oekolampads.* Quellen und Forschungen zur Reformationsgeschichte, no. 21. Leipzig: M. Heinsius, 1939.

STAEHELIN, FRIEDRICH, *Humanismus und Reformation im bürgerlichen Raum.* SVRG no. 159. Leipzig, 1936.

TOON, PETER, *God's Statesman: The Life and Work of John Owen.* Grand Rapids: Eerdmans, 1973.

VOSTÉ, FR. IACOBUS-MARIE, "Cardinal Cajetanus Sacrae Scripturae Interpres." *Angelicum* 11 (1934): 445–513.

WALSER, PETER, *Die Prädestination bei Heinrich Bullinger im Zusammenhang mit seiner Gotteslehre.* Studien zur Dogmengeschichte und systematischen Theologie, no. 11. Zürich: Zwingli-Verlag, 1957.

WENDORF, H., "Joachim Camerarius: Herbergen der Christenheit." *Beiträge zur Kirchengeschichte Deutschlands* 2 (1957): 34–78. Edited by Lau.

WICKS, JARED, "Thomism between Renaissance and Reformation: The Case of Cajetan." ARG 68 (1977): 9–31.

WOLF, HANS H., *Die Einheit des Bundes. Das Verhältnis von Altem und Neuem Testament bei Calvin.* Beiträge zur Geschichte und Lehre der Reformierten Kirche, no. 10. 2nd. ed. Neukirchen Kreis Moers: Verlag der Buchhandlung des Erziehungsvereins, 1958.

Scripture Index

Name Index

Subject Index